'In the 1980s and early 1990s, East Asia economic development was hailed as a miracle. Economists saw it as a model the world could follow: its visionary leadership, its egalitarian values and its future-oriented industrial strategy. For Maureen Sioh, this model has an underside, grounded in the legacies of colonial traumas. These traumas repeat themselves, producing a far more anxious and complex postcolonial legacy than most recognize or acknowledge. In this provocative and passionate book, Sioh brilliantly explores economic development as an ongoing struggle for survival and human dignity. In doing so, she addresses the core questions of global economic development: What are the lasting legacies of colonialism? How can we know what development is? Is economic development only about wealth generation?'

Steve Pile, *Professor of Human Geography, The Open University*

'This book is a tour de force, convincingly demonstrating that the psyche is not trivial or secondary but central to economic decision-making. Focusing on postcolonial Malaysia, Sioh brilliantly maps the wounds of trauma and anxiety in economic crisis and 'miracle'.'

Ilan Kapoor, *Author of Confronting Desire: Psychoanalysis and International Development and Professor of Critical Development Studies, York University, Toronto*

'Economic growth, development, progress ... belying these self-evidently rational aspirations are unconscious drives for the repair and restitution of psychic wounds running deep within the postcolonial world. Exploring the libidinal economy of the Malaysian state, Sioh expertly brings into relief the anxieties and trauma that surreptitiously play out in the seemingly staid realm of economic policy. *Colonial Trauma and Postcolonial Anxieties* is an important work, marking the beginning of a turn in political economy to the therapeutic.'

Earl Gammon, *Senior Lecturer in Global Political Economy, University of Sussex*

Colonial Trauma and Postcolonial Anxieties

Colonial Trauma and Postcolonial Anxieties argues that economic decisions reflect unconscious anxieties about survival and dignity experienced in a cycle of repeat trauma tracing back to the original trauma of loss in colonialism.

Readers will understand how emerging economies evaluate the costs and benefits of key economic policies in the postcolonial era using a psychoanalytical framework.

While there are psychoanalytic studies of the economy and finance from a Western perspective, there have been no sustained psychoanalytic studies from the perspective of East Asian economies, the fastest growing in the world. Scholars will also find the methodology combining archival research with field studies, including rare interviews with senior decision-makers useful in their own research since it is rare to find studies of social theory that are empirically rich.

This book will be of interest to policymakers and scholars of political economy, international development, human geography, postcolonial studies, psychoanalysis and area studies (Southeast and East Asia). The book can also be used as a text for graduate and upper level university courses.

Maureen Sioh is an Associate Professor in the Department of Geography at DePaul University. She trained as a hydrologist and has worked in China, Thailand, Cambodia, Malaysia, Singapore and with First Nations communities in Canada. Her early research focused on water quality. Concerned with the subjective process of how communities made decisions when confronting environmental issues, her research evolved to postcolonialism and then to economics and psychoanalysis. She is the coauthor of *Global Libidinal Economy* with Ilan Kapoor, Gavin Fridell and Pieter de Vries.

Routledge Research on Decoloniality and New Postcolonialisms
Series Editor: Mark Jackson, Senior Lecturer in Postcolonial Geographies, School of Geographical Sciences, University of Bristol, UK.

Routledge Research on Decoloniality and New Postcolonialisms is a forum for original, critical research into the histories, legacies, and life-worlds of modern colonialism, postcolonialism, and contemporary coloniality. It analyses efforts to decolonize dominant and damaging forms of thinking and practice, and identifies, from around the world, diverse perspectives that encourage living and flourishing differently. Once the purview of a postcolonial studies informed by the cultural turn's important focus on identity, language, text and representation, today's resurgent critiques of coloniality are also increasingly informed, across the humanities and social sciences, by a host of new influences and continuing insights for different futures: indigeneity, critical race theory, relational ecologies, critical semiotics, posthumanisms, ontology, affect, feminist standpoints, creative methodologies, post-development, critical pedagogies, intercultural activisms, place-based knowledges, and much else. The series welcomes a range of contributions from socially engaged intellectuals, theoretical scholars, empirical analysts, and critical practitioners whose work attends, and commits, to newly rigorous analyses of alternative proposals for understanding life and living well on our increasingly damaged earth.

This series is aimed at upper-level undergraduates, research students and academics, appealing to scholars from a range of academic fields including human geography, sociology, politics and broader interdisciplinary fields of social sciences, arts and humanities.

African Epistemologies in Higher Education Research
Kolawole Samuel Adeyemo

Decolonising Political Concepts
Edited by Valentin Clavé-Mercier and Marie With

Colonial Trauma and Postcolonial Anxieties
The Haunted Choices of Economic Development
Maureen Sioh

For more information about this series, please visit: https://www.routledge.com/Routledge-Research-on-Decoloniality-and-New-Postcolonialisms/book-series/RRNP

Colonial Trauma and Postcolonial Anxieties

The Haunted Choices of Economic Development

Maureen Sioh

Routledge
Taylor & Francis Group
LONDON AND NEW YORK

First published 2024
by Routledge
4 Park Square, Milton Park, Abingdon, Oxon OX14 4RN

and by Routledge
605 Third Avenue, New York, NY 10158

Routledge is an imprint of the Taylor & Francis Group, an informa business

British Library Cataloguing-in-Publication Data
A catalogue record for this book is available from the British Library

Library of Congress Cataloging-in-Publication Data
Names: Sioh, Maureen Kim Lian, 1962- author.
Title: Colonial trauma and postcolonial anxieties : the haunted choices of economic development / Maureen Sioh.
Description: Abingdon, Oxon ; New York, NY : Routledge, 2024. | Series: Routledge research on decoloniality and new postcolonialisms | Includes bibliographical references and index. | Identifiers: LCCN 2023047428 (print) | LCCN 2023047429 (ebook) | ISBN 9781138217492 (hardback) | ISBN 9781032732428 (paperback) | ISBN 9781315440286 (ebook)
Subjects: LCSH: Economic development--Malaysia--Psychological aspects. | Economic development--Singapore--Psychological aspects. | Economic development--East Asia--Psychological aspects. | Postcolonialism--Malaysia--Psychological aspects. | Postcolonialism--Singapore--Psychological aspects. | Postcolonialism--East Asia--Psychological aspects.
Classification: LCC HC445.5 .S576 2024 (print) | LCC HC445.5 (ebook) | DDC 338.9595--dc23/eng/20231228
LC record available at https://lccn.loc.gov/2023047428
LC ebook record available at https://lccn.loc.gov/2023047429

ISBN: 978-1-138-21749-2 (hbk)
ISBN: 978-1-032-73242-8 (pbk)
ISBN: 978-1-315-44028-6 (ebk)

DOI: 10.4324/9781315440286

Typeset in Sabon
by KnowledgeWorks Global Ltd.

Parts of this book have appeared in the following publications:

Kapoor, I. and G. Fridell, M. Sioh. 2023. *Global Libidinal Economy*. Albany: SUNY Press, 141–147.

Sioh, M. 2018. "The Logic of Humiliation in Financial Conquest." In *Psychoanalysis and the Global*, edited by I. Kapoor, 25–47. Lincoln: University of Nebraska Press.

Sioh, M. 2017. "In the Skin: Intimate Acts in Economic Globalization." In *Writing Intimacy into Feminist Geography*, edited by P. Moss and C. Donovan, 48–57. London: Routledge.

Sioh, M. 2010. "Anxious Enactments: Postcolonial Anxieties and the Performance of Territorialization." *Environment and Planning D: Society and Space* 28 (3): 467–487.

Sioh, M. 2007. "Pricing Race, Circulating Anxieties and the Fate of Malaya's Currency Reserves at Independence." *Cultural Critique* 65 (Winter): 115–139.

Sioh, M. 2004. "An Ecology of Postcoloniality: Disciplining Nature and Society in Malaya 1948-1957." *Journal of Historical Geography* 30: 729–746.

Contents

Preface *x*
List of Abbreviations *xii*

Introduction 1

1 Colonial Trauma and Postcolonial Anxieties 10

2 The Foundational Fantasy of Colonial Ecology 28

3 Dismantling the Colonial Foundational Fantasy 43

4 Trauma and the Wound of Race in the Malayan Emergency 59

5 Anxiety and Pricing Race at Independence 73

6 Postcolonial Anxieties and Performing Territorialization 91

7 The Logic of Trauma in Financial Crisis 105

8 Anxiety and Economic Policy in Resurgent East Asia 119

Conclusion 136

Bibliography *144*
Index *165*

Preface

I remember the sunlight, so bright that I have to squint my eyes. I can still feel the unforgiving heat now that the forest has been cut down to make way for hundreds of thousands of hectares of oil palm so that the unpaved tracks we drive on are unshaded. I remember the small pockets of *kampungs*, newly settled and provided with running water for the first time – the reason my father is here as senior engineer and I am tagging along. My childish presence, in a Western country, would probably have had my father charged with child endangerment, for who takes a child on fieldwork in areas still under military curfew? Those scenes would come back to me again and again over the years in Thailand, Cambodia, China and even Canada, with its cold, unfamiliar boreal landscape when I carried out my own fieldwork studying the links between erosion and water quality. It would lead me to ask if I was asking the right questions as a professional. What counts as development and what drives its practices? This book has its genesis in those trips to the early Federal Land Development Authority (FELDA) schemes and my attempts to find answers decades later.

Steve Pile, wise as ever, tells me that this book is my origin story. But it isn't just my story; it overlaps with those of millions around the world, each of us trying to make sense of the complex and frustrating story of "development," driven by the desire to be accorded human dignity. Or as a former student from South Korea reminded me, "this story, it's yours and mine too." So let me take this moment to thank the many students over the years who shared their stories and helped me see development through their eyes. I also thank the librarians at the Public Record Office (now the National Archives) at Kew Gardens, the Royal Commonwealth Society Archives at the Cambridge University Library, the British Library Newspaper Library (now the British Newspaper Archive) then in Colindale, North London and the Rubber Research Institute of Malaysia in Kuala Lumpur. I should note that many of the CO documents in the bibliography have been collated and published in Anthony Stockwell's excellent Malaya volumes as part of the British Documents on the End of Empire series. I was not aware of their publication at the time I carried out my archival research. I am grateful to my interviewees in

Chapter 8 who shared their time and knowledge. I also extend my thanks to Lee Yoke Har for her help in understanding the political terrain in Malaysia.

I am a solitary person, but I could not have completed this book without the help of my two Sarahs who kept me sane over the years. Thank you, Steve and Dylan for being my sounding boards for every harebrained idea and, importantly, for checking in on me during my travels to ensure I was still alive. I am especially grateful to Steve for talking (texting?) me down from clawing the walls in the final panicked days before the submission of my manuscript.

Most of all, I thank my father who is not here to see this book. You taught me by example that development is the work of millions engaged in the everyday tasks of making and telling this frustrating, heartbreaking, banal (because it seems we keep repeating our mistakes) yet somehow, utterly magnificent story.

Hutang budi di bawah mati

List of Abbreviations

ADB	Asian Development Bank
AIIB	Asian Infrastructure Investment Bank
BMA	British Military Administration
BRICS	Brazil, Russia, India, China, South Africa
CMIM	Chiang Mai Initiative Multilateralization
FELDA	Federal Land Development Authority
FMS	Federated Malay States
GLC	Government-Linked Corporation
INA	Indian National Army
MCP	Malayan Communist Party
MPAJA	Malayan Peoples' Anti-Japanese Army
MU	Malayan Union
NDB	New Development Bank
NEP	New Economic Policy
PAS	Malaysian Islamic Party or *Parti Islam Se-Malaysia*
PMGLU	Pan-Malayan General Labour Union
SMP	Second Malaysia Plan
SWF	Sovereign Wealth Fund
UMNO	United Malays National Organisation

Introduction

The mist hangs over the wetlands as we speed past. Even in the sealed air-conditioned space of the car, the sour smell of the anaerobic wetlands comes up to me from the depths of memory. It is just after sunrise and I am on my way to the airport—the end of a difficult trip in a difficult time in the country. For this is in the midst of the Asian financial crisis, the most serious economic crisis in the modern history of the region. The Malaysian economy will survive the crisis, as will its neighbors to varying degrees and in varying timeframes. Singapore will vault into the ranks of the "first world." The wetlands I passed that morning will soon be drained and buried under urban sprawl. Across the causeway, its neighbor Singapore's iconic skyline will be engineered on land reclaimed from coastal mangroves to triumphantly announce its arrival in the ranks of the "first world." In both countries, the story of the disappearing wetlands will mirror the countries' struggles to master economic growth in the march to take their place in History. If, in the years to come, a soil scientist were to take a core sample, the complex web of ecological relationships long buried under the paved surfaces will have to be pieced together from the sedimented layers exposed to daylight. Constructing this story will involve choices as it does with all stories. For our stories reflect choices made at critical junctures of what is unearthed from our buried history.

In 2008, the Commission on Economic Growth (13), in the midst of a global financial meltdown, posed the question asking what we actually knew about economic growth. This book takes up that question to trace the economic choices we make in reaction to symptoms that we do not always recognize. The idea for the book came from years of the same reaction to my presentations from many people. These were either appreciative or hostile, sometimes deeply, but the commentators could not, or chose not to, explain their reactions. Those who were appreciative would sometimes thank me but as one woman put it, "I am not sure what for." So the reactions were emotionally invested yet inarticulate and ambivalent. My presentations and this book focus on Malaysia over a 70-year period from the independence struggles leading up to the first decade of the twenty-first century, although Chapter 8 widens the lens to take in Singapore and

DOI: 10.4324/9781315440286-1

the broader region. This period bookends two traumatic events, the birth of the independent nation-state and the financial crisis in 1997–98. The consequent anxieties can be mapped in the economic policy choices that followed. I have chosen to bracket the 13 May 1969 riots, which arguably can be seen as a separate traumatic event, as a continuation of the racialized independence struggles which left serious unresolved political and psychological schisms. Beginning in the 1990s, the "East Asian Economic Miracle" (World Bank 1993), of which Malaysia was a part, generated a great deal of interest as a model to be emulated by other developing countries even as Western countries who acknowledge their economic gains still see them as moral failures for a variety of reasons ranging from authoritarian tendencies, to corruption, to a lack of intellectual originality. These criticisms detract from them being accorded the respect that usually accompanies economic success in the West where money transforms its possessors into icons who then pronounce on social issues; witness the awe accorded the pronouncements of our technology titans .... I address these criticisms in the book, but for now, I want to draw attention to two features common to the criticisms—the emotionally charged nature of the criticisms and their inherently essentialist cast.

If economic choices appear to belong to the domain of rationality, then their outcomes are a function of skill and informed choices. Yet in the case of East Asian countries, Western commentators and East Asian governments have consistently transformed economic decisions into cultural battlegrounds. In the context of economic development, the key questions become why some states succeed in galvanizing their economies and how they do it. Implicit in this line of questioning is that material accumulation is a self-evident endpoint in itself. Instead, I argue that nation-state actors evaluated the costs and benefits of key economic policies in the postcolonial era reflecting on unconscious anxieties about survival and dignity tracing back to the trauma of colonialism. The emotional force surrounding these decisions on the part of their proponents and detractors can be better explained by examining the contests and negotiations that take place in the parallel but buried just below the "skin" narratives that foreground issues of race and identity. Group conceptions such as race may be cultural constructs but they are important because development has come to be viewed as the potential of a group or region to progress (Kasese-Hara 2004, 545), one might add, to "full human status" (Johnson 1982, 52). And development is still commonly equated with economic growth. Conversely, if one's group/nation fails economically, the taint of failure sticks to individual members of the group. This raises the stakes for economic growth. The title of the book references hauntings, as I argue that economic choices are haunted by the trauma of colonialism. The latent anxieties that are the legacy of colonialism may be denied in public discourse, but these can be glimpsed in the language in which economic policies are fought.

In 2022 Malaysia completed its election which ended in a hung parliament. The architect of the economic vision that transformed the economy of the country in the 1980s and 1990s, the 97-year-old former prime minister Dr. Mahathir Mohamad, lost his seat in an election where the youth vote[1] was predicted to hand the electoral majority to more progressive forces but unexpectedly almost delivered the election to the ethno-religious party Perikatan Nasional (PN) coalition, which came second with 73 seats and is dominated by the Pan-Malaysian Islamic Party (PAS). Malaysia's political dysfunction, five prime ministers since 2018, ultimately a function of its inability to move beyond race-based politics, has hampered economic growth and prompted Dr. Mahathir to emerge from retirement in the hope of prioritizing an economic agenda to take Malaysia out of the middle-income trap. But the dysfunction is not recent in its making. As activist lawyer Siti Kasim (2022) noted, the result was decades in the making. This book is not meant to be a historical or geographical survey of Malaysia. Rather, I've used certain significant economic moments as illustrations of how the political economy and psychic structures of decision-making co-evolve from the history of the region. In my narrative, political pathologies are a function of the phenomena of colonialism, development and globalization experienced as repeat trauma.

From the perspective of the pathologies of successful (although not always acknowledged as such in the West) economic growth policies in East Asia, much of the Western focus has been on China. But from the perspective of developing countries, the size of China makes it an unlikely model to emulate.[2] The smaller East Asian countries provide more realistic models of success and failure for small and less powerful countries everywhere. Moreover, Malaysia's experience as a country whose attempts at industrialization were built on its agricultural economy, unlike Japan and other East Asian emerged and emerging economies, and its problematic accommodations with racial tensions, makes it even more emblematic of the dilemmas facing many developing countries, including South Africa that has used it as model (World Bank 1997; Khanna 2008; Mamdani 2008). These tensions have continued to dog subsequent governments since independence, including the 2022 federal election and the 2023 state elections.

My book examines the ways in which economic policies are embedded in specific configurations of territorialization in colonial and postcolonial Malaysia. I am particularly interested in the postcolonial anxieties of psychic legitimacy that accompany the humiliation of being colonized. I define psychic legitimacy in the case of the nation-state to be the unchallenged acceptance by both participants and observers of a state's status as a confluence of group identity with a territorial claim, in other words, its cultural ownership of a space. Chapters 2–4 and 6 focus on contests over physical space, Chapters 5, 7 and 8, particularly with the onset of Globalization 2.0, focus on financial space as the key territorial claim for cultural and psychic legitimacy. A brief note on terminology used in the book: I define an event traumatic if it evinces extraordinary widespread aggression. And while violent conflict is easily recognized as trauma because of the potential for physical injury and death,

I have included in that category events that resulted in high levels of material loss which threaten survival, such as the original moment of colonization for the non-White population in the country as well as financial crisis. I also included the less obvious category of widespread humiliation that results in loss of dignity and threatens psychic survival. I use the term race rather than ethnicity as it highlights the biologically determinist aspect of the colonial carryover that is still in use in Malaysia today. For most part, I use the term colonialism rather than imperialism because Malaysia was directly and officially ruled by Britain. The term imperialism usually refers to the indirect control of countries but in terms of the long-lasting psychic impact of control, even for China which was never officially colonized, the container term of colonialism seems appropriate. I refer to the political entity as Malaya until 1963 after which the new entity consisting of peninsular Malaya, Singapore and the states of Sabah and Sarawak on the island of Borneo became Malaysia. Singapore was forced out of the federation in 1965 to become an independent nation-state. I use the term developing country to refer to economically striving non-Western countries such as Malaysia in the 1970s and 1980s but use the term emerging economy from the 1990s onwards in keeping with contemporary media usage. While the chapters on the colonial period use the regional term Southeast Asia, the book's focus on economy also influenced my decision to stick with the container term of East Asia when referring to a regional category in Chapters 7 and 8 with reference to the World Bank's (World Bank 1993) controversial but seminal document, *The East Asian Miracle*. Finally, the term "Western" is used in reference to colonial authorities, Europeans, Anglophone commentators as well as representatives of global institutions such as the International Monetary Fund (IMF) and World Bank that tend to represent the Anglophone and Western European perspective.

Argument

This book focuses on how nation-state actors evaluated the costs and benefits of key economic policies in the postcolonial era using a psychoanalytical framework. While the book is indebted to political economy and postcolonial approaches to development and the nation-state, it differs from the former approaches in going beyond analyzing how induced material scarcity causes violence by examining why cultural articulations of the economy are so deadly. I argue that economic decisions reflect unconscious anxieties about survival and dignity which can be traced back to the trauma of colonialism. These anxieties are triggered whenever the nation-state undergoes an experience that recalls the original trauma of loss. Recent work in critical development by Kapoor (2018), Gerber (2022) and Kapoor et al. (2023) features scholars using various psychoanalytical frameworks, usually Lacanian and Zizekian, to interrogate unconscious desires on the part of Western actors in their role in development projects. Building on these important contributions, I turn the focus to the perspective of actors from developing countries/emerging economies to interrogate the basis of their economic choices using Malaysia as a case study. While psychoanalytical frameworks tend to imply an equation between unconscious and irrational, in my application I suggest that economic decisions are forms of storytelling that fall between conscious and unconscious motivations, just as what is termed irrational may prove quite rational in a libidinal calculus. The economy is the battleground for physical survival. But even for those fortunate enough to escape the quotidian struggle for physical survival, the economy is the battleground for psychic survival. Anxieties of raced and masculine identities are deeply implicated in economic phenomena. In the fast-changing world of globalization with its unstable moral signposts, economic success is perceived to be the only reliable guarantor of respect. These are the stakes driving economic growth.

Viewed through the psychoanalytical framework of the libidinal economy as a set of affect-driven decisions, the Malaysian state's economic decisions reflect how anxieties about survival and dignity are negotiated in international relations and the global economy. Securitizing the nation-state for less powerful countries in our anxious times is increasingly defined financially so that now exchange rates become the synecdoche for the "sovereign border" because a country's autonomy disappears if its exchange rate collapses (see Chapters 5 and 8). Today, the new defenders of the realm are the economic decision-makers who reflect the proper performance of hegemonic identity in the global hierarchy.

In this book I argue that the defining trait of postcoloniality is anxiety, rooted in the trauma of the experience of race under colonialism. These anxieties manifest themselves in the state's economic decision-making. Through colonialism, race is transformed into a narcissistic wound, not as an abstract concept but one literally embodied. This then is the wound that the postcolonial subject seeks to escape through the "lactification" of economic success. While terms such as Third World and postcolonial are seen as outdated, the cultural connotations and power relations live on with different accentuations. Thus, to employ a postcolonial lens in development is a recognition that development and its successor project, globalization, are (im)moral economies based on cultural value systems. As such, economic gains and losses are signals beyond simple material gains and losses because they reflect on identity. While the East Asian governments, including Malaysia, claim their policy pronouncements belong to the realm of economic rationality, in practice, their policy responses constitute a normative moral economy enabled through the agent of the state to challenge the existing international hierarchy. A psychoanalytic approach allows us to interrogate the emotionally charged unofficial discourses underneath the economic debates. Even Singapore and South Korea with Gross Domestic Products (GDPs) that qualify as developed economies evince the anxieties of poorer countries, for the perception of economic sustainability is still linked to intangible cultural capital. This perception translates into economic credibility during a crisis and affects exchange rates as I show in Chapter 7. In other words, the intangible capital is absent in the context of postcolonial and non-white countries who still fight that credibility battle every day.

The book's central argument is made in the following steps: economic decisions reflect unconscious anxieties about survival and dignity which can be traced back to the trauma of colonialism. As such, economic contests are "felt in the skin," given that economic contests are manifestations of unconscious contests over identity issues of race and entitlement. Hence, the goals of economic decisions are to create a safe space for psychic, rather than simply material, survival. Because the survival of race comes in the guise of the survival of the nation-state as even current Western political contests such as the election of President Trump and Brexit in 2016 have shown; economic gains and losses translate into narcissistic injuries. And race, as with any essentialized identity, feeds into the powerful appeal of capitalism because of its proven capacity to buy respect, hence the drive for economic growth.

Scope

Colonialism and globalization have always been about material dispossession, which at a collective level broadly translates into have and have-not countries. However, because colonialism was as much about race as capitalism, the postcolonial nation-state would always be about race as well. The book's focus on state-level decision-making highlights the enduring significance of race in the contemporary political economy of development and globalization. During the main period covered in this book, from the 1950s to the first decade of the twenty-first century, social power goes from being vested largely in military success to economic success. Thus, controlling economic space becomes the synecdoche for sovereignty. I work with the concepts of trauma, anxiety and psychological defense mechanisms to analyze the reproduction of capital as territorial displacements of the libidinal economy. A particular contribution of the book is to analyze the use of humiliation through practice and language not just to enforce but also induce economic self-discipline. Methodologically, I use a mix of archival official and unofficial documents such as diaries, letters, personal communication, newspapers and magazines. Chapter 8 also uses unstructured interviews. A brief word on the organization of the book; all the chapters use a similar theoretical framework so as to underscore the cycle of repeating trauma and its links to the ensuing defense against anxiety. The theoretical review providing the overall framework for the book is covered in Chapter 1 rather than fragmented throughout the book since historical contexts change but certain themes and motifs recur throughout the period covered in the book. However, I provide brief theoretical signposts in the relevant chapters for clarity even if this creates some redundancy.

Chapter 2 covers the origins of the colonial libidinal economy by providing a brief historical background to Malaya's colonial encounter in the nineteenth century. This is the first stage in the construction of a colonial ecology where nature and natives are constructed as benign and passive objects to agentic Western subjects. The relationship dynamic is accomplished through transforming the physical environment in the form of plantations and the attendant social relations to support the plantation mode of production. By the 1930s, a recognizable set of patterns of social, political and ultimately, cultural relations came into place which placed the superior colonizer above the inferior colonized. The colonial project became a fact of life replete with attitudes, rules and hierarchies that acted as intellectual and psychological gateways.

Chapter 3 looks at the psychic fractures resulting from the Japanese defeat of the British in Malaya in World War Two. The defeat followed by the violence that persisted even after the war ended in 1945 led to the declaration of a State of Emergency in 1948 by the colonial government. This chapter covers the rise of anti-colonial resistance emboldened by the British defeat in the war. The Malayan Communist Party (MCP) shifted their resistance against the Japanese toward the British reoccupation of Malaya and Singapore after the war. Chapter 3 examines the unraveling of the narrative of passive native and benign nature existing for the economic and psychological benefit of the colonizer. Instead, the reoccupying British confronted the reality of recalcitrant natives and a forest that, in obstructing colonial aims, became an enabler of the recalcitrant natives. The transformation was reflected in the switch from using the term "forest" to "jungle" reflecting the popularization of the expression the "law of the jungle" to describe social relations in colonial Malaya.

Where Chapter 3 focused on recalcitrant natives and an enabling nature, Chapter 4 covers the resulting narcissistic rage of the colonizers on being challenged. The Emergency was a violent contest over the narratives of racial superiority embedded within the assumption of economic entitlement. During this last successful Western-led counterinsurgency, the reoccupying British incarcerated or resettled almost a quarter of the Malayan population categorized along racial lines. The Emergency was a traumatic moment for all residents of Malaya. By challenging the economic entitlement of the colonial authorities, the Communists were refusing to accept the racial hierarchy. In doing so, they narcissistically wounded the British who reacted by projecting their rage onto the local population in the form of the everyday violence of bombing, shelling, public exhibitions of mutilated corpses and mass incarceration in the concentration camps euphemistically described as "New Villages." In the process of fighting the Emergency, the raced body itself was constructed as a wound, out of which would come the anxieties of postcoloniality.

Chapter 6 covers the lesser known but ultimately more significant front of the decolonization war. For the Malayan elites who relied on the British for protection, the trauma of the Emergency resulted in the fledgling Malayan government's decision to exchange its export income in US dollars for sterling resulted in a loss of value for the Malayan currency. Among the Malayan elites, the decision to go along with British plans for Malayan currency reserves reflected a disavowal of the manifest colonial order that allowed Britain tribute of Malaya's export income in return for limited independence rather than a future governed by the Communists whose defiance of the British only emphasized the shame of the complicity of the Malayan elite. In effect, negotiations over currency exchange rates became a negotiation on how to price racial dignity.

The Emergency was the traumatic moment which gave birth to the Malayan state in 1957, out of which came the Malaysia in 1963 and Singapore in 1965. For the Malayan elite, recuperating power after political independence required a plausible performance of the right to power. Chapter 6 examines the scopic politics that reterritorialization took in the postcolonial Malaysian state in the 1960s–1970s. Legitimacy for anxious governments of newly independent countries was predicated on delivering economic growth. The trauma of the Emergency and the struggle for political independence followed by the Indonesian *Konfrontasi* from 1962 to 1965 and then the 13 May 1969 race riots created latent anxieties about the psychic legitimacy of the state. Focusing on the FELDA agricultural schemes, I show that the Malaysian government's defensive policy response focused on legitimizing power through a performance of its citizens that would construct the postcolonial nation within landscapes that were affirmative *because* they were economically productive.

The transformation of the global economy in the 1980s saw Malaysia, along with others in the region transformed from "developing" to "emerging" economies. But the economic "miracle" (World Bank 1993) also increased private sector debt to foreign investors and, as with much of the overheated and interconnected East Asian economies of that period, Malaysia was affected by the collapse of the economic bubble in the 1997–98 East Asian financial crisis. Chapter 7 focuses on the Malaysian and Western responses during the crisis. The Western focus became a vitriolic and racialized referendum on identity in the form of its criticism of Asian values, a term that became the shorthand category for referencing the cultural underpinnings of state agency in economic policy. Western anxieties of economically and geopolitically ceding its premier international position exposed the long denied racialized dimension of the global economic order.

In the aftermath of the 1997–98 financial crisis, Malaysia, as with other East Asian countries, recognized that sovereignty could be lost overnight. More significantly, in attributing the loss of sovereignty to a lack financial autonomy, the diagnosis called for carving out financial space as a buffer from predatory speculation. Chapter 8 tracks a few of the East Asian defensive strategies ranging from Malaysia's pivot from export-orientation to domestic consumption, Singapore's build-up of reserves via their government-linked enterprises (GLCs) including their sovereign wealth funds and finally, the creation of the Chiang Mai Initiative (eventually the Chiang Mai Initiative

Multilateralization or CMIM) which created a pool of credit available to its members in a liquidity crunch. The CMIM was created as an alternative to the Asian Development Bank (ADB) that caved in to US pressure to deny credit to affected countries in 1997–98. The CMIM, in its initial formation, still required operating within IMF guidelines, but its significance lay in providing a template for alternative financing eventually taken up by China's better resourced and independent of Western control banks.

In this book, I try to highlight that history and psyche are in constant dialectic and that this has produced certain configurations of social relations. I map certain historical moments of hegemony being created, meaning that in them we can see the production of certain modern "truths" about racial and national hierarchies in international relations and political economy. Colonialism, development and globalization all involve inequality and as such, these phenomena entail narcissistic injuries for different groups of actors. They masquerade as progress but are, in reality, realized through acts of aggression and humiliation. The high psychic costs destroy human potential and actually obstruct progress. The "homelessness" of globalization is a staple of popular media coverage, yet the homelessness engendered through the destruction of a safe space through colonization and its legacy has received little coverage. This book is the result of my search for a narrative that could convey the anxieties and consequences of this search for a safe space. It is my hope that in choosing to retell the stories of colonialism, development and globalization differently, we also tell another way of being. Until we make different choices, we cannot hope to find a different pattern. The contribution of psychoanalysis is to help us recognize and understand why we are driven to accept and repeat the cruelties of the past even when we find ourselves on the losing side. This book is a challenge that we can recognize and reject those cruelties.

Notes

1 The voting age was lowered to 18 from 21 for the first time since political independence in 1957.
2 And even China has used Singapore as a model of economic development (Lee 2000, 595–603).

1 Colonial Trauma and Postcolonial Anxieties

Introduction

The fugue is a musical form best associated with the composer Johann Sebastian Bach and refers to "a composition in which three or more voices enter imitatively one after another. Each voice has a theme, which is an answer to the voice that precedes it until all the voices have been answered" (Tucker 1983, 731). But the Shostakovich fugue differs from this form in that "[t]he repetitions are both obsessive and probing, not reassuring as they are in Bach; and those nearly undetectable background chords create an eerie, almost frightening sensation of extreme depth beneath the etched surface" (Lesser 2011, 109–110). The "answers" do not offer any resolution. Instead, barely audible chords induce anxiety thereby eliciting the powerful emotional response in the listener. This book aims to highlight the barely audible chords of colonial history in the depths of a country's political unconscious that haunts its postcolonial economic response. The postcolonial condition is, to invoke Philip Larkin (1977), "a special way of being afraid" that influences decision-making for the political elites of Malaysia. The issue for any non-Western country after World War Two was how to achieve economic growth to catch up with their former colonial rulers. In the Introduction, I suggested that discussions of the Malaysian economy can only be made sense of in terms of its embeddedness in global capitalism, national sovereignty and race relations. While global capitalism as a factor is taken for granted, the other two are rarely seriously factored into progressive scholarly discussions of non-Western capitalism, references to which are seen as opportunistic, or at best, inadvertent distractions by non-Western elites to excuse their failures. Yet, as we shall see in the following chapters, decisions on military alliances, currency exchange rates, agriculture, land tenure, and investment inherently appealed to unvoiced anxieties about the cultural hierarchies of entitlement for which sovereignty and race are used as shorthand signifiers.

Addressing economic growth brings up the obvious problem of how a nation-state goes about it. But this in turn brings up the corollary of what is economic growth for. The answer is not simply increasing a country's income but what its use signifies. This approach helps to explain prestige investment

DOI: 10.4324/9781315440286-2

projects as well as money-losing investments which are not always the consequence of incompetence. This, of course, is not to say that I condone individual greed. Related to the initial question of how to go about economic growth, is who to blame for the lack of it. The significance of the answer to this question ranges from whose moral obligation it is to fund development efforts to the unspoken underlying assumption of the essentialized abilities of different groups to achieve development. For if the West underdeveloped the rest, then the White Man's Burden becomes the White Man's Privilege, and the West forfeits its moral right to lecture everyone else on their shortcomings. Concurrently, the West also incurs the obligation to help rather than a privilege that it extends to the rest of the world while accruing moral credit. The answers to the above questions reframe policy issues: whose opinions matter and, therefore, who gets to decide the goals of development? In a libidinal economy of psychic exchanges, decisions in one arena are linked and traded off emotionally against decisions in others such as the draining of the wetlands in the Introduction, deforestation, military conflicts, plantation expansion, overseas investment and currency manipulation. Historically, each decision can best be understood as parts of a fugue in which historical action calls forth a response picked up by a subsequent action. All the while, barely audible chords that lie below the surface leave something over that cannot be captured—even as they elicit the most powerful response.

What follows is a survey of the theoretical concepts that constitute my framework of the libidinal economy to explain the dynamic construction of latent affects and hierarchies that legitimize economic policies. Broadly, I define the libidinal economy as a process of anxiety-driven exchanges. I construct a model of how the libidinal economy works through three concepts: trauma, anxiety and performativity and their relationship to a fourth concept, identity. A brief clarification here on terminology: in psychoanalytic literature and social theory more generally, identity, self and subject are often used interchangeably. I use the term identity mostly in referring to self-recognized factors such as culture, race, class, gender and nationality that distinguish one individual or group from another based on Rycroft's (1995, 76) definition. The subject is used when referring to an active agent as in the case of an individual acting on a perceived identity as is the case with Teresa Brennan (1993). The term self as used by Heinz Kohut (1973) is analogous in some ways to Brennan's subject because both are conceived as the active agent in the relationship with the other but with certain significant differences for the purposes of my argument. Brennan's subject arrives at its superior identity through constraining the range of options available for the other's identity. I have chosen to apply Brennan's schema to how mobility/immobility in space is a key part of the process of how the relative identities of subject and object are derived. In the case of Kohut's self-selfobject relationship, I am interested in the way the self arrives at a satisfied coherent identity through the perceived approval of the other, its selfobject. In that sense, when I reference Kohut, I apply his ideas to the narrative of the relationship whereas

I tend to reference Brennan when I am examining how interactions in space define relative identities. Obviously, the two schemas have not been used in isolation but have productive overlaps since in this book the construction of an inferior selfobject often was a condition of literally constraining the entity in space. Finally, I refer to the colonial state as the self but the postcolonial state as selfobject. My rationale in those categorizations is that the definition depends on the main power relation. In the colonial era, the state is the dominant subject. In postcoloniality, the Malaysian nation-state is in the less powerful position relative to Western actors in economic and international relations. I expand on Brennan's and Kohut's ideas in greater detail later in this chapter.

A recurrent theme throughout the book is the trauma of humiliation, which creates compliance in colonialism, development and globalization by shaping an anxiety-haunted identity—what Edward Said (1989, 207) referred to as a fear of "secondariness." Beginning with a brief review of discursive analysis in postcolonial thought as a departure point for my model of the libidinal economy, I build on concepts of trauma and anxiety derived from Freudian psychoanalysis, clinical psychology and Butlerian performativity. My model of the libidinal economy links trauma, anxiety and identity to explain the powerful emotional force driving economic decisions. The theories reviewed are not used in their "pure" form, but simply underwrite my narrative of the Malaysian economy. As in my use of the fugue metaphor, the perceptions and practices engendered by these theories repeat certain themes while altering emphasis, but the overall outcome is to build upon each other to "materially enable and politically mobilize" (Thomas 1994, 67). And the spaces in my story—plantation, forest, battlefield, even virtual ones such as financial markets—have fluid and porous boundaries that are recalibrated as events in one space affect another.

My central argument conceptualizes identity, in the form of the raced body, transformed into a narcissistic wound due to the trauma of colonialism.[1] Collective memory then triggers anxiety and defensive responses during the postcolonial era. Colonialism is traumatic through violence, territorial dispossession and humiliation. The gendered concept of castration here is referenced in the trauma of the original colonial wound and the consequent anxiety. For when the memory of the trauma is triggered by situations in globalization that have similarities, so that they are akin to repeated wounding, anxiety results. The defensive mechanisms entrained by the victim's anxiety lead to disavowal, alienation, self-constraint, introjection of perpetrator's values and attendant self-hatred, which is then projected onto weaker groups. In the case of nation-states, its victims can be racial minorities, immigrants, labor, LGBTQ people or weaker neighboring countries. So, I use the term "victim" reservedly in the context of a nation-state or other group identities but I justify its use when that group experiences trauma as a function of its disempowered position relative to another group. The above contests are justified, resisted and negotiated through performing and staging identities in the scripted discourses of colonialism, development and globalization. As in the musical fugue, the central theme of humiliation features as repeated trauma but in altered configurations in each era.

Discourse, Legitimizing Identity and Authority

The contemporary international hierarchy evolved from a common understanding of the complex rules that govern the value, access and distribution of material wealth. Michel Foucault (1972, 1980, 1994) explained how assumptions, values, concepts and procedures form a "coherent corpora" (1972, 6, 11) to construct meaning—a discourse. This organizes subjects by categorizing and placing information in relation to each other to present social conventions as natural truths which then justify exclusion and hierarchy. Foucault (1972, 6, 11, 14, 220, 227; 1994, 3–16, 218) notes that our tacit knowledge of where we are placed within that hierarchy is constructed through our respective cultures and time. His concepts were developed in the West but through colonization, development and globalization they are relevant for the postcolonial world (Hook 2004c, 213). The resulting narrative, far from being one of choices at different points, becomes "autochthonous" facilitating individuals in discovering meanings lying within language (Foucault 1972, 14–15, 227). The key to preserving power is to control the narrative that validates the significance of a piece of information (Foucault 1972, 224). In colonial, development and globalization discourses, "truth" is manifested in the form of a racialized meritocracy for economic success.

Edward Said's (1978) classic study *Orientalism* extends Foucauldian discourse to question how ideas acquired the status of natural truths during the period of high imperialism.[2] I mainly focus on Said even as I accept the criticisms of his work because I have taken the broad outlines of his postcolonial critique as a starting point. I direct interested readers to Moore-Gilbert (1997), Gandhi (1998), Kapoor (2008) and Hiddleston (2009) who all provide excellent and comprehensive discussions of postcolonial theory. Colonialism is a concrete process of invasion and seizure of material resources, but it is also a cultural project justifying the former that is possibly more damaging if it succeeds in promoting acquiescence among the colonized (Hiddleston 2009, 2). Understanding the discourse that justifies the value, access and distribution of resources in the postcolonial world requires questioning how relations of power were produced in the colonial world, by which Said (1978, 32) meant how ideas acquire authority during the period of high imperialism. During this period, Said argues one could mention the word "Oriental" and be sure that certain associations would be understood by it. Similarly, today, one could designate a place or a people as "developing" to conjure up certain images. Said (1978, 3) argues that the epistemological distinction between East (developing) and West (developed) becomes the starting point for elaborate theories concerning the Orient, in which difference translates into hierarchy. Discourse—recurrent, systematic tropes and asymmetries in representation—ran through colonial texts which constructed the Orient ontologically as an essentialized inferior Other to the West.[3]

Significantly, for my study, Said (1978, 3) writes that historically, "Orientalism was the corporate institution for dealing with the Orient—dealing with it by making statements about it, authorizing views of it, describing it, by teaching it, settling it, ruling over it." This echoes Foucault (1995, 138) in that it is a multiplicity of often minor processes, of different origin and scattered location, which overlap, repeat, or imitate one another, support one another, to converge and gradually produce the "blueprint" of a general method. The anatomy of discipline is in the coherence of details that create an overall method of control. Said made the distinction between manifest and latent Orientalism, where the former consists of codes and laws, while the latter is a corporate identity that influences the unconscious sense of the way things are or should be (Said 1978, 206–207). Said (1978, 7) notes that the importance of any knowledge is gauged by its proximity to economic decisions, but following Gramsci, he is more interested in the kinds of knowledge that allowed control through consent rather than outright force. This is especially relevant in the context of colonialism because of the long-standing conundrum of how so few dominated so many. The acceptance of evaluative judgements about oneself constitutes hegemony and the subsequent damage depends on the extent to which a subject population acquiesces with the external judgement of itself. I want to return the focus to economic decisions because they are cultural decisions too and have particular force in the contemporary world. Today, racist discourse on intellectual capability combines with neoliberal discourse so that those who fail economically are deemed even more culpable for having caused their own misfortune due to personal choices, which, in turn, are attributed to innate intelligence.

The paradigm of economic growth has come to define much of contemporary writing about the non-Western world albeit, with globalization, of the whole world. Where in the past colonial "attitudes" or "perceptions" implied personal prejudices, Said's reading of Orientalism shifted the parameters of the issue to a discourse by acknowledging the *systemic* aspect of such attitudes to *collective* identities whose asymmetries in representation underpin the presumptions of authority of those in power to legitimize institutional practices (Thomas 1994, 19), a presumption still relevant today. To call something postcolonial reframes its history in terms of the relations between colonialism and nationalism (Breckenridge and van der Veer, 1993, 1). This is not to essentialize national identity but to remind us that the nation-state, with its ties to race through colonialism, is still the unit through which subjective cultural evaluations, not to mention geopolitical and economic agreements, are negotiated practically. While Said's critique of Orientalism has been criticized for ignoring the nuances of history (Spivak 1988; Young 1990; Bhabha 1994; Jasanoff 2005), vicious discourses are no more ineffectual for their apparent contradictions. The political significance lies in the material consequences of these subliminal assumptions for ascribing blame and allocating rewards. An alertness to the unsaid helps resist its influence. Today, one can designate a country as developing or emerging and immediately conjure up images of poverty, inefficiency, corruption or not playing by the "rules," the last assumed to be universal and fairly applied. Orientalism supplied colonialism with a vocabulary, which was transmitted through generations by repetition and institutional embeddedness, living on in the discourses of globalization and international relations. Through its economic policies, Malaysia, as with other developing countries, was not just attempting to escape poverty but also the external representations of its categorical inferiority. The emotional urgency of postcolonial arguments emerges from the undercurrents of the unconscious anxiety of the once-colonized of an inherent "dreadful secondariness" (Said 1989, 207).

This history of key Malaysian economic moments is about how hierarchies based on difference evolve and translate into the realm of economic practice. The conflict over access and rights to resources opens questions of how certain categories of people became denigrated, and how denigration was used to justify denying these groups access to material wealth and control of their lives. I am not suggesting that discourse unilaterally determines what can be said about a country but that a whole network of interests, not always overt or even conscious, is involved on any occasion when developing countries or emerging economies are discussed. The dominance of the discourses that turns the Orient into a negative place lies in their "knitted-together strength" (Said 1978, 6), that is, the very close ties between socio-economic and political institutions domestically and internationally, which have continued across the postcolonial divide. In the same manner that Orientalism as a political doctrine could be willed over the Orient because the Orient was weaker, neoliberal economics today can be imposed as policy and practice on emerging economies. In common with the doctrine of the Civilizing Mission, experts from the World Bank and non-governmental agencies such as the Gates Foundation are seen by the West as a moral credit to themselves because of their altruism.

Bhabha's (1994) criticism of Orientalism argues that Said asserts too much intentionality in power relations, instead, shifting the focus to unstable and hybrid identities. Moore-Gilbert (1997) suggests that Bhabha especially offers a critique that is a form of *cultural and psychological guerrilla warfare* regardless of intentionality but goes on to argue that if resistance is unconscious, then undermining power can never be used strategically (137). Moreover, the most potent weapon of power is denial and historical re-invention in nationalist narratives to erase humiliating memories of colonization (Gandhi 1998, 4). I argue that the shame that underwrites the continuities across the postcolonial divide manifests itself as a form of overdetermined self-sabotage. Historical amnesia as a function of shame is reinforced by the spread of capitalism allowing more people into the "have" part of society thus creating the conditions for inter-class complicity. If colonial societies effectively disbarred most of the non-white population from an equal stake in protecting colonial property, in globalization, capitalism has replaced God as the all-forgiving entity whereby economic success becomes the one reliable criterion of worth. Therefore, even those on the losing end of capitalism may choose to support it because, following from the first point, money creates a fantastical form of democracy whereby status is theoretically available for purchase rather than as a function of birth or cultural capital. This book analyzes Malaysia's economic policies as attempts to appease its anxieties of belatedness.

Trauma and Anxiety: The Psychodynamics of Postcolonial Identity

If discursive analysis explains how we arrive at meaning through custom, we still need to explain the emotional force attached to certain meanings. According to Jean Francois Lyotard (Cooper and Murphy 1999), every economic exchange has an incommensurability not captured in political economy. This incommensurability is most apparent in counter-intuitive decisions that can best be understood as a libidinal economy. While Sigmund Freud originally tied all adult choices back to the infantile experience of trauma, even he acknowledged that factors beyond familial relations could play a role: "We cannot do justice to the characteristics of the mind by linear outlines like those in a drawing or primitive painting, but rather by colors melting into one another as they are represented by modern artists" (Freud 1965, 99). Freud (1959, 1962, 1965, 84–85) went on to extend the psyche to groups including nations. His great insight was to recognize that the processes that create a discourse may be buried so deeply that even when challenged with contradictory evidence, the discourse survives because of the psychic investment (Kahn 2002, 8–9). Psychic resistance then allows us to persist in patterns of destructive behavior (Freud 1966, 355). Psychoanalysis, by focusing on how the inner world of the unconscious frames the public calculus of decision-making, allows us to examine how ego ideals are extensions and implementations of power (Hook 2004c, 241). And it does so because complicity with power in one's own victimization requires psychological cooptation. The key to successful governance is to train personal choices to correspond to the requirements of power so that we appear to choose subjugation (Rose 1996, 116). I move on to outline a framework for understanding the psychodynamics of the power relationship.

To understand how economic framing became the preeminent means of identity construction through colonialism, I turn to Teresa Brennan's (1993) thesis of the foundational fantasy. For the masculine subject to be the locus of active agency, it must be anchored by the constrained and passified feminine object, a condition Brennan names the "Foundational Fantasy" (22). She positions the Western ego as an active, self-contained, and invulnerable subject, who arrives at that identity through the psychical fantasy of controlling the passive object as a fixed reference point (91–117). Brennan's (22–24) object is feminine, but it could be replaced by the native or nature—the point is that the masculine subject's identity is created with respect to a reference point it controls. The consequence of this dependence breeds *ressentiment* in the subject (111), which translates into narcissistic rage. Since this is a condition of aggression, the subject is always anxious of retaliation, thus driving the quest for further outlets for aggression which end in territorial expansion (Brennan 1993, 8). Objectification of the other requires establishing a spatial boundary between subject and object, as we see in Chapters 2, 3, 4 and 6 of this book. Furthermore, in this schema, the less powerful will identify with the powerful subject (52–56). But Brennan (1993, 61) also points out it is possible to occupy the dominant position in economic and/or institutional life while occupying the passified position in a different hierarchy. This condition is echoed in contemporary East Asian states, aside from China, which have economic status but struggle to change their position in the geopolitical hierarchy. I now move onto the dynamics of the subject-object relationship.

Departing from Freud, Heinz Kohut (1973, 619) differentiated between sexual desire and narcissism, instead viewing narcissism as an essential process in the creation of the self. If the other is the target of desire, anger, love, or aggression, that other is a selfobject, which he defined as a structure that accounts for the experience of continuity, coherence and well-being of the self. The selfobject can be music, culture or nature, and it can be archaic or contemporary (628). Its psychic function as a support for the vulnerable self is to provide an approving mirroring response (ibid), but it can also be the basis of extreme rage. The selfobject is meant to the basis for a narcissistic transference, but Kohut (1973, 477, 628, 756) argues that if the subject's prior experience has not allowed for transformation of the narcissistic cathexis into a healthy self-esteem, then deprived of an "approving mirroring response" from the selfobject, the grandiose self will experience a narcissistic injury and respond with extreme rage. It is important to recognize that the selfobject also seeks recognition from the self, and in the case of disempowered groups that do not have that approval forthcoming, they do not have the option of retaliating; they can only project that rage onto weaker groups or internalize the rage. The need to recalibrate the self over time triggers recognition of past trauma. But unlike Freudian psychoanalysis, which interprets the process linking latency to response as anxiety, that is, a reminder of past wounding rather than actual wounding, Judith Herman (2015) conceptualizes repeated trauma as part of *real* ongoing wounding. In colonialism, development and globalization, the colonized selfobject struggles to emerge into selfhood and in the process transforms into a recalcitrant selfobject that enrages the grandiose colonizing/Western self eliciting further trauma. Yet Kohut's (1973, 620) message is optimistic since he suggests that acknowledging narcissistic forces allows them to be transformed into realistic self-esteem. And he sees the path of transformation going from ego autonomy whereby one is aware to ego dominance where one uses one's awareness to shape one's goals; what Kohut (1973, 621–623) described as "man as effective participant on the stage of history." This is the crux of the policy challenge Malaysia along with other East Asian countries face—staying aware of the geopolitical dangers of Western narcissistic rage so that they can shape strategic responses while staying indifferent to external evaluations of themselves.

If economic success becomes a means of identity construction, then economic challenges become threats to identity, particularly group identity. For a group to exist, the fate of the group must become part of the individual's fate. But for this to happen, its members must understand what a group stands for and who qualifies for membership (Freud 1959a, 24–25, 72, 86). The appeals to race and ethnicity lie in the ease with which members are identifiable. The libido then attaches itself to the people who have a common investment; the libidinal tie is narcissistic. The individual is loved and protected in compensation for group loyalty (Freud 1959a, 44). But if identifying as part of a group makes individuals less vulnerable, they also take on new anxieties based on the group identity. Perceived injuries against the group become a personal injury, even as competition with other groups consolidates group identity (Freud 2004, 23, 48). Group identity requires sublimation of individual aggression which must now be projected onto an external object (Rose 2004, xii). Freud (1962, 23–27) also postulated that we derive intense enjoyment from the contrast. In this sense, the phenomena of racism and colonialism gave historic substance to the language used today in competitive discourses of development and globalization. Emerging as winners in economic competitions become a means of satisfying the impulse for contrast and exerting superiority; conversely, disrupting this contrast will be perceived as aggression by the status quo. Peter Gay (1994, 6–7) reminds us that acts of aggression must be culturally commensurable if they are to register as such. While violence is easily recognizable as aggression, it doesn't serve as an ego ideal in modern societies the way success in capitalist competition does. Groups need competitors to fix their identity, but they also require their competitors to recognize, acknowledge and desire them to maintain their ideal self-image—in Kohutian terms, to provide the approving mirror. Desire for total control is a common denominator of all forms of totalitarian control (Herman 2015, 76). Simple compliance is insufficient to justify oppression; its perpetrators need affirmations of love and gratitude from their victims (Herman 2015, 75). East Asian countries' adoption of the export-oriented manufacturing model of development first made them the ideal approving mirror in a racialized capitalist narrative that featured the West as the dominant subject. But the slow decline of Western manufacturing from the 1970s onwards and the rise of its former protégés as competitors trampled on the self-image of the omnipotent West setting the stage for emotionally charged economic competitions such as the Asian values debate (Chapter 7) and the current tech war between the US and China.

The Dialectics of Trauma

In everyday understanding, trauma is a physical wound or rupture of skin causing a catastrophic reaction in the entire organism (Leys 2000, 19). Psychic trauma, the experience which an individual is unable to resist and assimilate need not feature physical wounds but still produces long-lasting effects in the form of anxiety that triggers defensive behavior (Rycroft 1967, 187–188). Herman (2015, 33) defines the common denominator of trauma as the experience of "intense fear, helplessness, loss of control and threat of annihilation." Yet as a defensive mechanism, the victim will disavow the experience only to have the sedimented memories return to haunt it in the form of numbing, hypervigilance, overreaction, flashbacks and guilt (Leys 2000, 2). One of the paradoxes of trauma is that, from a psychoanalytical perspective, the past may be so deeply buried in our unconscious that we are not aware of its existence yet the ease with which trauma is triggered contradicts this assertion. Like the Shostakovich fugue at the start of the chapter, the faint chords are always present, eliciting a greater emotional response than the main melody. Our challenge is to track how this elaboration comes to pass.

Part of the trauma diagnosis is that it could not be resisted. In other words, for the purposes of this study, the trauma diagnosis already allows for the dimension of disempowerment inherent in societies being completely reorganized in colonialism, development and globalization. This is not to say that countries have no agency in international relations but that highly unequal power relations make non-compliance by less powerful countries unlikely. Moreover, the shame of not being able to resist compounds the trauma. And while the implicit threat of losing status through social change may be experienced ultimately as a trauma, the incremental nature of the changes means that they create an amorphous anxiety so that victims are confused as to the source of the threat (Herman 2015, 34–37). Yet there is an additional step that is the signature of trauma: Herman's (2015, 39–41) assertion that someone "got away" with something reinforces the sense of helplessness and humiliation because the perpetrator is usually too powerful to challenge, thus driving its victims to look for scapegoats. This situation is symptomatic of political trauma. She (20) defines repeat trauma as a situation in which damage can be inflicted repeatedly and can arise through economic, social, legal or psychological barriers creating coercive control (74, 116).

For Freud (1959b, 67–68), the original trauma is the loss of the mother as an object of desire. Subsequently, this trauma is repeated when the subject is threatened with the loss of the penis (which he termed castration anxiety), of the object's love, and ultimately, the super-ego's love (Freud 1959b, 55–70). But the recognition of trauma can be long in surfacing. He (65) suggested that trauma was constituted by two experiences: the original trauma which could not be assimilated by the victim, and the second event that triggers the memory of the first which only then comes to be understood as traumatic. The interpretation involves latency and retrospection through which the first act comes to take on meaning—the return of the "outlaw" repressed (Freud 1959b, 86). Hence, trauma is unstable because of the unconscious motives that confer meaning which changes over time. My use of latency is adapted from Freud because I have used the concept in conjunction with Herman's concept of repeat or complex trauma. In this usage, the latent period between each wounding allows for adaptation to a new social equilibrium.

Colonial and postcolonial trauma and their attendant pathologies are dialectically related across space and in time. In Chapter 8, interviewees responded to questions about their decision-making by reflecting that that personal and national/collective histories are intertwined. Herman (2015, 74) reflects that the perpetrators of trauma escape censure because they are aware of social norms and can maintain the appearance of morality. But in colonialism, development and globalization, the perpetrators **create** the social norms through corporate ensembles involving economic, cultural and intellectual institutions backed by force. Among the formerly colonized, long after political liberation, people who have been subjected to coercive control bear the psychological scars of captivity (Herman 2015, 95). Repeat trauma is a slow drip that destroys the sense of the agentic self. Inequality is traumatic because of the humiliation of lacking basic needs but also because of the lack of respect and constant emotional labor of accommodation to those in power. Colonialism, development and globalization function as repeat trauma which trigger anxiety entraining the defensive mechanisms of disavowal, alienation, projection and introjection.

Conversely, for those used to being in power, the challenge or steady erosion of entitled privilege in the social compact comes to be experienced as trauma. More interestingly, as we are seeing even in the Western world now, it is not necessarily only those directly impacted who are displaying symptoms of trauma but everyone who can **imagine** themselves as potential victims of the phenomenon as a function of shared identity. In postcolonial pathology as manifested in the West, former colonizers cannot acknowledge the interdependency and the fact that Western prosperity is built on colonial oppression because this would undermine the hegemonic narrative of a morally superior, and thus deserving, successful West. This is why identity battles feature so prominently in political battles that showcase economic contests such as the Trump supporters in the US, Brexit supporters in the Britain and Asian values debate in the Asian financial crisis (see Chapter 7). Trauma, for Bollas (2011, 174) and Herman (2015, 1–2), operates on the logic of a population's unconscious need to believe in a social compact, what Herman refers to as the "dialectic of trauma"—because it involves both victims and witnesses. But she goes further in arguing that shattered expectations mean that each person only retains a fragment of the scene—knowledge is not only illusory, it is also partial. It is even more difficult to find a language to articulate the "unspeakability" of trauma because trauma attaches shame to its victims (Herman 2015, 2). My challenge in this book is to track the postcolonial consequences despite the stigma of colonialism being attached to the victims rather than the perpetrators. For denial, repression and disassociation operate on political and social levels as well as the individual level so that trauma has an "underground" history (Herman 2015, 2). This line of questioning is controversial, as I noted in the Introduction, because when trauma is consequence of human actions, we cannot be neutral and avoid blame. Precisely because colonialism was a massive project undertaken by a corporate effort, its consequences are problematic to address because they implicate many people and for better or worse, throw light on the head start that some have that makes beneficiaries reluctant to highlight their privilege. Equally disadvantageous in addressing the consequences of trauma is the victim's shamed disavowal of the experience.

Below I review the steps to establish control through trauma taken from Herman's (2015) study and apply it to a political context. The key aim is to instill a sense of helplessness so that the victim comes to introject the victimizer's values. Capitalism, with its emphasis on competition and survival of the fittest, is well suited for creating trauma through pitting groups against each other. In Chapter 8, I describe how the US and the IMF pressured Japan to withhold emergency loans to affected East Asian countries in the 1997–98 financial crisis. The final step in total psychic conquest is forcing victims to violate their own moral principles and betray each other (Herman 1992, 83). This is the most important step because it creates suspicion and prevents solidarity, but just as importantly, it creates self-hate which further disempowers victims. In Chapter 4, I describe the "land for life" campaign created by the British to sow distrust among the Malayan population during the Emergency.

The Logic of Trauma

The anxiety of humiliation and the desire for dignity are acted out in the global economy by investing economic decisions with savage competition beyond the endpoint of pure material accumulation. The term anxiety, derived from "angst" —"angustiae' and 'enge" which in the original German and Latin words mean "narrow place" and "straits" has a twofold origin—as a direct consequence of the traumatic moment and as a signal anticipating the moment repeating itself (Freud 1965, 118, 1966, 493, note 9, 340–341). The narrowing of options also recalls Brennan's condition of objectification. Freud (1959b, 12, 62–63) linked anxiety to trauma through memory which he signaled using the word "heritage." Freud (1959b, xxix–xxxi) traced trauma to the libido through the process of narcissistic wounding when confronted with a loss of either the love object or self-love (Freud 1959b, 58, 65–68). He distinguished between realistic anxiety, which he termed "intelligible" as a signal to expect physical injury from an external threat, and neurotic anxiety which is "free floating" and attaches itself to any possibility that threatens the loss of love (1965, 103, 110, 116). This book is about the costs of appeasing the anxiety of potential humiliation and the passionate craving for dignity. Frantz Fanon (1967, 19) foresaw the consequences of appeasement as a bifurcation into social alienation for the desiring anxious subject on the one hand and the scapegoating of even weaker populations on the other. Anxiety arises as a reaction to a state of danger and is reproduced whenever a similar state recurs and the ego is reduced to state of helplessness in the face of excessive need (Freud 1959b, 72). Castration then becomes a psychological category for referencing trauma, threat and anxiety. The fear of the Father is depersonalized into the super-ego, while the fear of castration transforms into social or moral anxiety (Freud 1959b, 56, 1965, 77). And fear of expulsion from the group and its protection corresponds to introjected parental authority (Freud 1959b, 69–70). Yet, even if the symptoms are consciously perceptible, their predeterminants escape consciousness (Freud 1966, 345, 448).

Freud's distinction between real and neurotic anxiety is less likely to hold the lower down the economic food chain for countries where the threat to material and psychic survival are intertwined. Fanon (1967, 134) famously described living in a dominant culture as "meaning that was already there, pre-existing, waiting for me," underscoring the fugue-like reciprocity between psychology and politics. Within the framework of the libidinal economy, I argue that developing countries/emerging economies respond to the anxieties triggered by the unequal international relations, in which rules are devised elsewhere, by manifesting the following cycle of trauma. Western narcissistic rage at being challenged on their place in the foundational fantasy results in trauma inflicted on the colonized/developing country/emerging economy. Victims then respond with (1) projection of their perceived failures onto racial minorities, poorer citizens or weaker neighboring countries, (2) disavowal of the inequity of the rules, (3) alienation from their own values, (4) identification with the idealized aggressor and introjection of the aggressor's values and finally, in closing of the cycle, (5) the performance of activities that signal success within those values.

Projection

Heinz Kohut's (1973, 644) concept of the selfobject offers a different defensive response from Freud, that of narcissistic anger, of which rage is an extreme version. Rage is activated because the recalcitrant selfobject is not seen as an autonomous source but as a flaw in a narcissistically perceived reality, over which the narcissistically vulnerable person had expected to exercise control. Thus, the other person's independence or (in)difference is experienced as offensive. But the selfobject also offers a canvas upon which negative traits that cannot be reconciled within the self are projected. And Bollas (2011, 81) reminds us that under intense emotional pressure such as envy or anxiety, any individual's or group's negative traits will be projected externally to coalesce into stereotypes. This is the crux of Western behavior to challenges, real or perceived, to its authority in colonialism and globalization. Given that Kohut (643–645) posits that narcissists must exert absolute control over their environment and unconditional availability of the approving mirroring for the maintenance of self-esteem, they will destroy opponents who dare to outshine them because this contradicts the self-image of the grandiose self. Global power competitions create intense anxiety because the only identity that counts is that of an economic winner, since that is the prerequisite to winning in other arenas. Anyone can experience narcissistic injury and react with rage but only the powerful can inflict trauma on the less powerful while the latter must bear their trauma as best they can. Postcolonial countries such as Malaysia recognize that the outlet for their narcissistic rage must be weaker groups such as poorer countries or domestically, labor unions and minority groups.

The key that narcissistic rage is involved is an obsession with the situation, which Kohut (1973, 642) attributes to the narcissist's inability to recognize their opponent as an independent entity. We see this in Chapters 3 and 4 in Britain's response to the demand for political independence by Malaya and again in Chapter 7, in the success of the East Asian countries from the 1990s onwards. Kohut (637–638) suggests that narcissistic rage occupies a very specific position in the spectrum defined by an obsession for revenge because of an archaic fixation, whereby narcissistic rage is as much a reaction to a past relation rather than the one ostensibly at hand (628, 635). In the case of decolonization and East Asian economic successes, Western reaction can be interpreted through a historic sense of entitlement. Similarly, the East Asian reaction to narcissistic wounding is also triggered and constrained by past relations. Bollas (2011, 176) goes on to hypothesize that extreme reactions occur as part of an unconscious restructuring of past trauma in which the subject puts others through the unconscious terms of extinction of the self. In this logic, aggressive narcissists identify only with those aspects of their identity that provide them with admiration and sense of superiority (Bollas 2011, 82). In Chapter 7, I argue that Western contempt and ridicule of Asian values is a reflection of narcissistic rage at the economic challenge, but I suggest it is also a function of the West projecting its own anxieties of the social upheaval that accompanied the transition from a manufacturing to service economy in the 1970s onward that inaugurated contemporary globalization and continues today.

Disavowal

Frantz Fanon (1967) argued that colonial anxieties were anchored in the socio-economic realities of powerlessness and its attendant humiliations experienced by the colonized. Capitalism inevitably creates winners and mostly losers rather than fulfilling the promise of uplifting all. Thus, within the fantasy of global capitalism, incommensurable factors that cannot be reconciled within the "rules" of the system must be disavowed. Žižek (1997) saw disavowal, in the case of capitalism, as the logical outcome of an ideology that ignores the unpleasant realities of inequality and oppression which are the necessary conditions of capitalist success. But he suggests that the disavowal is accepted by those disadvantaged by capitalism only if the ideology succeeds in the displacement or distortion of their "authentic longings" for a better life (Žižek 1997, 28–29). In the case of emerging economies, the ideological hegemony of the global capitalism succeeds when the longing to be conferred "full human status," in Johnson's words (1982, 53), persuades its victims to collude in its arbitrary rules and adopt historical amnesia. By accepting the ahistoricism and seemingly political neutrality of capital, developing countries in the 1960s and 1970s and now emerging economies disavow their concerns about the global economic system that disadvantages them. Thus, disavowal contains within it the idea that props up power. This can take the following forms: a discourse of power needs to get away with taking advantage of the oppressed; from the perspective of the oppressed, the disempowerment works not simply because they are taken advantage of, but also because they know what is being done to them and have few avenues to challenge their oppression. Moreover, they must collude with the oppression, thus further disempowering the subject through the shame of collusion.

Alienation

Alienation within the capitalist mode of production is defined as a situation when that the worker invariably loses the ability to determine their life and destiny through their relationship with other people as well as from the value of the goods and services produced with their labor (Hayes 2004). Psychological alienation is described as the estrangement from oneself and from others (Rycroft 1967, 6). Alienation is a product of anxiety as a legacy of trauma. The self splits to distance itself from its inferiority. But alienation then creates further anxiety and by shaping an individual or groups' actions, creates their identity. Fanon described alienation through colonial experience as a mutilated body: "My body was given back to me, sprawled out, distorted, recolored, clad in mourning ..." (1967, 113). Less poetically, the practical consequence of disavowal and alienation from what is happening before one's eyes is ego withdrawal resulting in constrained options (50, 60). But there are limits to ego withdrawal before the subject runs out of options. In the language echoed by Brennan (1993) 35 years later referencing gender, Fanon described the racialized body's movement in the world as "fixed" by white eyes, so that the victim of racism instead will seek admittance into the "white sanctuary" to escape externally imposed constraints (1967, 51, 116). In economics, this is evident in the assumption of achievement only through certain pre-determined pathways, which for non-Western countries in the 1950s to 1960s meant pursuing Walt Rostow's (1960) Stages of Growth model of industrialization and in the 1980s adopting the neoliberal strategy of open markets and minimal state intervention. Alienation results in inability to judge so that those who are also victimized are seen as one's enemies while the perpetrators are seen as allies. But the colonized, politically or psychologically, as Nandy (1983, xiv) points out, are not simple-hearted victims, they fight for survival consciously, by default or in self-contradictory ways. I take up this point when I discuss conscious performativity rather than unconscious introjection of Western ego ideals.

Introjection

Introjection is the internalization of the values of someone more powerful, which requires the repression of one's own desires. Introjecting the values of someone who does not have one's interest at stake is to understand one's self in negative terms. Citing Lacan, Adamson and Clark (1999, 181) define desire not a biological drive but a seeking of recognition from the other. Thus, humiliation is the experience of the other's negative evaluation of oneself; it is not necessarily the gaze we encounter but how we think we appear to the other. This is particularly true of the ego ideal. Anxiety manifests itself in the form of both what is feared AND what is desired. The stereotyped self becomes abjected (humiliated) while simultaneously desiring and introjecting the characteristics of the ego ideal. Thus, the development or postcolonial subject reconstructs this abjected self image each time it imagines itself incorporating the values of Western, capitalist modernity such as those of the international financial system. For the purposes of my study, a logical extension of this insight is that economic success becomes the antidote to abjection—above a certain financial level, one is white. Fanon (1967, 47) referred to the analogous cultural process of "lactification," in which a better command of language and cultural symbols, made one "whiter." Today, the ultimate symbols of power are money and technology. Thus, when East Asian economies followed a capitalist, technology-intensive trajectory in accumulating wealth as part of the strategy for challenging the international hierarchy, they can be perceived as engaging in a lactification process. Malaysia's trajectory was complicated by the need to appease a racial constituency which demanded economic policies that favored labor-intensive practices.

Performing Agency

Globalization, as an economic phenomenon, builds on the legacy of colonial discourse that inscribes the non-West in a passified role. Even if psychoanalysis exposes a person's unconscious motivations, translating that awareness, however partial, into a conscious strategy for challenging power is the true political test. Any attempt to escape the passified role by formerly colonized selfobjects is perceived as wounding by the Western self. For emerging economies, the challenge to changing their position of passified selfobjects is compounded by the threat of the inevitable rage of the wounded grandiose Western self. Judith Butler's (1990, 1997) theory of performativity offers a pathway for resistance. Butler used the Althusserian concept of interpellation to argue that a subject "exists" not only by virtue of being recognized, but by being recognizable (1997, 5, 28). Arguing that identity is not ontological but continually created as an illusion "through language, gesture, and all manner of symbolic social sign" (Butler 1990, 270), she described this as a "discursive constitution" (1997, 19). This is especially helpful for fledgling nationalist projects such as the Federal Land Development Authority (FELDA) schemes described in Chapter 6. Thus, interpellation as a form of identity constitution "assumes its specific proportion in time" requiring our tacit acknowledgement of historical hierarchy (Butler 1997, 2). She concedes that identity construction need not be conscious for it to work as it succeeds through its embeddedness within a mesh of signification that exceeds self-knowledge (1990, 310, 1997, 28, 34). Butler's conception of interpellation is organic: it refers to *cumulative* existing circuits of signification in that each act of recognition reinforces the process; it is *combinatory* because interpellation simultaneously appeals to several circuits of recognition. Butler (1990, 272, 310), like Foucault, argues that it is by endlessly citing the conventions and ideologies of the social world that we naturalize artificial conventions, but her formulation as a *dialectic* between performer and performance, a form of social fugue, opens a space for the process of intervention and adaptation in a positive identity construction as we see in Chapters 6 and 8.

Identity constitution through interpellation, thus, requires a mutual acknowledgement of the same social structures. Name-calling rests on certain conventions invoked at the moment of utterance, whether the person has the authority or whether the staging is right (Butler, 1997, 3, 36). In contrast to Fanon who argued that racialized bodies took on meaning that pre-existed them, Butler's contingent identity is hopeful because it can be changed and helpful in terms of constructing an agentic identity. Using Butler, I show in Chapters 6 and 8 that that in striving for positive recognition, developing countries/emerging economies attempted to insert their identities into the existing symbolic orders of capitalism and technology. Even partial self-awareness allows strategic misrecognitions of identity by subjects. This strategy allows subjects to manipulate what aspects of the interpellative process they *choose* to recognize. Shifting identities can be conflicting, but we can choose to emphasize some of them to our advantage. Negotiating better opportunities involves *conscious* appropriation and compromise. Less powerful countries have learnt the hard way that economic destruction, at worst annihilation, is the price of open insubordination to the global order. I argue that the key factor in actively using a psychoanalytical framework to understand policy strategy is recognizing that the East Asian emerging economies consciously interjected themselves as a middle-ground between the powerful West and the rest of the world even as this new relationship creates different geopolitical challenges. But to do so required that they understood and acknowledged the psychological ecosystem of international relations.

Conclusion

The world as social system is given expression by people who can reproduce a historical situation (imperialism) or subvert and change it. We miss the point when we criticize East Asian countries for merely reproducing capitalist relations. They are simply acknowledging, consciously or not, the shorthand signifiers of the cultural hierarchy in contemporary international relations and the global economic order. Yes, they are reproducing capitalist relations, but their goal is to subvert race relations that have condemned them to poverty for the last 250 years. Reproducing capitalist relations is simply the price tag. East Asian countries also see the need to find a common language if they want to change how they are seen by the desired other and capitalism is that common language. The second point I want to make is that if identity is to change, it must seem "autochthonous" (Foucault 1972, 14–15, 227). Butler (1997, 12) adds that actions require a venue or theater by which their performative effects may be materialized. Thus, the scale of transformation coupled with staging and theatricality are important for transforming assumptions, for it is the quotidian and ritualized forms that legitimize identity through habit performed on physical stages such as the FELDA schemes or virtual ones such as foreign exchange markets. Rather than Fanon's alienated self, I argue that in Malaysia, as with other East Asian countries, we are seeing a mutual constitution of agentic identity through the creation of a symbolic order that they can subscribe to by being consciously aware of the limits of performativity in negotiation.

Notes

1 While raced bodies have a class position, under colonialism, race formed the key signifier of identity. White working class men could change status if they were economically successful, but even Asian elites were still subordinate to their white counterparts.

2 Imperialism does not have to include the direct rule and conquest of colonialism but Said (1978) used both terms interchangeably to refer to the period of European political and cultural dominance from the mid-18th century onwards when large-scale conquest, administration and social and economic transformation of the non-European world by Europeans took place.

3 The first real challenges to equal status by non-white countries have been met by Western countries with great hostility. Geopolitically, this was and is evident in the reaction to Japan's and now China's economic success.

2 The Foundational Fantasy of Colonial Ecology

Introduction

The town of Teluk Anson, now Teluk Intan, was the site of an incident in the early years of British colonialism in Malaya that signifies a second and equally crucial encounter in which the first was embedded; the introduction of the railway through colonialism. According to a version of this tale, on the morning of the maiden trip of the train on the railway, British officials and local dignitaries were watching as the train approached the stop when a bull elephant stepped out and locked its tusks on the engine in an effort to stop this "monster" encroaching into its territory. The early trains were small and the outcome was not predictable, but after an agonizing passage of time the elephant collapsed, dead from a crushed skull. The grisly evidence of this incident is preserved in the town museum in the form of the cracked skull. The story has entered folklore and I heard various versions as a child.

This incident is suggestive of several interpretations. On that day in which the elephant halted the train, the indigenous briefly forced the Empire to a standstill. The tale can also be read as irrational nature confronting rational Western technology. And while details of the tale vary, the elephant was a bull elephant in all accounts I have heard. I think this point is suggestive of a once neglected aspect of the colonial encounter now seen as a male/colonizer encounter with the female/colonized other; the impotence of the native male to stop the colonial penetration that feminized colonized space. The technological arrival of the train also signals the arrival of capitalism in Malaya, interestingly, courtesy of the revenues raised by Chinese tin miners whose taxes paid for the early railways, rather than British investment (Voon 1971). I have interpreted this story as one of how the empire/capital nexus came to depend upon each other for their mutual survival and legitimacy, tracing the implications of this nexus for the construction of the agentic Western self and the passified native/nature selfobject in colonialism's foundational fantasy. I argue that the process of capital intrusion and resource appropriation by British colonialism was paralleled by the discursive construction of the colonized selfobject through the processes of physical reconfiguration and territorial constraint.

DOI: 10.4324/9781315440286-3

Any attempt to deal with the signification of the tropical rainforest in the colonial world must also deal with capitalism, which was at the center of colonial economies, and its diffracted image of nature—the plantation. Through colonialism, plantation agriculture came to be the new nature of the Malaysian environment, more recognizable than the disappearing forests. In colonial Malaya, as in many other European colonies in the nineteenth century, the transformation of the environment and the imposition of a new socio-economic hierarchy were legitimized by the rhetoric of modernization. Because the plantation system in Southeast Asia was not associated with slavery as its counterpart in the Americas, its existence is still perceived to be an unproblematic progressive force. Yet the plantation system had far-reaching consequences for Malaysian society because of the subsequent physical and demographic changes warranted by the economic changes, as well as the way nature and natives were captured and incorporated into the social imaginary. The plantation both reflected and instilled many ideological and philosophical attitudes toward nature and race: attitudes physically manifested through the changes wrought on the physical environment and through the plantation system's division of labor. The needs of the plantation economy reorganized Malayan social relations and plantation economies became plantation societies. In Chapter 2, I argue that a recognizable pattern of social, cultural, political relations and, ultimately, psychological relations came into place almost literally as places on the social hierarchy were mapped onto physical space. Adopting the plantation model, to a certain extent, commits a society to following certain pathways of relating to each other and to the state. In Malaya, this resulted in a society that justified repression and discrimination against certain groups in terms of sacrifices that are prerequisites to economic success.

Framing the Fantasy

Chapter 2 provides a brief historical background to Malaya's colonial encounter. I cover the introduction of plantation agriculture, which induced a scarcity of arable land and transformed agricultural production driven by subsistence needs to one driven by surplus demand. Labor requirements of the plantation system also resulted in large-scale immigration creating ethnic tensions among the non-white population, a legacy that continues to overdetermine contemporary domestic politics. These changes were accompanied by a discourse that constructed nature and native populations as inferior to the modernity of Westerners to justify the former's material dispossession, which in time would transform into a racialized hierarchy and a psychic shift in identity. The chapter is framed conceptually in three ways which are explained in greater detail in Chapter 1. Starting from the premise that the arriving British come from a place of unstable identity as a function of a Europe transforming through the Scientific and Industrial Revolutions, I reference Kohut's (1973) self-selfobject relationship to argue that for both material and psychological reasons, colonial identity needed native populations and nature to provide a narcissistic experience that would bolster its psychic coherence. I use Kohut's (1973, 628, 637–638) term selfobject when referring to native populations and nature. Kohut (1973, 629) sees a selfobject as providing essential support for the vulnerable self through "approving mirroring responses," which become the basis of self-esteem.

Next, citing Teresa Brennan's (1993) concept of the foundational fantasy, I argue that the colonizing British conceived themselves as the superior active geopolitical and economic agents of modernity, contingent quite literally through replacing heterogeneous nature, the Malayan rainforest, with monocultural plantations and spatially constraining native populations in reserves and plantations. This superior Western identity relies on scientific rationality manifested through use of technology to control its environment. Brennan (1993, 91–117) argues that the Western ego as agentic, self-contained and invulnerable arrives at its identity through the psychical fantasy of controlling the passive other as a fixed reference point. In Brennan's (52–53) schema, an objectifying projection is a condition of subjectivity because it is only through creating the fantasy of a fixed inferior (nature and natives) that the Western imperialist can overcome the anxiety of its own unstable identity. In colonial Malaya, constraining nature and native was achieved through physical transformation and standardization through the plantation system that replaced the biodiverse rainforest with monoculture and restricted native population access to space and financial investment and, finally, codifying and rationalizing these practices through legal jargon, albeit, always underwritten by force.

I now want to turn to how the above practices are organized to produce a "coherent corpora" (Foucault 1972, 6, 11) to construct the "truth" that governed the value, access and distribution of resources in the colonial world (15). Foucault (1995, 138) suggests that it is "a multiplicity of often minor processes, of different origin and scattered location, which overlap, repeat, or imitate one another, support one another, distinguish themselves from one another according to the domain of application, converge" and gradually produce the 'blueprint" for control. Recall that Edward Said (1978, 206–207) argues that the dominance of the discourses that turns the Orient into a negative place lies in their "knitted-together strength" (6), that is, the very close ties between socio-economic and political institutions, Orientalism supplied colonialism with the vocabulary transmitted through generations by repetition and institutional embeddedness, living on in the standards and values. By the 1930s, the needs of the plantation economy had transformed Malayan society to become a fact of life replete with attitudes, rules and hierarchies that acted as intellectual gateways to fulfill the psychic function of the selfobject as an "approving mirror" (Kohut, 1973, 629) for the colonial self.

Constructing the Foundational Fantasy of Colonial Ecology

The British foothold in Malaya began on the island of Penang in 1786, followed by Singapore in 1819 and then Malacca in 1824 (see Winstedt 1988; Turnbull 1989; Nonini 1992 for a historical overview). British possessions in Malaya were administered by the Government of India until 1867 when they were made a Crown Colony and administered by a Governor. There was a lull in territorial expansion until 1874 when the British assigned an advisor to the Sultan of Perak in the wake of civil unrest within both the local Malay and the Chinese immigrant populations. Ramasamy (1994) has suggested that the British may have been looking for an excuse to intervene as their plans to develop land commercially depended upon political stability and consolidation. Between 1874 and 1914, British residents or advisers were appointed to the courts of Malay rulers in nine states. By 1914, all of Malaya was under British rule with the Malay sultans providing legitimacy as figureheads in the administration (Winstedt 1988; Turnbull 1989). In the wake of British plans for agricultural development, a mutually reinforcing spatial and racial division evolved in Malaya. In this section I briefly sketch the evolving spatial division of Malaya according to the main racial groups: the Malays, Chinese, Indians and British. Such a division developed in tandem with the resource-based capitalist economy during the colonial period leading up to World War Two. I note here that there are also indigenous forest dwellers known in Malaya as the *Orang Asli*. Many of them still live in forest reservations and interaction with the rest of the population was, and still is, limited (Williams-Hunt 1952; Noone 1972; Endicott 2015). However, my main concern is with the interactions between the Malays, Chinese, Indians and British and the competition for arable lowlands. As competition for valuable land increased, it was precisely this competition that led to conflict between the different groups.

The British rulers instituted a new system of land tenure that was based on individual ownership and which allowed Malays to dispose of their lands without the consensus of their community. In addition, the new classification of land use based on occupied land, lands allocated for transport and lands suitable for agricultural enterprise or mining effectively meant that the British reserved the right to three out of the four categories of land use by decree. After 1875, all land not previously occupied and thereby covered by *adat* or customary law, became state land to be disposed of by the state (Maxwell 1883; see Brookfield et al. 1991 for a summary of colonial land tenure laws). While it is debatable whether widespread non-compliance by the non-European population with this new legal system would have halted British acquisition of the best lands, it is useful here to recall Said's (1993, 69) point about Joseph Conrad's awareness of the need of a justificatory regime for greed. In this case, disguised by imposing new property laws, the ritual and order embodied in the new legal system imparted a sense of propriety and provided the vocabulary to justify what was essentially theft. Through the loss of tax revenues engendered by this transformation of land tenure, the power of the Malay rulers over their people became symbolic. The rulers would pay a high price for inviting the British into alliances against local enemies. The changing form of land tenure was significant because of the accompanying transition of agricultural production from self-sufficiency to surplus. Over the course of 80 years, native populations were slowly constrained within the boundaries set by the new land legislation.

Rubber and Malaya

After British colonization of Penang, Singapore and Malacca, immigrants from southern China were imported to mine tin and grow export crops such as pepper, nutmeg, gambier and sugar cane (Jackson 1968; Morgan 1996). These immigrants were organized as *kongsis*, based on the region of origin in China, each headed by a *Kapitan* who arranged for their immigration. In fact, the Chinese rather than the British pioneered plantation agriculture in Malaya. While the early definition of a plantation was land cultivated for export purposes, in the twentieth century the term "estate" was often conflated with plantation (Jackson 1968, xiv). In this study, I have taken the term "estates" to refer to plantations over 100 acres; smaller acreages are smallholdings (*The Malayan Agricultural Journal* 1939, 214). The early Chinese settlers, who possessed little capital and intended to return to China, opted for crops that yielded quick returns. Chinese cultivators were useful to colonial authorities because they cleared the forest and expanded the agricultural frontier while paying taxes to the British (Bird 1967; Jackson 1968). Chinese agricultural settlements were organized separately from both the Malays and the British, nor were they allowed on Malay land or to trade with the Malays (ibid). These agricultural communities were the first step in creating a rural Chinese population that existed beside, but separate from, the Malay population. This segregated system meant that the different ethnic groups had very little interaction with each other. Early plantations were extensions or fringes of the forest rather than an alternate form of green space. Texts written in English from the mid-1880s to before World War Two by travelers or colonial civil servants, or about that period by later authors, used the terms "forest" and "jungle" interchangeably (Clifford 1929; Bird 1967; Winstedt 1988; Aiken 1994). The advent of rubber cultivation would upset this balance. The porous boundaries were replaced with ones hardened and coded by difference—racial demographics, land tenure laws and type of vegetation. The most dominant trope was that of economic potential. European perception of the landscape was always inflected through the needs of Empire so that cash-cropping was the lens through which they visually recorded Malaya (Bird 1967; Thomson 1984). But Bird's early form of public relations for the needs of empire underscores the knitted together strength of the discourse that transformed Malayan nature and native populations into selfobjects for the colonial self.

European plantations in Malaya followed in the wake of the railroads and were initially dedicated to coffee but they were unsuccessful, and it was only with the advent of rubber that European commercial agriculture took off (Jackson 1968). In the nineteenth century, the high price of wild Amazonian rubber was enough to persuade countries which possessed tropical colonies to cultivate rubber (Brockway 1979; Hecht and Cockburn 1990). The difficulty lay in getting the rubber seedlings; not surprisingly, the Brazilian government made it a crime to remove wild rubber seedlings from Brazil. It was not until 1877 that rubber seedlings were shipped to Singapore; of these, nine were planted in the garden of the British Resident in the state of Perak. The issue of whether the seeds were shipped out of Brazil illegally is still controversial today. The British denied this charge (Wickham 1908; Ridley 1955; Wycherley 1960). The British emphasis on denying any association of illegality with the initial shipment of rubber seeds underscores Edward Said's (1993, 69) argument that imperialism needed the justification of high purpose. In the age of high imperialism, commercial enterprise would seek to distance itself by any means *rhetorically*, if not in practice, from the ugliness of profit since commerce was now part of the project to exploit the earth's resources for the benefit of the human race. Brennan (1993, 91–117) reminds us that a condition of superior Western identity in the age of the ego is a denial of vulnerability and dependency. With reference to Kohut (1973) this denial was necessary to preserve the imperial perception of the morally superior grandiose self whose good fortune was independent of its selfobjects. The first Malayan rubber planters in 1895 were Chinese and British, but because rubber takes five to six years to mature, investment in rubber required capital to which European planters had easier access (Headrick 1988, 245). Thus, European planters were in a better position to take advantage of this new crop.

To promote European-owned plantations the colonial government introduced land use legislation in 1896 which alienated new agricultural lands from non-Europeans (Brookfield et al. 1991). The idea was to standardize the laws of ownership and transfer to regulate administration of lands, an important issue in a country undergoing rapid development of commercial resource extraction. But in terms of realizing Brennan's (1993) foundational fantasy, this had the effect of literally constraining native populations in spaces that became visual signifiers of their inferior status. The colonial government tried to encourage cultivation by granting large blocks of land rent free (to Europeans), offering loans on easy terms, bringing in more immigrant labor and extending roads and railways to improve communication and transportation to the isolated plantations (Ramasamy 1994, 91). When floating a company on the market, the directors were apt to use the proximity of railways lines as a selling point (Gow, Wilson and Stanton Ltd. 1906). Non-Europeans were not allowed to buy land fronting transportation corridors, thus increasing marketing costs for smallholders (Ramasamy 1994, 14). Additionally, the "Lalang Clause" allowed Europeans to alienate land that appeared idle to the disadvantage of both the Malays and the Chinese (Sioh 1998, 151). The use of the term "alienation" has double meaning here: in its official meaning of removing from access but also the psychic separation of homeland from the native population through the magnitude of the physical transformation brought about by the scale of the European operations. For example, in 1899, the acreage of rubber in the state of Selangor was about 500 acres (Jackson 1968).[1] By 1909, the figure stood at 84,871 acres owned by Europeans. European companies bought out old Chinese plantations of sugar, gambier and nutmeg while the colonial government redefined many smallholdings as uncultivated so that they could take over the land which was then sold to European planters (Ibid). The combined processes of land alienation through new legislation and large-scale commercialized agriculture radically changed the physical landscape. The preceding description of policies and practices recalls Foucault's (1972, 6, 11, 15) assertion that it takes a "coherent corpora" to construct the "truth" that governed the value, access and distribution of resources.

By 1910, rubber had virtually displaced all other crops, whether for cash or subsistence, occupying 62 percent of the cultivated land (Headrick 1988, 199, 246; Ramasamy 1994, 12). The great rubber estates became the "leading feature of Malaya's ecology" (Jackson 1991, 5). Remade nature became part of the suite of selfobjects that provided the approving mirror to the grandiose colonial self. However, the value of rubber to its producer depended on the scale of the operation, which, in turn, was usually a function of race. The colonial administration restricted sales of rubber from smallholders through the Stevenson's Scheme to prevent prices from collapsing during price slumps which set quotas on how much rubber per acre each planter was allowed to sell (Drabble 1991, 38–46). This system favored the estates by allowing them a much higher quota per acre than the smallholdings. The quota of rubber allocated to smallholders versus estates was calculated from the overall acreage of smallholdings compared to estates. The follow-up to the Stevenson's Scheme, the Rubber Regulation Scheme, allocated 36.8 percent of the export quota to smallholders whereas production capacity may actually have been as high as 47.8 percent of Malaya's total rubber production capacity (McHale 1967, 79–81). Because smallholdings frequently interplanted rubber with other crops, the acreage dedicated to rubber was underestimated; hence, the volume of rubber the smallholders were allowed to sell was also underestimated. While this may seem an inadvertent mistake on the part of colonial officials, it does highlight the point that even the definition of what constituted a plantation was open to interpretation. Needless to say, the interpretation that prevailed benefitted the group with the most power. Finally, the lack of access to long-term credit and new technology ensured that the Chinese planters could not maintain their successful positions for long. By 1938, Asian-owned (mainly Chinese) smallholdings accounted for 1,264,678 acres to 2,031,969 acres of European owned plantations (*The Malayan Agricultural Journal* 1939). Putting Edward Said's (1978) Orientalist critique in conversation with Heinz Kohut's (1973) framework for identity construction, we see that constructing the position of the grandiose imperial self was a corporate endeavor marshalling financial, legal and scientific resources to provide the practical and rhetorical tools to realize and rationalize that position.

Colonial Financing

So far, we have covered the material and legal tools for constructing the foundational fantasy. I now turn to the role of finance in constructing a practical psychic cordon around the colonized. Since even few European individuals could afford the outlay for a rubber plantation, many of the new efforts were owned by British agency houses such as Harrisons and Crosfield, Guthrie and Company, Boustead and companies such as Dunlop (Voon 1976). The lack of access to credit was a fundamental aspect of constraining native populations from entering the lucrative plantation sector or expanding their position. This set the stage for the corporate style agriculture that continues to dominate Malaysia today. In the early 1900s, responding to a demand for rubber from American tire manufacturers, companies were floated on the London stock exchange to raise capital for planting and production. Although European capitalization is well recorded, what is less well known is the extent to which European capital based in other colonies, notably India and Ceylon, also invested in the Malayan rubber industry (Voon 1971, 3). The success of the Malayan rubber industry then made it possible to raise further capital from American investors. Malayan planters persuaded investors outside Britain to support their efforts in Malaya because there was anticipation that, as a wild source, the Brazilian supply of rubber was undependable.

The fastest way for Western capital to enter the rubber industry was to take over existing estates. The European owner of an estate who may have been experiencing problems with cash flow would float his company on a metropolitan market with the help of merchant firms such as Harrisons and Crosfield (Voon 1971). In the Malayan rubber industry, the pattern was for the vendor to yield financial control to the new majority shareholder. The vendor would be bought out partly through cash or stocks in the new ownership, staying on as the manager of the estate. In the case of the consolidation of several estates, the previous owner might be offered a directorship in the company or become the visiting agent on behalf of an agency house managing the estates for shareholders. To rationalize their holdings, European companies frequently bought up adjoining Asian smallholdings (Gow, Wilson and Stanton Ltd. 1906; Voon 1971, 1976). Voon's (1971) research showed that control was concentrated in the hands of a few men who sat on several boards of directors. This was especially true of sterling companies registered in Britain rather than dollar companies registered in the US or rupee companies registered in India and Ceylon. Of the 221 directorships controlling the largest companies, over 50 percent were taken up by 40 directors represented on more than one board. Former and current civil servants also featured prominently on the boards (Gow, Wilson and Stanton Ltd. 1906). And the same names appeared again and again on the various boards owing to the prominent role played by agency houses. The revolving door policy between public and private sector personnel was a key aspect of the "knitted together" strength, in the words of Edward Said (1978, 6), that underwrote British colonial power in Malaya. The pattern of strength did not change until after independence and the intervention of a racially based nationalist policy of agricultural expansion which will be discussed in Chapter 6.

Science and Empire

Botany formed the final strand in Said's (1978, 6) "knitted together" strength of the symbiotic relationship among capital, science and imperialism in the plantation sector. While eighteenth-century plant transfers were unsystematic, by the second half of the nineteenth century the Linnaean classification system gave scientists a means of redirecting raw material to suitable locales in other colonies based on their understanding of plant types matched to environmental conditions (see essays in MacKenzie 1990). Significantly, Linnaeus himself was interested in botany as an adjunct to the political economy of Sweden (Koerner 1996). Science would provide the vocabulary to make the strongest case for the power relationship in the colonial foundational fantasy. Deepak Kumar (1990, 52) claims that while early scientific activity was amateur and disorganized, and that funding by East India Company promoted results not means, from 1791 onwards British government policy supported economic botany research. The early projects were carried out through the botanic gardens and, at least in India, began with crops for local people. Eventually the gardens would focus on cash crops, and research would be coordinated through institutions and societies as well as gardens in both metropolitan centers and colonies (ibid, 60).

Government-funded research institutions, such as Kew Gardens, England, acted as clearing houses for seeds of potential crops from all over the empire, and scientists arranged plant transfers across the colonies (Mackay 1996; Miller 1996). The development of botany made the spatial reorganization of nature conceivable but territorial expansion allowed that reorganization to become a reality. Europeans could ecologically colonize new lands because their prior military and political colonization gave them the opportunity to do so. Europeans were able to treat their colonies as giant experimental gardens, and because of the scale of the area available to them, they were able to overcome the physical limitations of climate and soil conditions simply by moving a failed experiment to another colony (Brockway 1979), even as new legal codes on land tenure and denial of access to financial investment placed further limitations on non-Europeans. Information pouring in from various parts of the empire was organized to direct plans and policies for the colonial project. Science would no longer just serve in exploration and cataloguing but in directing investment; it would serve to remove risks from investors. Metropolitan scientists took precedence over colony-based European scientists causing tension in the division of labor between the two groups as the former focused on analysis while the task of the latter was to provide only samples (Kumar 1990, 62). The former gave meaning while the latter provided samples and data, thus setting the stage for future scientific relationships. Scientific research in the service of capital was an expansive corporate effort: metropolitan and colonial scientists, the institutes they worked for and the learned societies and journals they created, constituted a network nurturing crops and research until the time when the private sector was ready to take on the new crops.

The natural sciences fed the Victorian need to order the world through their emphasis on taxonomy, but science also literally fed the capitalist need for resources, what David Arnold (1998) described as the "economic intentionality behind plant transfers" (4). Crops derived from botanical studies to feed the engine of the industrial revolution and imperial enterprise were routed through Kew Gardens and its junior partner gardens around the globe. Kew's place in the dense web of interlocking interests between the rise in status of botanical science and its service to Empire is described by Brockway (1979), MacKay (1996) and Miller (1996). In particular, Brockway's study focuses on the awareness of the economic potential of botanical knowledge by Kew's directors Sir Joseph Banks, Sir Joseph Hooker and his son, Sir William Hooker. Kew directors Joseph Banks and William Hooker hired plant collectors to obtain specimens and seeds from all over the globe. This action was made possible through the directors' personal ties with government agencies and aristocratic patrons (Miller 1996). Hooker established cooperative arrangements with the Royal Navy, the Colonial Office and the India Office (Brockway 1979, 82). Plants with economic potential were studied and bred at Kew before being sent out to colonial gardens. Among Kew's most illustrious contributions to imperial expansion were tea, cinchona (for the treatment of malaria) and rubber. Kew's directors nominated the directors of colonial gardens, and those gardens were often staffed by botanists trained at Kew (Brockway, 1979). The most famous of colonial botanists was Henry Ridley at the Singapore Botanical Gardens.

Economic Gardens

While Kew was the best known of the economic botany gardens, others like Buitenzorg (created in1819) in the Dutch East Indies, Peradeniya (created in 1821) in Ceylon, Calcutta (created in 1787), Trinidad (created in 1927) and Sydney (created in 1788) were also important for their roles in the imperial economy (*Agricultural Bulletin* 1910). The Singapore Botanic Gardens, created in 1888, played an important role in the rubber industry that came to dominate the Malayan economy (Wycherley 1960).[2] Early botanic gardens were even known as economic gardens, rather than the emphasis on science (Ibid.). The earliest gardens in the Malayan Peninsula were the Penang Botanic Gardens. These were created in 1800 from Sir Francis Light's ambition to create spice gardens that would break the spice monopoly of the Dutch. The Penang Gardens had a checkered history and only existed at intermittent periods (*Agricultural Bulletin* 1910). The Malacca Gardens were established from a gift of land by a Chinese planter in 1886 only to be abolished by Sir Charles Mitchell ten years later, whereas the 1903 economic garden at Batu Tiga, Selangor was said to contain "a very complete series of plants likely to prove useful to planters" (*Agricultural Bulletin* 1910). The shaky survival of the gardens traces the efforts of colonial science to make itself an indispensable part of the alliance of science and capital, but the ability of gardens to secure funding even with uncertainty underscores capital's recognition that it needed science. Colonial gardens served as the first easily observable point in establishing the corporate cohesiveness (Foucault 1972, 6,11) of material accumulation and ordering in the project of commodification of botany and its alliance with Empire. Their survival in various parts of the Empire can be twinned to this project and can be seen in the jealous competition between the colonial scientists in Peradeniya, Ceylon and Malaya to claim responsibility for the success of rubber, one of the great demonstrations of science serving empire (Ridley 1955). In tandem with the establishment of economic gardens was the establishment of amateur societies and clubs such as the Agri-Horticultural Society founded to lobby the colonial government for proper research funding for agriculture (*Agricultural Bulletin* 1910).

Rubber cultivation took off in Malaya with the appointment of Henry Ridley as Director of the Singapore Botanical Gardens in 1888 (Wycherley 1960). Ridley was an excellent example of the scientist as empire builder. He was as indispensable to the construction and functioning of Empire as the soldiers and administrators. Even in the days before the popularity of rubber, he handed out rubber seeds in the hope that people would plant the rubber if only as an ornamental plant. He was convinced that once the economic importance of cultivated rubber emerged, there would be a shortage of seeds unless he took precautions ahead of time. Among the numerous innovative processes that Ridley and his staff at the Botanic Gardens in Singapore contributed to the success of the rubber industry were: ways to export seeds to ensure a high survival rate; a non-destructive method of tapping through refining the timing of the tapping and age of the trees, important in considering the economic viability of estates; the sheet method for drying, smoking and curing rubber which reduced processing time and impurities; remedies for plant diseases and pests; fertilizers and identifying new locales for estates that would ensure the success of the investment (Ridley 1955). All the abovementioned innovations reduced risks involved in cultivating rubber and reduced wastage, thus improving profit margins for planters and investors. But crucially, the role of science in the success of the rubber industry was also important in reifying the superiority of European to native planters and dispelling the opprobrium associated with the accusation of theft of the original rubber seeds.

Labor Requirements

The last ethnic group to be discussed in the context of the capitalist agricultural economy of colonial Malaya is the Indians. The expansion of plantation agriculture created a new demand for labor which could not be satisfied locally. Racial stereotyping at the time meant that Europeans were considered totally unsuited for manual work in the tropics (Livingstone 1994). On the other hand, the Malays who had access to their own land would not put up with the dreadful conditions on the plantations, and there was competition for Chinese workers from Chinese plantations which drove up the relative cost of labor (Stubbs 1989, 51; Ramasamy 1994, 32, 37). Tamil workers from southern India had moved to Malaya through the 1830s and 1840s, but the large-scale movement of Tamils did not take place until the mid-1850s (Sandhu 1969). The Indian Passenger Acts of 1857 and 1859 and the Indian Act of 1877 improved conditions for recruiting Indian labor (see Sandhu 1969, 75–141 for a summary of various Indian Acts and Parmer 1960 for a history of colonial labor policies). This laid out conditions of wages, price of foodstuffs on estates, working hours and punishment for absenteeism or desertion. This echoes Foucault (1995, 138) in that it is a multiplicity of often minor processes, of different origin and location which by overlapping, repeating or imitating one another, converge and gradually produce a "blueprint" of control. Even so, labor shortage in Malaya persuaded the colonial authorities in Malaya to add the 1884 Indian Immigration Ordinance which subsidized the British India Steam Navigation Company leading to lower fares and establishing medical officers to ensure fewer losses due to mortality. Thus, Malaya became a frontier society with almost half of its population made up of new arrivals in socially subordinate positions who came to work the land but were alienated from the fruits of their labor.

Subsequent complaints about the estate system were strictly from the point of view of the owners and managers and revolved around the inefficiency of the system whereas complaints of ill treatment by labor were dismissed. During the peak recruitment period in 1926, 165,377 Indians arrived in Malaya (Sandhu 1969, Appendix 1). Racial stereotyping depicted Tamils as ideal labor for plantation work because they possessed "all the right qualities such as docility, submissiveness, malleability and little self-reliance" (Ramasamy 1994, 23). The indentured system was a severe one; beatings, malnutrition, overwork and disease took their toll on the new immigrants (Sandhu 1969, 75–152). Estate laborers were sold rotten food at high prices at the estate shop that was sometimes owned by the manager (Ramasamy 1994, 44). A chief cause of the high mortality rates was malaria; the Anopheles mosquito's habitat increased with the opening up of the forest. Eventually, the rise of Indian nationalism on the subcontinent drew attention on the inequities of the indenture system, and in 1910 it was replaced by the *kangani* or recruiter system. This improved recruitment rates but not work conditions (Sandhu 1969, 84). de Silva (1982, 336–338) contends that the subsequent discrimination in wages for Indian labor in comparison to Chinese labor who earned two-and-half to three times more (Ramasamy 1994, 36) was a function of the recruitment system. Chinese laborers were contracted through clan and society organizations whereby the contractor's cut was a percentage of the wage negotiated giving the contractor an investment in maximizing wages. The Indian *kangani* was employed by the estate and, therefore, had no interest in negotiating a better wage on behalf of the laborers he recruited. The 1922 Indian Emigration Act allowed an Agent of the Indian Government to inspect estates, depots and other places of Indian labor settlement or employment as well as to improve the male-to-female ratio of workers but still failed to improve living conditions (Arasaratnam 1970, 24–25). Efforts to settle on a fair fixed wage collapsed with the advent of the Depression. Immigration to Malaya was stopped, and between 1929 and 1932, 215,234 Indians were repatriated (Sandhu 1969, Appendix 4).

Early Indian labor protests about the inhuman conditions that they were expected to endure were manifested in desertions (Arasaratnam 1970). And far from the passive selfobjects of colonial fantasies, from 1912 onwards, both Indian and Chinese workers struck as a means of improving the labor conditions. Strikes appeared to cease during the Depression, but with an economic resurgence and accompanying demand for labor, strikes resumed from 1933 onwards culminating in the Klang strikes of 1941. These strikes began on 8 February 1941 and lasted until May 1941 involving over 20,000 workers from every estate in Selangor (Reid 1941). Labor troubles took on racialized overtones as striking Indian workers tried to prevent Malay workers from crossing the picket lines. Striking Indian women workers positioned themselves so close to the Malay men that they were unable to cross the line for fear of committing *khalwat* (ibid). According to Muslims, *khalwat* refers to the sinful act of a person being in close physical proximity to a member of the opposite sex who is not the person's spouse or a close relative. Stenson (1980; also see Chapter 3) argues that Indian labor unrest from 1938 onwards was subsumed within Indian nationalist protests leading to the erroneous conclusion that there was no labor conflict during the period. Indian protests in Malaya were interpreted as in support of the Indian nationalism rather than class protest. In part, this interpretation may have arisen because Indian nationalists protested the conditions of Indians abroad as part of the mistreatment of Indians everywhere because they were a subjugated people in their own country. But this is a false dichotomy. Ramasamy (1994, 49) records that appeals to racial solidarity couched as nationalism were sometimes the device for uniting workers and *kangani* in Malaya to strike for better working condition and wages. In this situation, while not exactly a member of the elite, the *kangani* deserted their traditional alliance with capital. But generally, Indian nationalism has been postulated as a device for co-opting the poor to fight on behalf of the elite (Grove 1990). Moreover, the Indians were taking their cue from successful Chinese strikes in 1937. Over 30,000 workers struck and while the strike was broken through the use of the police and army, some concessions were obtained. The passage of the Aliens Ordinance in 1933 cut off the supply of Chinese labor and, paradoxically, improved the bargaining position of the ones left in Malaya. The rise of the Malayan Communist Party (MCP) as an organizational force also helped Chinese workers to coordinate their demands. The recalcitrant native selfobjects were breaking out of their imposed spatial immobility as well as in terms of upward mobility. World War Two would see the recalcitrance transform into outright rebellion against their colonial rulers, both Japanese and European.

Conclusion

British encroachment and eventual colonization of Malaya in the nineteenth century resulted in material losses for the local population as land alienation and legally formalized land tenure induced scarcity of arable land. Moreover, cultivation now focused on surplus production in monocultural plantations rather than food crops. As the demand for rubber in the modern economy grew, the scale of cultivation expanded and accelerated with the introduction of rubber plantations. The introduction of plantation agriculture also created a need for labor which resulted in an immigrant population because the local Malays had the option of refusing plantation work since they could subsist on crops grown in the reserve lands. Colonial labor demand, then, was for the kind of worker socialized for plantation work from lack of options because of their impoverished circumstances. Participation in a monetized economy was essential for plantation labor who had to purchase food but eventually, the Malay peasantry also found that participation was no longer discretionary as they needed to pay taxes. Not only was land appropriated for Europeans but high capital investment for the new plantation agriculture effectively shut out non-white participation because of the difficulty in accessing financing. Lastly, the input of colonial scientists was crucial in advancing the expansion of European-owned plantations. By reducing risk and wastage in cultivation, they improved profit margins. The productive nexus between colonialism, capitalism and science produced a "coherent corpora" in Foucault's (1972) words, which would produce the "truth" of how resources should be distributed in the colonial world with the colonizer accruing most of the resources. The changes necessitated by the plantation economy transformed social relations and turned colonial Malaya into a plantation society. By the 1930s, Malayan society reflected attitudes, rules and hierarchies that acted as material and intellectual gateways which fulfilled the psychic function of the providing selfobjects to support the colonial self (Kohut, 1973, 629). Malayan plantation society realized the foundational fantasy of colonialism in which the identity of the colonizer as a superior agentic subject was only made possible because of the reconfiguration of nature and the losses imposed upon the native populations. The reconfiguration of space so that it is physically unrecognizable and the demographic changes and social reorganization that were all conditions of the plantation economy can also be understood as a psychic loss in terms of the rupture from, and loss of, traditional ways of life. But because the losses from colonization happened gradually and violence was sporadic and limited, it was not conceived as trauma at the moment of occurrence. Freud's (1959b, 86) analysis conceives of trauma only as recognizable through retrospection. Hence, for the majority of non-white Malayans, colonization would only be recognized as traumatic through the Emergency.

Notes

1 This figure of 500 acres probably covered both Chinese and European plantations as rubber was only introduced as a commercial crop in 1895. The statistics in the following sentences are from Jackson (1968, 237–248).

2 In a special centennial commemoration of the Singapore Botanic Gardens, P.R. Wycherley reviewed the work of gentlemen scientists such as James Collins whose work led to Sir Charles Markham's recommendation of the collection of *Hevea brasiliensis* rubber from Brazil. Note the use of the term "collection," rather than the harsher description of theft used by Brazil.

3 Dismantling the Colonial Foundational Fantasy

Introduction

On the eve of World War Two, the Malayan landscape reflected the physical changes wrought by capitalist agriculture, which sited people largely based on class and race. And far from accepting their place in space and the social and economic hierarchy, labor unrest on the estates characterized the 1930s and 1940s in Malaya. Contrary to the peaceful colony image the British wanted to project, it appeared that many Asians, other than the elites, did not approve of the division of labor and access to resources. In addition to labor troubles, educated Malays were also complaining of being crowded out of Malaya (Muhamad 1938; Roff 1967). The war inaugurated a new phase in the contest for space. Chapter 3 is the first of two chapters devoted to analyzing the Malayan Emergency as the moment for contemporary Malaysia when the trauma of colonialism was laid bare through the military uprising by the Malayan Communist Party (MCP). In Freudian terms, this marks the second traumatic experience through which the first, the colonial encounter, is assimilated and understood as trauma (Freud 1959b, 65). The experience of colonization now takes on its significance as trauma—the return of the "outlaw" repressed (Freud 1959b, 86). I make three related arguments within the framework of the libidinal economy. First, British losses in World War Two shattered the illusion of the invulnerable colonizing subject. Second, the postwar struggle, known as the Emergency, to keep colonial control of Malaya's resources, saw nature and the native populations transformed from the approving mirror of empire to recalcitrant selfobjects that triggered narcissistic rage in the colonizers. Third, through the human-perpetrated violence, the word "jungle" became a repository of the anxieties and fears of a world of military and political uncertainty and the key sign in the struggle to dismantle the colonial foundational fantasy. Conversely, by taking the site of the conflict to the estates, the MCP mirrored a similar strategy not just in highlighting the resource angle of the conflict, but in psychologically deconstructing the colonizer's identity by exposing its vulnerability.

Chapter 2 described the construction of the colonial self-selfobject relationship. In Chapter 3, I frame the struggle over space and the dismantling of

DOI: 10.4324/9781315440286-4

the foundational fantasy applying Heinz Kohut's (1973, 620–644) concept of the recalcitrant selfobject to Malaya's native populations. The story covers the sequence of events to show the growing recalcitrance over time, whereby British vulnerability increases with the selfobject challenges so that the flaws in the "narcissistically perceived reality" (Kohut 1973, 643–644) accumulate. Continuing on from the labor strikes in Chapter 2, I cover the destabilizing of the colonial foundational fantasy first through the British defeat in Malaya by the Japanese and then the onset of the decolonization struggle, the Emergency. I describe the violent struggle as it played out across Malaya to show the significance the forest took on as physical and psychological control moved back and forth between the colonial state and their challengers, the MCP. The third and final section of the chapter examines how the MCP moved the locus of the Emergency from the forests to the estates thus exposing colonial vulnerability.

Destabilizing the Foundational Fantasy: Malaya in World War Two

Malaya fell to the Japanese troops with the British surrender of Singapore on 15 February 1942 (Winstedt 1988, 247). Resource-poor Japan was convinced of its need for the Greater East Asia Co-Prosperity Sphere, the Japanese title for conquered territories, to secure the resources it needed to grow. Resource-rich Malaya was an important prize in this plan. The reason for the easy Japanese victory is still a subject of controversy, but in another example of policy based on stereotypes, Britain had assumed that the Japanese made inferior troops because they had not managed to bring the war with China to a successful conclusion (Sabine 1942). And if they could not defeat an Asian force, how could they possibly defeat a European one? The repercussions of colonial defeats in Asia may not have impinged psychologically on the European powers in their moment of defeat, but a signal of its importance was noted by Asians, and unsurprisingly, by the ultimate racist, Hitler (1953, 149) himself, who upon hearing of Japan's entry into the war, remarked: "[I]t was also a turning point in history. It means the loss of a whole continent, and one must regret it, for it's the white race which is the loser." The British and other Europeans who had not been evacuated before the fall were interned in Singapore (Collinge 1944). The consequence of Britain's defeat was the loss of an economically important part of the empire, but more damaging in the long term was the loss of the psychological aura of invulnerability. In Malaya, the Japanese administration coerced and persuaded some Malays and Indians into their administration with eventual political independence as the reward for cooperation. Local elites may have cooperated with the Japanese as much out of fear as for the hope of getting rid of their European colonial rulers but support was not unanimous (BAM Photos Collection 7/34 and 7/37 1946). Unlike the British, the Japanese governed Malaya as a single central administration (Cheah 1983, 22–23). And although the Japanese still took the senior administrative positions, they favored a pro-Malay policy for other administrative positions relying on a Malay District Officer (previously held by the British) at the district level and the *penghulu* and *ketua kampong* at village level. These policies broke the psychological barrier for Asians in leadership positions and would contribute to Asians resisting a return to the prewar status quo. In contrast, the Japanese were extremely harsh in their treatment of the Chinese population in Malaya as opposed to their more conciliatory stance in Indonesia. One reason was that the Twenty-fifth Army that conquered Malaya had come directly from China where it had encountered fierce fighting. The *sook ching*, or "purification by elimination," claimed between 30,000 and 40,000 Chinese lives (Cheah 1983). As a result of Japanese persecution, many Chinese families fled into the forests; others had already preceded them during the economic depression in the 1930s when the lack of both employment and land forced many families to practice subsistence agriculture as squatters on the fringes of the forests.

As the Japanese embarked on their own foundational fantasy through transforming the rest of Asia into the Greater East Asia Co-Prosperity Sphere, the MCP, once harassed and constrained to the margins of society, emerged to challenge the new colonial power. Shortly before the fall of Malay to the Japanese, the MCP had approached the British to offer their services if the British would cease persecuting its members (Chapman 1949). The British refused until 18 December 1941 when they agreed to an alliance with the MCP. After the fall of Singapore in 1942, the MCP renamed itself the Malayan Peoples' Anti-Japanese Army (MPAJA) and retreated into the forest to continue resistance against the Japanese. The Japanese responded by raiding Chinese villages with the cooperation of Malay guides and informants (Cheah 1983, 70). Throughout the war the urban landscape was the scene of most of the atrocities. Executions had to be public spectacles because the Japanese used them as part of the regime of fear to discipline the population since they were a minority trying to control the majority, and spatial discipline was part of the strategy to establish the Japanese foundational fantasy.

As Japanese forces moved into Malaya and thousands of Indian troops under British command were taken captive, the Japanese attempted to recruit troops from the ranks of the captured (Bhargava 1982, 13–15). Class divisions prevailed Indian officers were unwilling to "go over" but many among the rank and file did. These men, together with women who subsequently signed up, became the Indian National Army (INA) (Gordon 1990; Ghosh 1997). The 40,000-strong INA was never used to its maximum capacity but its recruits were important in organizing estate unions after the war, the real multitude of recalcitrant colonial selfobjects (Stenson 1980, 101; Cheah 1983, 49). As the war progressed and the British reorganized their war effort, British officers, known as Force 136, were parachuted into the forests where they collaborated with the MPAJA (Chapman 1949). Jain (1970, 302–305) contends that Indian estate laborers also joined the MPAJA or the INA as an alternative to being sent to work on the Siam Death Railway. Britain bought the allegiance of the MCP through a deal that provided the MCP with arms, supplies, money and training in return for which they would take orders from British officers. Although the power relationship still favored the British, their dependence on the alliance with the MCP dismantled the facade of imperial invulnerability that was already under strain from the Japanese threat.

In summary, the Japanese Occupation of Malaya lasted only three years, but it was critical in terms of framing future political contests through its effect on the prewar organization of Malayan society. It demolished the idea of European invincibility and entitlement. In doing so, the war inspired a generation of Asian nationalists dubious of European entitlement. Moreover, the Japanese policy of promoting Malays and Indians to positions of responsibility provided the training ground for the psychological challenge to European supremacy after the war while their harsh treatment of the Chinese population galvanized resistance and laid the foundations for the military challenge. Indian and Malay nationalists obtained training in bearing weapons and administration that would serve them well in their postwar political agitation. The newly armed MCP acquired proficiency in guerrilla warfare and surviving in the forests, skills that would serve them well during the Emergency. But racial antagonism between the Malays and the Chinese also deepened as a result of the pro-Malay and anti-Chinese policies of the Japanese resulting in a racialized postwar settling of scores which negatively affected postwar anti-colonial opposition. Lastly, the Japanese ruled Malaya from a central administration. This action prepared the psychological ground for the concept of a united country.

Shattering the "Approving Mirror"

Japan surrendered to the Allies in August of 1945, but the British Military Administration (BMA) (1945–46) only reoccupied Malaya in late September. This time lag was crucial in the subsequent political turmoil. Not only had the British lost prestige by losing Malaya to the Japanese in the first place, they were also not *seen* to defeat the Japanese physically in 1945 because surrender was a consequence of the bombing of Hiroshima and Nagasaki (Stockwell 1995a, lv). The restoration of European colonial territories signaled a new phase in the imperial project as Europeans largely depended on American support to reclaim their colonies. In retrospect, it is interesting to note that the European colonial powers were aware that the imperial order was changing and a new foundational fantasy was emerging centered on the US (Colonial Office 1942; Gent 1942a; Dening 1945b). While European colonialists had always been dependent on their colonized selfobjects to an unacknowledged extent, their dependence on the US was harder to ignore. The position of the invulnerable, agentic European imperial self of its foundational fantasy was transforming into a junior ally of the US and, as such, had to defer to its policies regarding the rest of the world. China was to be accommodated because of American pressure. But the early American ambivalence toward colonialism faded as the war progressed. It became obvious that the US would assume the imperial mantle. During the Potsdam Conference in July 1945, Britain's share of the Japanese empire was determined as the former European colonies of Southeast Asia as well as Thailand, despite Thailand's prewar uncolonized status (Stockwell 1995a, lvi). While the Europeans were still thinking in terms of carving up the world, albeit now sharing it with a new partner, the Americans, their former colonial subjects were very much aware that an era had ended. The events during the BMA period from 1945 to 1948 widened the perception gap between colonizer and colonized regarding the acceptance of colonial rule and set the context for the decolonization struggle.

The BMA faced shortages of all kinds owing to the disruption of supplies during the war. Part of the problems with supply may have had to do with an agenda that prioritized reopening mines and estates rather than concentrating on basic supplies such as food (Killearn 1947). To begin with, the comparison between the Japanese Occupation and the British Reoccupation showed the British in a favorable light providing the important approving mirror to the reoccupying British. Even working class Chinese, later the most active resistance to the British during the Emergency, were initially welcoming of the British presence. But as shortages in basic supplies continued, social discontent rose. Local people alleged that troops took goods without paying, looted and raped local women, while Asians working for the BMA complained that they went short of rations compared to European staff (Purcell 1945; Sabine 1942; Stubbs 1989, 75). In response, British Treasury officials argued that Malaya's resource wealth meant that rather than diverting money into the Malayan postwar reconstruction effort money would be better spent placating other parts of the Empire (Keynes 1945; Winifrith 1945; Tronoh-Malayan Group 1948). Finally, the greatest resentment was reserved for the British use of Japanese prisoners of war as troops to suppress both strikes in Malaya and nationalist struggles in the Dutch East Indies and French Indochina to prepare the way for the Dutch and the French to return to those countries (Dening 1946; Killearn 1947).[1] This act had a twofold negative significance: it came across as an act of betrayal to continue to deploy the perpetrators of trauma that the return of European colonialists was meant to oust. And it reinforced the vulnerability of a European colonial power that it had to rely on the Japanese who had originally defeated them, mindful that the Japanese defeat had been brought about by the Americans, not the Europeans.

Forging a New Hegemonic Identity

In 1943, shortly after the loss of their Southeast Asian colonies, the British foreign secretary, Oliver Stanley (1943), stated Britain's policy: "We are pledged to guide colonial people along the road to self government within the framework of the British Empire." Britain recognized that the world order had changed, and while it wanted to keep its colonies, the US would have to be consulted and placated (Cranbourne 1942; Gent 1942a,b; Atlee 1944; Colonial office and Foreign Office 1953). Moreover, both the US and China would have to be taken into consideration in power sharing in East Asia (Gent and MacDougall 1942). With regard to Malaya, the British saw their continued presence as integral to maintaining a social and political environment conducive to resource exploitation "[] we may readily assume that our resumption of control is the obvious and only reasonable arrangement" (Ibid). Malaya's practical usefulness as a dollar earner made it a significant prize in imperial stakes given its revenue contributions to imperial coffers and the British war effort (Stockwell 1995a, 93). The economic adviser for Malaya, Sir George Gater (1945), stressed Malaya's importance to the imperial economy:

> Malaya was before the war probably the most prosperous part of the Colonial Empire and, what is no doubt more important at the present, was among the most important dollar earners in the sterling block.

But the British and Americans clashed over the interpretation of the third Article of the Atlantic Charter which recognized the right of all people to choose the form of government under which they would live (Gent and MacDougall 1942). The US saw it as pertaining to the Far East while Britain did not. Anthony Stockwell (1995a) points out that Britain's policy for post World War Two Malaya was to try to appeal to as many constituencies without yielding any privileges to the point of offering the Malayan Union (MU) experiment that would have consolidated administrative control in preparation for an indeterminate independent future (Malayan Union Government 1947; also see Harper 1999). In 1946, the British first proposed the MU as a means of persuading the Malayan population to cooperate with continued British control, which would have opened citizenship in the Union to all races but was rejected by the Malays (Malaya 1946). The compromise over citizenship and the creation of Malay-dominated state governments in tandem with a powerful British central government drove the simmering racial and class conflicts into the open.

As the Japanese withdrew into the bigger towns to await the arrival of the British, their withdrawal became the tacit signal for the MPAJA to emerge from the forests. The British tried, with little success, to insist that the MPAJA stay in the forests until sufficient colonial troop strength had been amassed in Malaya to control them (Sweet-Escott 1945a,b). The British were also adamant that the MPAJA not take part in Councils of Government during the BMA (Blythe 1970). Recall that a condition of identity construction in Brennan's (1993) foundational fantasy requires spatially constraining and fixing in place the Kohutian selfobject, then it is easy to understand why constraining the MPAJA to the forests was a key aspect of returning to the prewar status quo. Unlike the urban areas, the British never really controlled the forests of Malaya. Before the Japanese occupation, British District Officers working in cooperation with local Chinese community leaders indirectly supervised the forest fringes and rural areas. But as wealthy Chinese fled Malaya during the war, they lost their influence over the Chinese community. This leadership vacuum and the psychological break entrained by the earlier British defeat by the Japanese made it easy for the MPAJA to influence the rural population. The aftermath of the war was as violent as the war itself as different racial groups took the opportunity to settle old scores (Miller 1972, 74; Cheah 1983, 80–81). Most importantly, it was a time of uncertain territorial control. MPAJA flags and banners raised in small towns and villages across the country visually challenged the colonial foundational fantasy.

The relationship between the MCP and the British broke down irretrievably on 15 February 1947 when the former used the anniversary of the fall of Singapore to inaugurate the founding of the Pan-Malayan General Labour Union (PMGLU). The event was significant in two ways: (1) the date reminded the British of their vulnerability to an Asian power and (2) it was a celebration of a recalcitrant selfobject that was growing in power. When the BMA refused permission for the celebrations, the MCP went ahead resulting in the BMA turning the police on the marchers in Malaya and Singapore. The decision by the BMA to suppress legal activities drove the MCP underground while the PMGLU encouraged its members to demand better working conditions. Strikes continued to multiply across the country affecting some of the biggest estates, mines and docks. In July 1946, 43,000 workers went on strike in Singapore. In 1947, 696,036 workdays were lost in labor action (Gamba 1962, 288). The political clash between the British and the MCP against a backdrop of labor strikes across the country was bound to result in a military struggle. The aftermath of World War Two in Malaya was punctuated by a series of disturbances that multiplied across the country setting up a serious political challenge to the reoccupying BMA and resulted in the declaration of a state of emergency on 16 June 1948 (Gent 1948b). This was declared in three stages and completed by 18 June 1948. The Government's campaign was conducted through a series of committees such as the Federal War Council and at the state level, the War Executive committee. Although a war in everything but name, it was never officially referred to as such because the British relied on insurance companies to compensate for the damage and loss of equipment which was eligible under civilian conditions but not in times of war.

Recalcitrant Selfobject I: The Forest

Recall that in Teresa Brennan's (1993) concept of the foundational fantasy, colonial self-identity is predicated on constraining and fixing in place a weaker, inferior other. Referencing Kohut's (1973) self-selfobject dynamic, this weaker, inferior selfobject, is essential for coherent self-esteem and identity. But World War Two and the Japanese defeat of European colonial powers forever demolished the illusion of an invulnerable colonizer. The onset of the Emergency signaled the beginning of the struggle for control over space in Malaya with the violence between state forces and Communist forces moving back and forth across the sites of conflict. The town of Gua Musang, seized by the MCP in 1947 and declared "liberated," and then retaken by colonial troops, came to symbolize the tenuous nature of control (Churchill N.d. circa 1950–51). The town of Tras was fought over 15 times before its final destruction by state forces as a decisive way of ending the struggle for control ("The Evacuation" N.d., circa 1951). Although state forces often succeeded in retaking control of a village or town, control was nebulous manifested by numerous ambushes on state forces and the subsequent difficulties of getting cooperation from the local population. Many towns designated problem areas during the Emergency had been symbols of resistance to the Japanese only three years earlier. This transformation in symbolism reflected the wider struggle to control both public allegiance and narrative. And unlike pre-occupation writers who used the signs "forest" and "jungle" interchangeably, writers dealing with the Japanese occupation, the Emergency and later periods almost invariably used the term "jungle."

The forest may have posed difficulties for both sides, but its role in leveling the advantages of numerical and material superiority gave the perception that the forest was on the side of the MCP by impeding the exercise of power through obscuring vision. Colonial authorities noted that four-fifths of Malaya was jungle (United Kingdom, Colonial Office and the Central Office of Information 1952) where the "30,000 square miles of forests afforded limitless opportunities" for ambushing (Purcell 1948). The forest gave attackers the opportunity to "melt away" into nothingness after an attack. A Police Mission Report (Maxwell, Ferguson, and Jackson 1950) described the situation in this manner: "The vast tracts of country covered by continuous jungle give the bandits opportunities to elude pursuit, to move from one area to another, and make sudden attacks on life or property, now at one point, now at another." In very dense forests or undergrowth, visibility could be reduced to three or four yards. A patrol of ten men would frequently find the lead scout invisible to the last man (Godfrey 1978, 8). For the reoccupying British, delineating hard boundaries and fixing in place rebellious natives as a precondition to maintaining the colonial foundational fantasy proved impossible when a large part of the country was hidden from their sights and beyond their control. The MCP operated in small groups of five or ten for mobility making it possible for them to hide from colonial forces many times their size. Attempts to engage the MCP in open firefights were usually fruitless as the MCP knew better than to be drawn into an open fight with a numerically superior and better-equipped opponent (Warner 1953). Arthur Campbell (1953, vi) who served with the Suffolk Regiment complained that the MCP were afforded "the protection of interminable jungles" referring to the forest as "[T]he jungle, the enemy" (Ibid, title of Chapter 2). As W.F.N. Churchill (N.d., circa 1950–51) put it, "In a war against guerrillas ... the jungle is very much on the side of the weaker—a cloak for the life and movement of the 'little' fellow." Limited visibility meant that Communist camps could be very close to nodes of power while remaining undetected. This sometimes had farcical consequences as in the case of a month-long firing campaign by colonial troops who later found that they were being overlooked by their target who were 500 yards behind them ('S' Troop 1956, entry 14/10/54). If not pushed back, the forest was always threatening to overwhelm roads, villages and estates, symbols of colonial modernity; war had come to the cities. The most spectacular instance of ambushing was the killing of the British High Commissioner Sir Henry Gurney on 6 October 1951 as he was being driven through a densely forested area (Stockwell 1995a, xxix).

Another factor by which the forest restricted the exercise of power is the way it reduced mobility. In a reversal of the foundational fantasy where the colonized selfobject is immobilized, it was colonial troops who found themselves immobilized in the forest. Forests do not favor big groups, and the logistical problems of command and coordination increased tremendously when companies comprising more than 20 men were involved (Godfrey 1978). The military advantages of sophisticated and heavy equipment were reduced because of the problems of mounting guns in cramped conditions and the hardship involved in conveying such heavy equipment over long distances and harsh terrain. Movement in dense forest could be as slow as 50–100 yards per hour (Ibid, 10). One infantry troop recorded a journey of three miles taking six hours ('S' Troop 1956). The struggle with swamps, leeches and undergrowth limited patrolling to about eight miles a day ("The Manchesters" 1951). The constantly changing speed also posed problems for navigation compounded by the inability to use maps (Godfrey 1978, 9). Colonial authorities finally addressed the obstructive forest by spraying it with chemicals (Bishop 1951; Kearns and Woodford 1952; Malaya [Colonial Government] 1953a,b; Woodford 1953). This approach failed because it was deemed too time-consuming given the size of the forest that needed to be destroyed, but it should be remembered that Agent Orange was actually pioneered in the Malayan campaign before it was used in Vietnam by the US.

If preserving the colonial fantasies of control rested on maintaining fixed spatial boundaries for the different races, in the actual combat, where the lines were drawn to delimit territory were blurred at the best since no one could say where the estate ended and the forest began. While initial Communist strategy focused on killing either Europeans or colonial collaborators in public executions (United Kingdom, Colonial Office and the Central Office of Information 1952, 7) the site of punishment later shifted from the body to a place—the estate or the mine. To colonial elites whether European or Asian, it seemed that they had lost control and the forest had reclaimed their estates for its own. Many estates were so isolated that there was no road access (Gidden 1950). A police report that suggested installing wireless communications on all the estates to overcome the psychological isolation and risk of having telephone lines cut was vetoed by the telephone company that feared loss of business (Maxwell et al. 1950). Initial attempts to fence in the estates were soon abandoned, as it was impossible to obtain sufficient barbed wire. Patrolling the perimeter of an estate or posting special constables as boundary markers were impractical given the scale of the project and the special constables themselves risked ambush as long as the estate perimeter was open (Swaine 1952). As population resettlement programs got underway and the police force expanded, estates found their pool of estate guards, known as special constables, depleted. These special constables had comprised a force of between 17,000 and 19,000-strong (O'Donovan 1948). Planters had to content themselves with creating safe spaces on the estates akin to fortresses through the use of the ubiquitous barbed wire, sandbags and searchlights. The planter's bungalow was probably the primary symbol of European presence in the rural areas. Patrick O' Donovan (1948) described it thus; "It seems a bit withdrawn from the exuberance—as though recalling Woking and games of weekend golf and strenuous evenings spent mowing the lawn while the radio played loudly through the french windows" ... in contrast, "there is a place beneath the bungalow for the night guard." The estate had transformed into a site of violent contestation with the planter no longer the uncontested ruler of his realm. Gunfire regularly sounded interspersed between the usual night time noises of insects and animals (Ibid). Travel in and out of estates required armored vehicles (Howe N.d.). Security forces rang on an hourly basis to verify that lines had not been cut. Almost all the estates could offer examples of a European killed on a neighboring estate a few days earlier. Estates had become sites of siege and the battleground in a war of nerves that drove planters to retire (Commercial Interests 1951c). Estates continued to be sites of contestations in the 1980s. The Sime Darby oil palm estate enroute to Meru village outside the town of Kelang was put on hold for almost 30 years because water mains were continually sabotaged (personal communication from the planter). This ties in with Herman's (2015, 20) definition of complex or repeated trauma as a situation in which damage can be inflicted repeatedly. Repeat trauma, a situation present in captivity, was the daily experience for almost all non-white residents of colonial Malaya. But this was a new experience for the British.

Recalcitrant Selfobject II: Class, Race and Gender

While the forests were cast as the theater of the war by the colonial state, the estates were the actual nexus of the violent struggle for most of the 12-year conflict. The estates, as the premier symbols of capitalist exploitation and the sites of numerous strikes by the workers, were natural targets for Communist attacks. The significance of rubber and the estates to the Malayan economy and the Malayan elite was considerable. During the 1950s, the decade of the most intense conflict, rubber accounted for 30–40 percent of government revenues, almost a quarter of the Gross Domestic Product (GDP), and between 50 and 70 percent of net export income (McHale 1967).

Although estates accounted for 57 percent of the output during that period compared to smallholdings, Europeans owned most of the estates whereas all the smallholders were Asian. The network of interests ranged on the side of protecting the plantation industry included planters, colonial administrators and international investors. As estates became the real nexus of the violence, the MCP achieved two aims: highlighting the estate as the symbol of their struggle against colonialism and capitalism and affecting the colonial economy directly by slashing rubber trees and disrupting production. Early in the Emergency, the MCP took control of estates with absentee landlords as a way of obtaining much needed revenue (Combined Intelligence Staff 1953a). They also took control of estates in the state of Pahang after their owners had abandoned them. It was hardly surprising that estates became sites of resistance in response to their other role as sites of exploitation. Housing was inadequate, described as "frayed huts that look as if they were built of unrolled cigars" (O' Donovan 1948). In addition, the unequal racial relationship as well as the drain of capital out of the country all provided good reasons for rebelling. Denis Warner (1953) suggested that local people may have cooperated with the MCP because they were scrupulous in paying for food and that their attacks bypassed the majority of the population since these were aimed at informers, police, troops and Europeans. Morris (1950) wrote, "The conflict in Malaya is with communism and not just with 3,000 bandits, and speed in improving labour conditions on estates in the manner proposed is in his [High Commissioner] view vitally important." He went on to criticize the planters for treating government-sponsored unions with suspicion, adding that "the High Commissioner fully understands that the lesson of experience demands vigilance, but the attitude on some estates in this manner is tantamount to playing straight into the hands of the MCP. He feels sure that your Association will wish to assist rather than hinder the growth of a sound trade union movement which with wise guidance, is one of the strongest anti-Communist weapons."

More worryingly, European planters' anxieties of danger centered on their servants whose subject positionality in the matrix of race, class and gender rendered them beneath the notice of those in power and, therefore, particularly useful in passive resistance. Their indispensability in running European households and conferred social invisibility brought sites of contestation everywhere. While these put servants in direct danger from retaliation by their employers, it also meant that planters' homes could become sites of potential resistance. The frontier had come home. Guerrilla wars show the effectiveness of the combination of a small group of armed troops aided by a considerably larger group of willing supporters whose aid may be largely in the form of passive non-cooperation with the enemy. And in a war of nerves, the anxieties triggered in the planters by the knowledge that even their homes were unsafe because of the presence of their servants served the MCP well.

The Malayan Emergency began as a class war, but race quickly became the dominant trope. Because the majority of the members of the MCP were

Chinese, officially, the British proclaimed confidence in Malay support for the colonial government against the MCP. In private the Intelligence Service admitted that they were concerned about Communist influence over Malays such as in the border towns of Dusun Nyor and Tomo (Combined Intelligence Staff 1953b). The actual number of MCP in the area only ran to 540 with 220 part-time members of the MCP fighting force and the Betong Salient area had a platoon only 56 strong but the MCP in the area was well funded by estate owners and laborers. In North Perak, the miners in Klian Intan provided food, recruits and money. Even after the resettlement of villagers had been completed on the Malayan side, forest settlements remained on the Thai side of the border as a source of help to the MCP (ibid.). And despite official denials of Malay involvement, the Government admitted Malay participation in all the states except for Penang. Their suspicion of their Malay allies extended to the Malay Home Guard. Additionally, despite a shortage of guards, estate managers refused to arm their largely Tamil workers who they claimed were "unsuitable" (Commercial Interests 1951c). This implies that either they felt that Tamils were biologically unsuitable for combat duty, or else they feared that their workers were not entirely loyal and arming them might be a temptation to use their arms against their exploiters. As O' Donovan (1948) described it, "the planter controls ... some thousand labourers, and some of them have already shown a steady desire to kill." Because planters felt that they could not depend on the loyalty of labor, re-housing labor on estates became paramount (Commercial interests 1951b). Certainly, Indian estate labor would have empathized with the MCP on issues such as wages and treatment of workers. Moreover, Indians, like the Chinese, as immigrants were discriminated against in terms of rights to residency in Malaya. To deny MCP support from estate labor, General Briggs proposed regrouping labor closer to the estate center where their movements could be monitored (Ibid). The boundary between estate and forest was seen as permeable as much for the psychological permeability as physical contiguity in that laborers were perceived by capital and the state as vectors through which the germs of communism penetrated the body of capital and the colonial state.

The MCP policy with regard to Malays was to try to emphasize similarity in aims between communism, pan-Islamism and Malay nationalism (Combined Intelligence Staff 1953c). Members of Angkatan Permuda Insaf (API), banned in 1947, formed the Ikatan Permuda Tanah Ayer (PETA) eventually taking to the forests with the MCP. The MCP always had an inter-racial military force as their objective and could probably draw upon 300 Malay MCP with more sympathizers. Colonial authorities justified their suspicion of communist sympathies among the Malays by citing coverage in the Malay vernacular press *Warta Negara*, *Majlis* and *Utusan Melayu* (Ibid). I would describe the three newspapers as nationalist and pro-independence, but at that time, the British equated nationalism with communism. Yet, displaying an equal blind spot with respect to the majority of the local population, scrutiny of captured MCP documents showed little awareness of the racial schisms among Asians or their own racism (Blades 1953a). The MCP assumed that Asian groups would unite to drive out the British colonialists without ever considering that for the Malays, the British may have been perceived as the lesser of two evils. An example is the MCP's interpretation of the Hertogh riots in Singapore. Referring to "the outbreak of war of racial liberation" during the Hertogh riots in Singapore in December 1950, they inferred passive resistance from the attitude of the Malay police constables but conveniently ignored the religious aims of the riots (Ibid).

We have seen so far that alliances during the Emergency fell along class and race lines although they sometimes cut across them owing to specific circumstances. Gender does not appear to have been an explicit category of difference in determining alliances during the Emergency. That women were involved in the Emergency is obvious, but it is more difficult to gauge the level of their involvement. Aside from the tendency to under-report women's involvement in military campaigns, gender would have been of minor interest in a class war where race quickly became the dominant trope. Women participated in military campaigns and were taken prisoners, killed in firefights and executed. The difficulty lay in finding secondary accounts that gave figures for women killed or taken prisoners separate from the total numbers. Women fought on the government side as well. And they took part in enough dangerous activities that the government, to save money, devised a policy so that the families of women who died in the line of duty on behalf of the Colonial Government could not claim pensions unlike the families of servicemen under Emergency Regulations issued on 25 October 1949 (CO 717/167).

Women supported the MCP in several ways: as armed fighters, couriers and camp support (performing traditional women's work such as cooking, sewing and nursing) but the largest number helped as the *Min Yuen* providing supplies to the troops in the jungle. And of course, most domestic staff in wealthy households were women who could steal supplies and convey them to the MCP.[2] Working-class women were also more mobile as a function of their work than upper-class women whose movements were far more circumscribed by convention. For example, servants would shop where they could get the best deal for their employers. Even less wealthy women like my mother thought nothing of sending servants into the villages or less savoury parts of town where she herself would not venture. Aside from social status, it was also a way of transferring risk to poorer women. This acceptance of risk as a part of life made it easier for working-class women to breach racial boundaries in space. In combination with class, social erasure due to color meant that non-white working-class women were considered part of the landscape. While wealthy Asian women were confined to their homes, Malay women restricted to their rural reserve lands, and poor Indian women were confined to the rubber and oil palm estates, working-class Chinese women who supported the MCP were in the best position to take advantage of their social invisibility. Until the later stages of the war, when Asians were brought in to help with Government strategy, skin color meant erasure and, hence, conferred invisibility and with it the advantage of traversing space. It should be added here that non-white men also availed themselves of this advantage but it was useful to a lesser degree. It was the permutation of gender, race and class, that gave these women the social invisibility and the accompanying relative freedom.

The MCP would take advantage of this social invisibility to evade the colonial constraints on communication. The most important position in the organization held by a woman was undoubtedly as coordinator of the MCP's communications network. Communications were key to the MCP because of the mobile and scattered nature of their units especially after the British banned sales of transmitting and receiving equipment (Barber 1971; Miller 1972). An earlier delivery system failed because they relied on a single courier to convey the messages from one post to another. However, this was easily disrupted by frequent police searches. In 1949, the Secretary General of the MCP, Chin Peng, appointed a woman, 24-four year-old Lee Meng, to reorganize the communications network (Abraham 1952). Lee Meng's decision to use a network of couriers who passed on messages over short distances, but who did not know the location of pick-up or drop off points other than the ones they used, proved to be very successful in evading government surveillance.[3] Lee Meng also used the widely accepted female pastime of window-shopping as a means for her couriers to meet under innocent-looking circumstances to pass information to each other (Barber 1971, 165–166). In addition to the couriers recruited by Lee Meng, some women conveyed warnings and reports of government troop movements to the MCP in the forests. Women used their bodies, strapping food, medicine and messages to their breasts and thighs (Miller 1972, 99). Supplies were also hidden in humble, homely goods such as the false bottoms of buckets, in the hollow bamboo poles supporting these buckets, in bicycle pumps and tire tubes, and in tins of talcum powder (Han 1956, 35–37; Barber 1971, 110). Lee Meng's eventual capture and trial became one of the most controversial episodes in the Emergency (Abraham 1952).

As the Emergency progressed, companies and sometimes even platoons were based on estates and housed in "tapper lines" or the planter's house, the latter presumably for the officers ('S' Troop 1956). Estates that were the sites of labor troubles made urgent claims for troops. Firing plans were sometimes scheduled on the estates themselves and relations between officers and planters were cordial and went beyond professional cooperation (Ibid). Planters who wanted arms were issued with police weapons (The Anglo-Java Rubber Company 1952). No doubt the cooperation reflected in part a colonial attitude that planters were in the frontline of the battle against communism. In this sense, estates were the material manifestation of boundaries set by the discourses of race, class and gender. Estates went from defensive positions to nodes of power from which the state launched its attacks and slowly reinstated constraints and boundaries that were essential to the foundational fantasy, now reaccentuated in the closing days of empire. Estates were the physical manifestations of divisions between labor and capital, Asians and Europeans and men and women. During the Emergency, the estates came to manifest a less obvious difference—between the European planters who stood and defended their territory for Empire and the Asian planters who either compromised with the MCP or abandoned the defense of their estates to others. Estates highlighted schisms along racial lines. For example, Asian estate owners had difficulty getting government protection compared to European estates and were sometimes forced to close because of this (Commercial Interests 1951e). Several Chinese mine owners admitted that they were paying the MCP up to $10,000 a month to be left in peace (Gurney 1948). In response to complaints from Asian estate and mine owners, General Templer (1952c) argued that "inevitably" almost all European estates met the preconditions of leadership, economic importance and proof of cooperation, while most Asian ones did not. Templer's remarks highlighted the racial cleavages that so influenced policy decisions in Malaya and continue to do so even now.

Conclusion

The advent of World War Two and the Japanese defeat of the British began the process of shattering the illusion of the invulnerable colonialist. Malaya fell to the Japanese in 1942. Although the Japanese Occupation of Malaya lasted only three years, it was critical in terms of framing future political contests through its effect both socially and psychologically in Malaya. It demolished the idea of Europeans' invincibility and entitlement. In doing so, the war inspired a generation of Asian nationalists already dubious of European entitlement. By the end of the war, moreover, the Japanese promotion of Malays and Indians to positions of responsibility provided the training ground for the psychological challenge to European supremacy after the war while their harsh treatment of the Chinese population galvanized resistance and laid the foundations for the military challenge. Indian and Malay nationalists obtained training in bearing weapons and administration that gave them the confidence to initiate postwar political agitation. The newly armed MCP emerged from the forests proficient in guerrilla warfare now used on their new military targets, the British. The racial score settling combined with renewed labor strikes and material shortages under the reoccupying BMA were early indicators that a reassessment of what colonial rule meant was underway (Daud 1977). In 1948, colonial authorities declared a state of emergency to quell unrest and the country was once again at war.

Through the human-perpetrated violence, the colonial authorities assigned the forest a code of violence—"the law of the jungle" (Gerald Templer quoted in Stubbs 1989, 148). The word "jungle" became a repository of the anxieties and fears of a world of military and political uncertainty and the key sign in the struggle for power. To return to Teresa Brennan's (1993) concept of the foundational fantasy and its role in a grandiose colonial identity, the attempt to contain the MCP within the forests was not only a military strategy but an essential psychological strategy in preserving colonial identity. In Malaya, this transition of signs from "forest" to "jungle" paralleled evolving meanings associated with the Emergency (Sioh 1998, 154) In this struggle, nature itself turned into a recalcitrant selfobject for the colonizers by leveling the power differential between the colonizers and their recalcitrant native selfobjects. Hence, the urgency of the project to reconstruct the forest as a frontier that had to be reterritorialized because this process was imperative to the reestablishing the grandiose colonial identity. The British were expecting to win the Emergency, but they were wary of ever being able to control the forest or its population (Maxwell et al. 1950). Conversely, by taking the site of the conflict to the estates, the MCP mirrored a similar strategy, not just in highlighting the resource angle of the conflict but in psychologically deconstructing colonial identity by exposing its vulnerability. While initial Communist strategy focused on killing either Europeans or colonial collaborators in public executions, the site of punishment later shifted from the body to the estate or the mine. The estate, once the symbol of rational production and progress wrested from the primitive forest, could no longer disassociate itself from the forest. It was no longer a symbol of colonial success but the site of its greatest fear, the end of empire.

Notes

1 The British response to the Japanese was a curious mixture of admiration for their "gallantry and devotion to duty" and resentment that their cooperation was a function of their obedience to the orders of their Emperor rather than an acknowledgment of defeat.
2 In her 1980 autobiography, *My House Has Two Doors*, author Han Suyin describes how her grocery bills were mysteriously inflated every month. This led her to conclude that some of her supplies were going to the MCP; her house was a meeting place for surrendered MCP who may have still had links with their former comrades despite the fact that her husband, Leon Comber, was a Special Branch (Intelligence) officer. Her experiences living and working as a doctor in Malaya over the course of ten years became the basis of her novel, *And the Rain My Drink* (London: Jonathan Cape, 1956), which follows her autobiography very closely.
3 Details for this section taken from notes in file CO 1022/3.

4 Trauma and the Wound of Race in the Malayan Emergency

Introduction

On New Year's Day 1970, the front page of *The Sunday Times* ran a story of 13 men who had been captured by the Malaysian Army from a camp in the forest outside the town of Kajang (*The Sunday Times* 1970). They were accused of being Communist sympathizers, especially since one of the group had been the Secretary General of the deregistered (and thus, illegal) Malayan Estate Workers' Union, punishable under the Internal Security Act often invoked during the military conflict known as the Emergency, which ran officially from 1948 to 1962 and only ended in practice in 1989. The men themselves argued that because they were jobless and starving, they preferred to hide in the forest rather than endure the shame of starving in public. The Army forced them back to the town. I do not know what happened to the men, but the story has haunted me over the years since I came across the newspaper clipping. I still cannot fathom the cruelty of forcing another human being to endure the humiliation of starving in public. When I've related this story, it has always caught the audience's attention. It strikes a chord of fear in listeners because it encapsulates a dimension and the dynamic of the postcolonial legacy left out of abstract theoretical analysis—the visceral fear and anxiety that consumes us when we are humiliated. Malaysia had been independent for almost 13 years by then but the trauma of the Emergency lived on.

This chapter analyzes the Emergency from the perspective of how trauma was inflicted on and experienced by the working classes in Malaya. The Emergency, declared on 16 June 1948 to defend British access to the resource economy of Malaya, lasted 12 years. At its peak, 6,000 guerrillas engaged an armed force 300,000 strong (Jackson 1991, 115). By the end of the Emergency, through the Briggs Plan, the British had resettled almost 600,000 Chinese and another 150,000 Indians, the latter under the estate regrouping program (Commercial Interests 1951b). Together, these accounted for 25 percent of the Malayan population and more than half of the non-Malay population. In a country already spatially segregated by race through employment opportunities, the Briggs Plan further entrenched spatial segregation by race.

DOI: 10.4324/9781315440286-5

Chapter 4 argues for the Emergency as the birth trauma of the Malaysian nation-state by focusing on the processes through which the British inflicted trauma upon the working classes of Malaya. The legacy of this psychodrama continues today in the racial politics that continue to define the country's economic policies and political landscape, including the recent 2022 federal and 2023 state elections.

Trauma constructed a consistent, if not always coherent narrative of the Emergency. The Emergency, an economic war for control of Malaya's natural resources, was officially recast as a Manichean fight of Good (the British and the Malayan elite) against Evil (the mainly Chinese Malayan Communist Party [MCP] and the Malayan working class) to disavow the greed underlying the colonial project. Just as significantly, racial anxieties underpinned the Emergency as a violent contest over economic entitlement embedded within the assumption of racial entitlement. But a legitimizing discourse alone cannot explain the viciousness and pettiness of the war. Colonialism, by creating an asymmetrical system of winning underpinned by racial privilege, sets up the colonizer for a narcissistic wound when the expected victories do not materialize. For the British, race was a mark of privilege but, crucially, one that could be lost resulting in a wound. I want to emphasize that I do **not** equate the experience of the colonizers with that of the colonized in terms of suffering but if we are to understand what drives the agonizing dynamic of race and political economy, we need to come to terms with how even the colonizers came to conceptualize potentially losing their racial privilege as trauma. After all, they had their victims in front of them as proof of the consequences of what race experienced as trauma would be like. For the colonized, with the exception of the elites, the quotidian violence and humiliation as a function of their racial identity transformed skin color, already a mark of inferiority in the colonial world, into a wound.

Trauma and the Wound of Race

The central framing of the chapter is through the concept of trauma. Psychological trauma is an affliction of powerlessness, which Judith Herman (2015, 33) defines as the experience of "intense fear, helplessness, loss of control and threat of annihilation." She goes on to add that trauma overwhelms ordinary systems of care that give people a sense of control, connection and meaning (ibid). Chapter 3 examined how British colonialists came to perceive the non-white population of Malaya as Kohutian recalcitrant selfobjects who inflicted further narcissistic wounding on the British following on the heels of their defeat by the Japanese. Chapter 4 now turns to the ensuing narcissistic rage by the British when confronted with the decolonization war of the Emergency and the trauma they inflicted on the colonized as vengeance. If the grandiose colonial self only identifies with the invulnerable, then shame at its own vulnerability must be projected elsewhere in "circuit of depersonalization" (Bollas 2011, 87) to find a "victim who will die his death" (160).

Most of Chapter 4 is concerned with *how* trauma is inflicted on its victims through violence and humiliation. For this reason, the chapter provides more detailed accounts of practices than in the rest of the book. I do so for two reasons: if the argument of the book is that if a population's repeated experience of trauma underpins that society's contemporary political dysfunction, then the accumulation of details provides support for the argument. Second, the Emergency was a brilliant public relations exercise by the British, so that unlike the Americans in Vietnam, there is little criticism of their conduct in Malaya. The "unspeakability" of trauma lies in the stigma attached to the victims so that trauma has an "underground" history (Herman 2015, 2). Moreover, the perpetrator's line of defense promotes forgetting through secrecy and silence and attacking the credibility of victim to ensure no one listens. The more cultural capital the perpetrators possess, the greater their prerogative to name and define reality (Herman 2015, 8). Colonial discourse, to invoke Christopher Bollas (2011) is a form of "psychic rendering" (115). This chapter aims to offer a corrective to this narrative slant by highlighting the underground history of the Emergency.

I analyze how trauma is repeatedly inflicted and reinforced through four **overlapping** pathways. The **first** pathway is to create an experience of extreme helplessness to the exposure to danger and humiliation through captivity (Herman 1992, 74–77), an extreme version of the conditions of Brennan's (1993) foundational fantasy mutated into Foucault's (1980, 68) "carceral archipelago:" as a punitive system dispersed yet covering whole societies. During the Malayan Emergency, punitive zones were distributed across the country as whole towns and parts of the country were declared under curfew, and civil rights suspended for the local population, who were then subjected to shelling and aerial bombardment. As Herman (2015, 77) notes, the victim must be made to feel that survival is dependent on the indulgence of the perpetrator since the use of force is capricious. **Second**, the staging of the violence was as significant a factor in its efficacy as the actual violence itself as a means of control so that the site of violence becomes embedded within a system of signs that conveyed the lesson to be learnt of the price paid for a crime committed—"a serious theatre of moral lessons" (Foucault 1995, 113). The **third** means of inflicting trauma is psychological: humiliating the victim such as the example in the opening paragraph of forcing the men to starve in front of witnesses, the disrespect inherent in parading dead and mutilated bodies, and denying the use of toilets. These practices constitute Herman's (2015, 2) "dialectic of trauma" whereby trauma involves not just victims but also witnesses to the victimization. **Fourth**, and the final means of inflicting trauma is to force the victims to violate their own values (Herman 2015, 83). This can take the form of causing victims to betray others or to disavow their own victimization. In the latter case, Herman (75) notes that the victim's compliance alone is insufficient. And Bollas (2011) notes that the victim's collusion in the act of disempowerment provides the victimizer with a reprieve from their "malevolent desire" (117). As we shall see in the case of the colonial conduct of the Emergency, betrayals were rewarded with land tenure in the "land for life" policy.

Trauma and the Carceral Archipelago

The idea that the forest was the theater of war (Chapter 3) was replaced by the reality that the entire country had turned into a theater of war. The colonial state metaphorically constructed the forest as an alien space through its policy of relocating forest dwellers in compounds surrounded by barbed wire that were euphemistically called New Villages. This section outlines the ways in which the drama of war was enacted on the stage of Malaya with the props of roadblocks, barbed wire, searchlights and concentration camps against the thudding overture of helicopters in the sky—the electronic eyes of the state. Through a series of textual, visual and legislative practices, the forest and New Villages were delineated as moral representations. The legislation enacted in tandem with the resettlement policies to immobilize and socially divide the population would see its legacy in the psychic landscape that characterizes contemporary Malaysian politics.

In Chapter 3, I recounted how the colonial state saw the Chinese squatters living on the edge of the forests as the main source of support for the Communists. In tandem with the strategy to drive the Communists into the forest, was the attempt to isolate them from their source of support by containing, enclosing and fixing individuals in spaces where they could be watched. This containment strategy resulted in the construction of the New Villages as part of the Briggs Plan (Commercial Interests 1951b). Squatters were forcibly removed from their villages, and their homes, livestock and crops destroyed. They were then relocated to a new area where they had to rebuild their homes with a small allocation of money within a fenced compound where they were placed under surveillance. The design of the New Villages was regular and geometric to enhance visibility in contrast to the settlements at the forest edge. The New Villages were examples of Foucault's (1995) architecture "that would operate to transform individuals: to act on those it shelters, to provide a hold on their conduct, to carry the effects of power right to them, to make it possible to know them, to alter them" (172). Not surprisingly, when casting about for land to resettle squatters from the edge of one forest, the colonial government sometimes excised forest reserves such as the Tampin Forest Reserve for resettlement purposes (Potter 1954a,b). But, in many cases, lack of available and suitable land meant villagers were resettled in unsuitable locations such as the swampy Bedok village in Singapore (Blades 1952). Well water was brackish resulting in insufficient water for drinking or agriculture. During high tide, huts were flooded and mosquitoes thrived increasing the danger of malaria and dengue. The Malaya Branch of the British Medical Association expressed concern at the "gross inadequacy of medical services in Malayan resettlement camps" with conditions that threatened epidemics (*The Daily Worker* 1952b).

The colonial state codified the fixing of people in space through elaborate inventories to establish presences and absences, thereby eliminating uncontrolled disappearances—unless the Government was responsible for the disappearances. House curfews of up to 22 hours literally fixed people in space.[1] A curfew was a restriction on movement outdoors, although it could be modified to restrict people to, or keep them out of, certain areas. Curfews were also humiliating in a sense that people were fined $50 for going to the outhouse, this at a time when $50 was a lot of money and most homes had no indoor plumbing (Templer 1952d). But I would suggest that humiliation was an important part of the punishment. The 4,000 inhabitants of Sungai Pelek were punished because a few villagers engineered an incident whereby sentries in the resettlement camp thought that they were being attacked, and in the ensuing commotion other villagers threw packets of food over the fence to waiting Communists (Malaya 1955). The authorities' reaction was to extend the 7.30-pm to 6.00-am curfew by another 1.5 hours, remove all surplus rice, cut rations and build a second perimeter fence. In addition to the now 13.5-hour house curfew, there was a 20-hour perimeter curfew and the villagers were made to pay the $55,000 to put up the second fence. In other examples, rural areas outside Kuala Lumpur and the town of Rawang had 24-hour house curfews imposed (ibid). The transformation of the symbolic significance of Rawang from site of rebellion during the Japanese Occupation to site of punishment during the Emergency was ironic: the decapitated heads of insurgents had been exhibited by the Japanese in the Rawang town center. Then, it was a cause for local pride that they resisted.

The most extreme version of fixing people in place was the firing plan. This began by outlining a grid of 20–24 map squares on a map. From battalion logs, it would appear that the government troops concentrated on areas such as Yong Peng and Segamat, both in Johore, that had once been sites of resistance to the Japanese occupying army (Third East Anglian Regiment 1960). Respected by local people, these were now seen by the reoccupation forces as trouble spots because resistance was now redirected at another occupier: the British. The economic costs of the forest operations were high. An example toward the official end of the war gives an idea of the numbers involved in an operation: four companies and nine platoons supported by the air force and tracker teams (ibid). Another operation mounted in a different part of the country involved five companies, nine platoons, air support and tracker teams. On average, it took 700 person-hours for every Communist killed (Cross 1971). The summary of a firing plan in this paragraph is taken from a campaign diary ('S' Troop RA, 1954–1956). The main activity of a firing plan was to shell the outlined area usually with a 25-pound gun. Firing would commence and continue non-stop for three to six days. A typical firing plan covered a 100 map squares with each square divided into nine portions lettered "A" to "I." One hundred rounds were fired three times a day engaging all the "Bs" at 0600 hours or all the "Fs" at 1500 hours. This meant that the whole area was covered evenly three times a day and after three days, forest residents would have experienced a round of shelling at least 150 yards away from them. Another method of covering the area was to shell it along diagonal lines thus eventually covering the area with a criss-crossed grid. The motivation behind shelling was more psychological than operational as captured Communist personnel claimed that it caused few casualties since shells usually exploded before they reached the ground ('S' Troop RA 1954–1956, 20 March 1955). However, the shelling did accomplish the aim of immobilizing the Communists who were forced to shelter under large trees. The army also argued that it worked for psychological reasons as it forced Communists camps to move on or surrender after enduring prolonged shelling ('S' Troop RA 1954–1956, 31 October 1954). Night firing was also favored as it was thought to be more stressful for the Communists who could not find cover in the dark. Royal Air Force jets synchronized bombing runs and strafing with the firing plans. When a meeting of Communists was rumored to be taking place around Tanah Hitam, shelling and strafing of the area commenced. The impact of the military struggles must have been extremely stressful for the local population as the armed forces rarely knew the exact location of potential targets.

Emergency regulations implemented on 13 July 1948 made fingerprinting and identification cards mandatory for anyone over 12 (Malaya 1948b). Initially, these practices were put in place for the Chinese who had to go to the police stations to be fingerprinted and photographed (Malaya 1948c). The practice of mandatory identity cards continues to this day. During the Emergency, household residents' inventories were pasted outside every house, and random house-to-house searches by the police or army encouraged a self-disciplining society. Inventories of individuals were replicated at the level of collectivities as presses, clubs and groups all had to be registered, while rallies and meetings were illegal. The Trade Union Ordinance of 1940 had already banned freedom of association between trade unions of government workers and trade unions of non-government workers (Smee 1954). A psychological dimension of the containment strategy was withholding of information by restricting publications, maps and radios.

But the New Villages in the Briggs Plan was the centerpiece of Malayan military and political strategy. The Plan depended on segregating the Communists from their main source of support, the squatters. Since this would channel the Communists onto the estates, estate laborers and Malay villagers also had to be regrouped as part of the strategy of isolating the Communists in the forests. Michel Foucault (1995, 141) argues that discipline requires enclosing bodies in space. In this manner, those in authority can control distribution of bodies and break up potential collectivities. Foucault went on to argue that because disciplinary space is partitioned into as many spaces as bodies, it allows easy visual surveillance of presences and absences (ibid, 143–144). The difference in terminology between resettlement and regrouping appeared to be related to the degree of civil rights associated with the different terms. At a conceptual level, the colonial state's tactics could be seen as an attempt to purify space physically and control bodies. In the New Villages, individuals would be confined in their huts and village perimeter through different kinds of curfews for households and areas. Individuals would be marked and recorded through fingerprinting, photographing and issuing identification cards for anyone over 12 years. The practice of random checks trained the population in self-surveillance. A binary grading system of "black" versus "white" areas served to separate the bad from the good, at least by the definition of those in power. Thus, the extension of the physical purification process would continue imaginatively through these disciplinary and textual practices on the newly incarcerated population to mark the spaces of the colonial state. Foucault's (1995, 138) argument that it is through a repetition of processes that overlap, imitate and support each other that a coherent method is built held true for Malaya during the Emergency. The domains of application of disciplinary practices were different—roadblocks, individual households, concentration camps—but they repeated and supported each other through numerous interventions in quotidian details to create a "blueprint" of control.

Trauma and the Serious Theater of Moral Lessons

A metaphorical extension of curfew was the designation of these civil-rights deprived areas as black, grey and white. Perhaps the most widespread form of moral representations was the designation of "black" and "white" areas with corresponding degrees of curfew and deprivation of civil rights (Malaya 1954). From the point of view of the colonial state, their impact was mainly psychological rather than practical. Another government tactic to eliminate uncontrolled movement of people was to designate only certain routes into, and out of, towns and villages (Malaya 1948b). Roadblocks multiplied across the landscape, and roads were designated "black" or "white" reflecting their status as off limits or not. Being seen near the forest was deemed an implication of guilt. People seen at the forest edge were assumed to be Communists or their sympathizers (Third East Anglian Regiment 1960). An area would be designated "black" as a form of hostage-taking. The transformation into a "white" area would be the reward for the local population providing information or, better still, killing a few Communists themselves. Triang was the last area in South Central Malaya to remain "black," the surrounding areas were redesignated "white" after a six-man Communist band surrendered (*Malaya* 1960, 20). The *Daily Worker* (1952a) shrewdly commented that the policy was to impose collective punishment until the government could induce individual betrayals. Among the punishments meted out to the residents of "black" areas were fines and paying for the forces billeted there (Haynes 1950a), severe hardship for already poor, landless peasants. The policy toward the landless peasants who were seen as the main supporters of the Communists was repatriation, resettlement in New Villages under government surveillance, or simply dispersal from their original homes where they were left to fend for themselves (Godfrey 1978, 4). Shelling "black" areas was a drastic means of creating sites of punishment. For example, in retaliation for an ambush that killed 11 men and wounded 11 more, troops shelled a resettlement area in Selangor, which killed four people including an 11-year-old girl and wounded three others (*The Daily Worker* 1951).

This strategy of taking sites of contestation and turning them into moral representations is exemplified by the village of Permatang Tinggi in the Bukit Mertajam district of Province Wellesley. Past incidents of rebellion by the villagers included the murder of government contractor, giving subscriptions, and allowing Communists to visit the Chinese temple just outside the village. When Assistant Resettlement Officer, Teoh Boon Hoe, was killed, 62 villagers were sent to detention camp and 21 deported from Permatang Tinggi (Templer 1953a). Seventeen villagers were arrested, including four children and the village was destroyed. The residents were also forced to pay a fine of $250 per shop and $150 per house under Emergency Regulation 17DA (Templer 1952f). The villagers' goods were confiscated and then publicly auctioned. Perhaps due to previous incidents, the British claimed that every policeman was searched before going on operation and coming off it, indicating that British were not confident in the impartiality of the police who carried out the confiscation. After all, given that the villagers' belongings were being treated like the spoils of war, it was understandable that the local police simply took the actions to their logical conclusion. Six months later the villagers were moved back to the old village and wired in (Director of Operations Staff for Templer 1952).

Perhaps the best example of the fate of victims of colonial narcissistic rage is the town of Tras. Mass detention was institutionalized in 1949 under Regulation 17(D). On 7 November 1951 the entire town of Tras, Pahang was detained for suspicion of having cooperated with the Communists who killed Sir Henry Gurney, the High Commissioner. Two thousand people, mostly old men, women and children were detained because 5 women and 15 men were suspected of being involved in the killing of Sir Henry Gurney.[2] Residents' belongings were sold off while Troops scoured the nearby forest and Brigand bombers roared overhead. Singling out Tras may have been related to the fact that British troops had fought in the village 15 times to retake it from Communists ("The Evacuation" 1951). The Secretary of State for the Colonies argued that the main reason for the destruction was to evacuate a bad area rather than "punish" the inhabitants (United Kingdom 1951b). In an example of schisms by class, the Malayan Chinese Association aided in the "color-coding" of villagers and detainees as "black," "grey" or "white" (Commercial Interests 1951c; United Kingdom 1951a). The point of describing the individual cases above is to show the degree of detail involved in punishing and disciplining the population. Punishment, while severe, in most cases did not result in death, thus depriving the victims of any moral upper hand inherent in martyrdom. This was an important strategy on the part of the government to wean support from the MCP by whatever methods but, at the same time, avoid surrounding the MCP and their potential supporters with any aura of victimization. The coding of "bad" attributes distributed in space was underpinned by a latent Orientalism in that spatial distributions of group characteristics were attributed to race—literally "color-coded." These conditions were then justified to the public as essential in preserving peace and freedom. Ultimately, these repressive measures became interwoven in the story of how Malaya became an independent nation-state. The question of why the measures to protect the privileges of the British colonialists should be conflated with the sovereignty of the nation-state of postcolonial Malaysia has rarely been raised, no doubt as a result of the censorship laws. But describing the racially biased institutional practices and rhetorical strategies the state deployed in dealing with dissent explains why social tensions are never far below the surface in contemporary Malaysia.

Meanwhile, labor regrouping on the estates, while promoted for safety reasons, had the consequence of making it easier to control labor movement and activities. The Anglo-Java Rubber Company (1952) reported that they had regrouped all their workers into two illuminated areas surrounded by barbed wire fences for 3,300 yards and 1,200 yards, respectively. Emergency regulations forbade workers to take food out of estates which meant in effect they could not work after noon (Lennox-Boyd 1955b). Local people resisted these oppressive conditions. At Mentakap, Pahang, tappers defied police orders not to take out food (Blades 1953d). When refused exit unless they left behind the food, they went on strike led by ten women, seven of whom the British later arrested. On another occasion, concentration camp residents led by a woman attacked police who tried to beat up workers who exited the camp gates without being searched after the police had opened the gates late. Although three tappers were beaten up in retaliation, the gates were never again locked as late as 7.00 am (Blades 1953c). The MCP interpreted these acts of resistance as gestures of solidarity (ibid), but these actions were more likely desperate attempts to deal with quotidian issues of survival. A more likely sympathetic action is that of the Kajang estate strikes by 4,000 tappers in 1951 (ibid). The Korean War took place concurrently with labor regrouping. This coincidence meant that as the estates cashed in on the high price of rubber by expanding their plantations, labor regrouping proved a useful exercise in reorganizing for a more docile labor force (Potter 1954a,b). Resettlement and regrouping meant that the increasingly desperate Communists attempted to buy or coerce supplies from Malay villagers. Under these circumstances, Malay villagers were occasionally moved to new locations. The conditions under which detention took place varied depending on race. Since the British were trying to maintain their alliance with the Malays, they couldn't afford to treat Malays who defied them too badly, instead choosing to regard Malay transgressors as ignorant or misunderstood. Preparations made for Malay detainees were more considerate and detainees were referred to as *siswas* or student ("Communism" undated).The policy of sending detainees to a camp far away from their original place of residence was common method of physically and psychologically isolating the individuals. Rather than outright incarceration, the camps focused on vocational training such as tailoring, carpentry and agricultural husbandry, and warders, staff and detainees lived in the same compound on 20 acres of grounds (Ibid).

Along with curfew, residents of "black" areas were restricted in the amount of goods they could buy, store, move and consume, and their movements by day and night and hours of business were circumscribed (Malaya 1954). Even after an area was redesignated "white," it was still subject to surveillance. Tins of food purchased in shops continued to have holes punched in them, while area curfews persisted even after house curfews were lifted. The strategy of areas being recategorized from "black" to "white" was a metaphorical equivalent of territorialization, and recategorizations were accompanied by maps of the area to fix the images in people's minds. Black areas redesignated "White" were represented on maps as "*berseh*" or "clean" (CO 1030/1). Maps and plans not only acted as charters of intervention, they also reified the characterization of the spaces they represented. Despite the acclaim accompanying the redesignation of an area from "black" to "white" the government was concerned that the MCP would see the "white" areas as a source of supplies now that the restrictions had been lifted. Certainly, the fanfare preceding the declaration of Klang and surrounding areas as "white" on 5 December 1954 was premature as the Communist underground organization was still strong. Perhaps the strongest admission of the ineffectualness of "white" areas was the recommendation that estates and "white" areas not abut the forest for fear of military and political contamination. Special Branch urged that "[W]henever possible, a "white" area should not be extended to the edge of the jungle" (Combined Intelligence Staff 1955). Nevertheless, every occasion of a "black" area recategorized as "white" became important propaganda. By November 1954, the Government was reporting that 1.7 million people were living in "White" areas, ignoring the remaining 4.3 million still living in "black" and "grey" areas (Archive: D.Inf.11/54/68 N.d. Emergency CO1030/1).

Successful territorialization for the colonial authorities translated into the removal of safe space so that "home" becomes an alien space for the non-white working class population. The goal of transforming the forest into a punitive space was not just physical alienation but also psychological alienation. Unlike the forest-dwelling *Orang Asli*, neither Government forces nor the Communists could survive in the forests on their own. Government troops could count on food drops during long tours of duty in the jungle but the Communists had to rely on what they could eke out. Captured documents indicated conditions so desperate that even the departure of one soldier eased the food distribution while a few departures allowed the unit to carry on as it relieved strain on food (Blades 1953b). A letter captured by Gurkhas near Mersing in February 1953 showed that the food situation was causing insubordination among the rank and file at the perceived inequality of food distribution. The letter continued for four pages on such seemingly trivial problems as a lack of tins to store food, which caused the food to go bad. Furthermore, the shortage of food caused hostility between the Min Yuen, their public supporters and the Communist troops because of the latter's belief that the former were starving them deliberately (ibid).

Food scarcity was a serious problem, but the MCP was also acutely concerned about the psychological effects of isolation in the forest. The Emergency proved the testing ground for the widespread use of helicopters in an army support capacity; they were used in casualty evacuation, reconnaissance and troop-lifting (Godfrey 1978, 1). Lastly, technology was important in overcoming psychological isolation in the forests. Wireless communication was crucial for "jungle squads," police stations and estates as there were no lines susceptible to be sabotaged by the Communists (Maxwell et al. 1950). For that reason, as much as any other, communication was a key factor in survival. Not only was communication essential for disseminating battle plans and party policy, but it was also crucial to keeping up morale. Loss of morale could result in troop defections. The MCP attempted to convey news of victories and celebrations such as the commemoration of the birthday of the Party (Blades 1953e). Unlike colonial troops, the MCP could not rely on technology to overcome the physical impediment of the forest to communication because of government restrictions on sales of radios and parts for transmission equipment. So Communist communications relied heavily on the population to act as couriers collecting notes, personal views, minutes of meetings and records of interviews for submission to the upper tier of the organization which were then published by sympathetic urban presses or Party-run presses in the forests (ibid).

The final acts in theater of moral lessons were deportation or execution. The number sentenced to death in 1953 stood at 169 (Blades 1953c). Traditional punishment centered on the body such as the exhibition of dead Communists outside a police station. The corpse of a 17-year-old girl, Lim Saw Hoon, and a man named Subramaniam were exhibited outside the Kulim Police station (Plummer 1953). Two Communists killed by the Green Howards were exhibited outside Telok Anson and the body of Liew Kon Kim (a prominent Communist) was paraded around villages in southern Selangor (*Manchester Guardian* 1952). All these practices harked back to the Japanese Occupation when exhibiting decapitated heads was a common means of instilling fear in the general population. The Japanese relied solely on a regime of fear because they were a minority facing a majority. Other acts centered on the body were execution by hanging and the practice of government soldiers taking back the heads of Communists killed in the forests (Jerrom 1952c,d,e,f). The latter act caused one of the major controversies of the war. While the state designated the forest the theater of war, to create a regime of fear successfully, the site of vengeance had to be visible. Hence, corpses were moved from the forest to the town. The executions, mutilation and exhibition of corpses recall Bollas' (2011, 160) point that narcissistic rage projection literally requires a victim who will die the death of the enraged subject. In the beginning, the Colonial government defended the actions as reasonable (Jerrom 1952b). After taking legal counsel in England they were advised that under International Law it was a war crime (1952c). The Colonial government then tried arguing that international law did not hold during a revolution (Jerrom 1952d). When advised that this was not true, their strategy moved to playing down the story (ibid). The concern, after all, was not moral but from the adverse publicity. In a Colonial Office memorandum, Jerrom (1952e) wrote:

> It seems to me that the specific instructions to Unit Commanders will be necessary and will have to lay emphasis on the extreme seriousness of the photographs from the propaganda point of view....

Jerrom (1952f) went on:

> This matter is not one in which we could safely take a high line without the risk of rejoinders – critics can always fall back on the bandits' head story and other unsavoury episodes.

Maintaining the moral high line was an important part of the justificatory regime for this war. By this point in history, the justification for colonialism itself as a stage along the indefinite road to independence was taken for granted. But prolonging colonialism needed justifying and here it came courtesy of the need to protect Malaya from falling into the hands of the MCP. Even more controversially, General Templer seems to have suggested in a letter that a regiment of Dyaks be used not just for tracking "but in their traditional fighting role as head-hunters" (Jerrom 1952e). I could not verify Templer's letter itself as it was not in the file in the archives. In addition, "minor" acts of punishment included whipping or caning (Malaya 1948a). Like hanging, the practice of caning continues to this day. A common method of torture was stripping prisoners and making them lie on a bed of ice (Blades 1953c). In the 1970s, two senior police officers, one in intelligence and the other in the regular force, corroborated this story in conversations with my father, although the actual method of torture was described as making prisoners sit on a block of ice. More than half the population of Malaya during the Emergency were treated as enemies. At the same time, contrary to the views of the Communists, the conditions for a popular revolution never existed because almost an equal portion of the population were allied with the colonialists even if they did not necessarily want colonialism to continue. In these circumstances, executions and exhibitions of their grisly results created a climate of fear and served as markers of the colonial state's power.

With regard to punishment by banishment, the state's right to banish people was never questioned, only who should be subjected to banishment. The colonial government also saw deportation as a useful way of ridding the state of "persons rendered homeless or destitute by the present emergency measures" (Commissioner General for South-East Asia 1948; Morris 1948). The Office of the Attorney General for the Federation of Malaya added that deportation would be a way of dealing with the destitute being looked after by the state who were mostly women and children (ibid). It is difficult to calculate exactly how many people were deported. Between 1949 and 1953, a total of 29,828 persons were detained. Of those deported, 14,946 were Chinese, 1,752 were Indians, 12 Ceylonese and 129 Indonesians (Haynes 1950a).

The libidinal dimension of the punitive practices during the Emergency were examples of Herman's (2015, 75) contention that simple compliance is not enough to justify crimes, and therefore, perpetrators need constant affirmations from their victims. This fits in with the trope of "the white man's burden" since the colonialists were only taking over someone else's country at their request. Instead, the recalcitrance of local people who refused to betray each other or even opted for self-sacrifice triggered narcissistic rage in colonial authorities. After all, self-sacrifice is seen as the ultimate act of defiance. For example, in an incident on 19 June 1953, two comrades were ambushed in a banana grove. This time, the wounded man, Leong Sang, blew himself and six approaching soldiers up to allow the second man to get away (Blades 1953c). The significance of self-sacrifice as an act of resistance lies in the willingness to deprive one's self to a greater extent than perpetrators can inflict upon you thus denying them psychological control. By the same token, self-sacrifice affirms integrity and self-control for victim (Herman 1992, 79). Acts of self-deprivation inherent in resistance become moral victories even in physical defeat. For this reason, "land for a life" exchanges was important in removing the aura of integrity from the Communists and their allies by sowing distrust and highlighting the cupidity of those who participated. And for those who participated, "land for life" exchanges were a way around the predicament of landlessness and poverty. General Templer (1953b,c) offered the villagers of Jabor Valley half an acre of land for every person who provided information leading to the capture or killing of a Communist.

Conclusion

British humiliation at losing to the Japanese during the war and displaced onto the economic struggle transformed the Emergency into a vicious war officially lasting 12 years and resulting in the incarceration of a sixth of the Malayan population. By challenging the economic entitlement of the colonial authorities, the Communists were refusing interpellation within the accepted racial hierarchy. But for the British colonialists used to being in power, the challenge to entitled privilege came to be experienced as trauma triggering a narcissistic rage which they projected onto the Communist-led insurgent population of Malaya. Psychologically, as the only organized resistance to the Japanese early in the war, the Communists subsequently bore the brunt of the shame of the British for their losses and the shame of local elites who relied on the British for protection. Chapter 4 has reviewed the ways in which colonial authorities literally and figuratively forced the Malayan population to "die their death" (Bollas 2011, 160) as punishment for the challenging the colonial right to rule but perhaps also as a way of working through their own shame at losing to the Japanese. Prewar illusions of a benign colonial rule were shattered during the Emergency in light of public exhibitions of mutilated corpses and mass incarceration of the non-white population in concentration camps euphemistically described as "New Villages." The emphasis on cutting off the Communists from their supply line in the larger population can be seen as an attempt to castrate the protagonists in the decolonization war and to reassert colonial racial and masculine authority. The New Villages may have been an attempt to reassert the colonial fantasy for the British, but it has also become part of the new postcolonial foundational fantasy of the Malaysian nation-state. The structural violence entrained in the struggle to defeat the MCP became the birth trauma of the Malaysian nation-state and one whose psychic legacy continues to determine the country's political landscape today.

Notes

1 This following section on curfew summarizes notes in file CO 1022/56.
2 *Straits Times,* 9 November 1951.

5 Anxiety and Pricing Race at Independence

Introduction

This chapter examines what factors lay behind the creation of the policies for Malaya's formidable currency reserves in the years leading up to political independence in 1957. Albert Memmi (1967, 85) suggests that economic privilege functions as psychological privilege in a relationship of equivalence. But I argue that the significance of economic privilege, after satisfying basic needs, lies in its ability to create psychological privilege, in other words, a precondition of psychological privilege rather than a parallel privilege. The Malayan government-in-waiting facing a large currency reserve chose to peg the Malayan currency to British sterling whose value appeared to be declining. The size of a country's foreign currency reserves affects its ability to qualify for loans or attract capital investment, in that the larger the reserves, the greater the international community's confidence in a currency. This, in turn, affects the cost of imports to a country and the price of its exports. More significantly for Western popular media depictions of decolonization, conventional wisdom holds that, once freed of external rule, ex-colonies are responsible for their poor decisions. Hence, the fledgling Malayan government's decision became a silent rebuttal of its claims to being a competent successor to the colonial rulers.

My departure point is to ask how we explain decisions characterized by the search for economic advantage without concomitant real gains, sometimes even with losses. I argue that the fledgling Malayan government's decision to exchange its export income in US dollars for sterling, which resulted in a loss of value for the Malayan currency, was less a product of poor economic judgement than of the racial anxieties that underpinned its understanding of what its currency reserves purchased. I am not claiming that the decisions had no material basis, but as we shall see later in the chapter, the negotiations took place domestically against the backdrop of the military conflict of the Emergency, and internationally, against the backdrop of the Cold War. Given the resource-based wealth of colonial Malaya, the influence of class conflict on the negotiations was apparent and the platform of one major combatant, the Malayan Communist Party (MCP). Less obvious, but equally influential,

DOI: 10.4324/9781315440286-6

was the influence of racial anxiety in determining the outcome of the currency negotiations. For Britain, this was an anxious time as the superpower torch passed on to their main creditors, the US. Henceforth, Britain's status vis-à-vis the US would depend greatly on its financial reserves. For the Malayan elites, whose inheritance of the country came through an independence war fought by the MCP, maintaining Malayan export income in sterling was the price of the political handover, which was not won through their own military prowess, the traditional indicator of entitlement. Thus, the racial dimension of the conflict was everywhere present yet never openly acknowledged. This chapter highlights the role of racial anxieties in one of Britain's key economic negotiations of the era: the fate of Malaya's currency reserves.

In neoclassical economics, decisions are assumed to be a function of the rational preferences of individuals based on maximizing profits, if not monetary, then some other tangible gain. Intuitively, if a party incurs a loss of income, then the decision leading to that loss is a bad one. Assuming that the party was free to choose, did the decision-maker lack the knowledge to choose wisely or was it because the "commodity" purchased through the economic decision was other than the one verbalized? The difference between the two situations is relevant to the underlying discourse of economic failures in developing countries, which are largely former colonies as well. In the first situation, the decision-maker lacks the intellectual capacity to make the right choice, thus reinforcing the trope of ignorant natives. The second situation requires a historically contextualized understanding of the decision-maker's perception of what it gains. For this was a time when the role of economic ranking, in the form of Gross Domestic Product (GDP) or Gross National Product (GNP),[1] as a chief overt indicator for international ranking gathered strength in the post-World War Two era as the brave new presumably post-racist decolonizing world looked for some other acceptable indicator of intrinsic superiority.

Chapter 5 examines the negotiations over the fate of Malaya's currency reserves as a function of racial anxieties in volatile post-World War Two geopolitics. From the rational perspective of neoclassical economics, the Malayan elite's decision to maintain its foreign exchange reserves in sterling was a bad decision. In Malaya, the choice to convert export income obtained in US dollars to sterling resulted in low economic growth and social tension, which culminated in the race riots of 13 May 1969. So, why did the Malayan elite choose to invest in sterling? Who benefited from this policy and what were the perceived benefits? Money is a symbol of value; therefore, currency pegs, as investment choices affecting the value of a currency are surrogate indicators of faith in a particular set of social relations. I begin with a brief theoretical review psychoanalytically framing the negotiations through the concept of anxiety followed by a historical overview of sterling as an international currency and the role of colonial economies in supporting sterling. I then situate Malaya's role in the sterling area at the end of World War Two before examining the negotiations over the control of Malayan currency reserves in tandem with the identity anxieties evolving concomitant with the decolonization struggle.

The Libidinal Economy of Currency Reserves

David Harvey (1982, 10) notes that the money commodity is the product of a historically specific social process, and its exchange value has two parts: inherent value and reflex value, the latter being what money will buy. He argues that the power that comes with money is in fact a great social leveler because a dollar is worth a dollar regardless of who possesses it (19). Yet racialized capitalism both in the colonial world and the contemporary developed world shows us a crude distinction in which the purchasing power of a dollar buys far less in the hands of non-white people in general. Money doesn't just give social value; it also takes on value from the social worth of its possessor, a process that was normalized and introjected by both the winners and the losers in colonialism. Money's reflex value is a function of historical and social processes; thus, we need to examine what conditions and intrinsic traits go into the processes shaping the commensurability of exchange values. If money is a storehouse of meaning that imparts social power, what underlying meanings are present in each set of value exchanges?

Harvey (1982, 18, 245) also notes that for money to function as social power, it must be guaranteed by a solid legal foundation that enforces the conditions of exchange. The bourgeois state then acts as a guarantor of contracts and individual freedoms through its legal monopoly on violence. The state as regulator of monetary value and conditions of exchange is manifested in the central bank, whose policies and practices link the domestic economy to its place in the international arena. But the state's position in the international hierarchy depends on its power to convince others of the legitimacy of its position and this goes beyond military enforcement. Chapter 5 links the factors that influenced the presumed social worth of the various national and international groups, including the MCP, at the currency negotiations. In pre-Independence Malaya, the contesting claims to Malaya's currency reserves highlight the struggle for the state apparatus precisely because a different leadership in an independent Malaya would have resulted in different monetary investment choices, which would have had repercussions far beyond the local level. But the alliances made that supported one investment decision over another rested on assumptions of who could be trusted and why. The currency negotiations in Malaya at the time are important for highlighting how the waning legal and moral force of colonialism was supplanted by an equally effective hegemony that persuaded the indigenous elite to maintain the colonial status quo through introjection of the social worth of the different actors. I frame my analysis in two ways: I analyze the hegemonic uses of essentialized racial and national representations in a calculus of value commensurability; and I link the driving impetus behind the negotiations to the identity anxieties of the time.

The Narrow Spaces of Decision-Making

Edward Said (1978, 7) admitted that the importance of any knowledge is gauged by its proximity to economic decisions, although he was more interested in the hegemonic influence of culture. But even if the importance of any body of knowledge is gauged by its proximity to economic decisions, these themselves turn on the unconscious knowledge of how things should be. Said (1978, 206–207) made the distinction between manifest and latent Orientalism where the former is a question of codes and laws, and the latter is a corporate identity that influences the unconscious sense of the way things are or should be (206–207). The significance of hegemony in the study of postcolonial predicaments depends on the extent to which a subject population acquiesces with the external judgement of itself. What it meant to be politically independent as opposed to substantively independent is a tension that bears revisiting because of the oftentimes complicity of colonized subjects with their rulers, now conveniently forgotten (Gandhi 1998, 10). Moreover, the study of the libidinal economy that governs the culture of financial decision-making is a still neglected area in the social sciences. In Chapter 1, I defined a libidinal economy as one of psychic exchanges where decisions in one arena are linked and traded off emotionally against decisions in others. Kapoor et al. (2023) and Glynos et al. (2012, 2015) address denial and the fantasies of desire and control in financial cultures but do not offer substantive analysis of the role of race or ethnicity even in the performativity of finance where the identity of the performer must play an important part. After all, the performance of debt negotiation, its incurrence and settlement incorporates the social position of both the debtor and the debtholder. This chapter builds on their work by adding race as a key factor in my analysis.

The negotiations over the fate of Malaya's earnings were framed in the rhetoric of debt and obligations incurred, but those obligations, and the direction of the obligations, themselves reflected the introjected subjective worth of the actors and the resultant social order of the time. As such, we need to examine the discursive construction of the social order underwriting the exchange value commensurabilities. While Janet Roitman (2003) doesn't directly address race as a factor in economic culture, her perceptive study of debt in Cameroonian society does question what kind of value transformations and parity exchanges take place in settling debts. For Roitman the condition of debt returns us to relations of dependency and the representation of *a just social order and who is entitled to the rewards* (221). In debt negotiations, value parities are determined by social hierarchy so that the higher the social standing of the individual, the greater the degree of debt forgiveness of the debtor. I expand upon Roitman's analysis in the context of the various anxieties at play in currency negotiations prior to Malayan independence.

Freud (1959b, 58, 62–68) linked anxiety to trauma through the memory of narcissistic wounding when confronted with a loss of either the love object or self-love Freud (1959b, 72). Anxiety arises originally as a reaction to a state of danger and is reproduced whenever a similar state recurs and the ego is reduced to state of helplessness in the face of excessive need. He distinguished between realistic anxiety, which is "intelligible" as a signal to expect physical injury from an external threat, and neurotic anxiety which is "free floating" and attaches itself to any possibility that threatens the loss of love (Freud 1965, 103–116). Castration then becomes a psychological category for referencing the terms of trauma, threat and anxiety, conditions that acutely faced the colonized population but because of the humiliating losses of World War Two and the passing superpower torch to the US also came to be perceived as relevant for the British in Malaya. One of the defensive mechanisms entrained in the face of anxiety is the introjection of the values of someone more powerful, which requires the repression of one's own desires. But introjecting the values of someone who does not have one's interest at stake is to understand one's self in negative terms (Fanon 1967, 41). The Malaysian elites' actions during the currency negotiations appeared accepting of the hierarchy of entitlement that was a legacy of colonialism. Citing Lacan, Adamson and Clark (1999 181) define desire as not a biological drive but a seeking of recognition from the other. Thus, humiliation is the experience of the other's negative evaluation of oneself. The stereotyped self becomes abjected (humiliated) while simultaneously desiring and introjecting the characteristics of the colonial ego ideal. Memmi foregrounded the attention to the idealization of race encapsulated by a visible marker, such as skin color or shape of eyes, that is representative of the colonized stereotype, to signify position in the "natural" order (1967, 84–89). For Frantz Fanon (1967), stereotyping creates a "dialectic between the body and the world" (111), which he argued overdetermined the stereotyped subject's conduct from within (115). His way out of the psychological constraints of the stereotype for the colonized was through the practical actions of violent revolution (Fanon 1963, 187–199), an option not taken by the Malayan elite. I want to highlight the introjection by the colonized of the characterizing dualities imposed upon them by their rulers, which ascribed positive traits such as martial prowess, courage and intellectual acumen to said rulers, an acceptance that after all made the task of their own domination easier for their rulers. This is not to argue that psychoanalytic categories are essential or universal. But as Derek Hook (2004a, 92) has pointed out, they do allow us to account for certain effects that do not conform to the mainstream calculus of economic or political rationality.

Malaya and Sterling

As the preeminent colonial power in the nineteenth century, British sterling was the principle means of exchange in international trade. Although gold was the official standard for valuing currency, the widespread use of sterling made it the defacto means of pricing other currencies in the same manner the US dollar functions today. As such, Britain should have needed to maintain large reserves in case customers needed to settle debts, since the inability to meet a currency call would have compromised the stability of sterling (Oppenheimer 1966, 90–96). The main domestic policy weapon for maintaining the value of sterling was the Bank Rate which was augmented by adjustments to the price of gold and restricting borrowing when the value of sterling needed to propped up (Oppenheimer 1966, 90–91). What is lesser known, as Krozewski (1996, 48) argues, is that Britain heavily relied on its colonies to maintain a positive current account balance and gold reserves to prop up the value of sterling. He is supported by Balachandran 1996, 47–100) and Oppenheimer (1966, 101) who argue that India carried sterling's value through its gold holdings. These reserves allowed Britain to maintain a free trade policy until the 1930s Depression when the sterling area emerged.[2] The sterling area consisted of countries with currencies linked to sterling rather than the US dollar or gold. Sterling on the other hand did not have a fixed exchange rate with the other two so that when the exchange rate swung the whole sterling area was affected. It is worth noting that the European sterling countries, unlike the colonies which had no financial autonomy, transferred some of their reserves to gold as sterling's value depreciated vis-à-vis gold. Because 60 percent of its liabilities was to sterling countries, most of which were also their colonies, Britain ran few risks of being called on its debts. At the outbreak of World War Two, Britain suspended sterling convertibility and free trade outside of the sterling area. These policies allowed Britain to manage transactions with the dollar area through a pooling system whereby the accumulated balances of the sterling area were used to offset trade imbalances between Britain and the US (Krozewski 1996, 48). This meant that sterling's value was being propped up by Malayan earnings, a relationship that took on increasing importance as British imperial power waned relative to the US.

The sterling exchange rate relative to the dollar declined after World War Two, and Britain ended the war with increased debt to the US. Aside from the US, most of Britain's debts were to the colonies. This meant that Britain could rely on not having to meet them, and foreign credit was important in maintaining confidence in sterling and, in turn, preserving what remained of Britain's great power status. The importance of Malayan contributions to sterling reserves has to be viewed in light of the adverse balance of payments (BOP) situation that had developed between Britain and the US during World War Two (Gardner 1969). In 1943, the US changed its wartime financial arrangement with Britain whereby industrial equipment was loaned to Britain and its allies, insisting that it must now be purchased. Under these new terms, Britain developed a considerable deficit with the US that continued after the war. In contrast, Malaya was one of the few countries in the sterling area with a positive BOP with the US. The nature of the colonial relationship was such that the Malayan Currency Board automatically exchanged Malaya's US dollar earnings for sterling; each Malayan dollar issued had to be covered 100 percent by sterling reserves (Oppenheimer 1966, 115). Malayan currency was then issued on the basis of the sterling exchange rate of Malayan $8 to £1, set by the British. But at a time when Britain needed to be sure that it controlled Malayan surpluses, it also faced its most serious challenge to its power in Malaya—the Emergency.

The direction of financial obligations in the relationships among the different political entities relevant to the Malayan currency negotiations during the Emergency can be summarized as follows. Britain was in debt to the Americans at the close of the war and attempted to reverse the rhetoric of obligation by emphasizing the US need for Malayan rubber and tin as well as the Americans' ability to build on longtime British connections in the East to create alliances against global communism. But this partially successful rhetorical reversal of obligations still relied heavily on Britain's debt to Malayan dollar earnings to prop up the value of sterling and contribute to Britain's debt servicing to the detriment of the Malayan economy. This second obligation inverted the long-cherished myth that the colonies were dependent on the largesse of the colonizing power. According to the conventions of Orientalist discourse, playing down the colonizing self's dependence on the colonized selfobject was an important aspect of the imperial identity of the "White Man's Burden" in which the colonies were seen as weak and needing rescuing, while the colonizers were strong and conferred protection (Said 1978, 36; Spurr 1993, 109–124). Colonial power relations demanded that the colonizer not appear dependent on the colonized. The Malayan Emergency, largely fought between the British and the MCP, provided the perfect bargaining counter for reversing Britain's obligations to Malaya. The MCP threat, framed by the British as ideological to the Americans and racial to the Malayan elite, allowed a new calculus of equivalence between dollars and dignity.

The Anxious Imperialist: Passing the Superpower Torch

Early on during the war, Britain, together with the other European colonial powers, recognized that the mantle of imperial power was passing and that the views of the new superpower would not always be congruent with European colonial aims (Dening 1945a,b,c). The key objective for the Europeans was to minimize the indignity of their subordinate status, which required at least maintaining economic advantages while accepting the inevitable political trade-offs ensuing in the transition from European to American imperialism. Britain then needed to neutralize the mild US antipathy to European colonialism and represent the anti-colonial wars in a light that was acceptable to the US (Dening 1945a,b,c, 1946) The US emerged from the war as the undisputed economic leader to the point that it could afford to shrug off temporary dollar discriminations by the sterling block in return for political support in its fight against the Soviet Union. There were two links between Malayan and American interests: the first was the perceived global nature of the communist threat; the second was the importance of keeping rubber and tin supplies flowing to the West, in particular the US which was Malaya's biggest customer (United Kingdom, Colonial Office and the Central Office of Information 1952). Since the US was the most powerful player, it had to be made interested in the Malayan Emergency. This was done in the Malayan case by situating the British position within the network against Communism. The recasting of the Malayan Emergency as "part of the whole duel between the Western Powers and Communism" (*British Survey*, 18) depended in large measure on using Orientalist vocabulary to describe the Asian stereotype so that, as Said (1978, 32) has argued, a few terms invoked the required negative associations. The British struggle against the MCP was recast as the fight against Moscow and Peking (Beijing), and Malaya became the domino that must not fall if the rest of the world was to be safe from Communism.

As early as 1948 Washington had approved of arms shipments to Malaya to augment the fight against the MCP (*The Times*, 27 August 1948). In attempting to reassure the commercial interests in Malaya that the Americans viewed Malaya as a high priority geopolitically, General Briggs said that Malaya had been put on the same priority as Korea (Commercial Interests 1951a). The Americans were far more interested in Korea, and later Vietnam, but they recognized the Malayan Emergency as part of the broader Cold War. In arguing for escalating the war in Korea, General James Van Fleet (1953) argued:

> I think they [Chinese] want to get out of the Korean War to build up their strength and shift their attack to places like Indochina and Malaya. This would only mean we would have to fight again some day against a stronger enemy in a place more to his advantage.

Malcolm Muggeridge (1952) in a series of articles about the Emergency, put the case succinctly:

> [I]t is not just a question of holding or losing Malaya, but of suffering a serious defeat in the global struggle between the free West and the enslaved East. Malaya is an integral part of the Western defensive system. If the dyke bursts, it will be more difficult to hold back the flood elsewhere (IV).

During the Cold War, many Asian countries, once seen as securely colonized, now once again became new territories to be recolonized, as frontiers between the West and Communist Russia and China. A new imperium was being mapped onto the globe, and recently decolonized countries constituted a danger zone because they were a transitional space between the US and USSR. The insurgent campaigns were not only a threat in themselves but seen as part of a larger take-over conspiracy by the communist powers.

Superficially, it appeared that the British needed the Americans more than the reverse, but they also felt that the US would be helped by the established

British hegemony in courting local elites (United Kingdom, Foreign Office 1949). At the same time, in an effort at preserving the illusion of independence from the US, the Colonial Office attempted to avoid synchronizing their policy statements on Malaya with American press releases (Jerrom 1952a). Reflecting Britain's anxieties of imperial castration on the international stage by the US, the British Embassy in Washington noted approvingly:

> There is a steadily improving climate here for the acceptance by the American press and people of a public expression of support for the restoration of peace and order in Malaya. Various recent events have contributed to that end. The gradual growth of knowledge that there were other Asian theatres of war besides Korea was given a sudden and important impulse by the Secretary of State's speech in New York. In the reaction to Mr. Eden's remarks there was no real inclination to dispute the argument that Malaya and Korea are parts of the same war against Communist aggression.
>
> (Burrows 1952)

Calculus of Value: Pricing Race

It is important to note that during this transitional period between the British Empire giving way to the American Empire, the establishment of a new political leader lagged behind the economic one. In the crucial postwar years, Malaya was the major dollar earner in the sterling area. In 1951 alone, 83 percent of Malaya's earnings went into the sterling pool (Edmunds 1949; United Kingdom, Foreign Office 1949). Britain candidly admitted at home that Malaya had to be protected because without it, "it would involve a surgical cut in British living standards" and "the sterling currency system, as we know it, could not exist. Britain would have to halve her imports from the U.S.A." (*British Survey* 1952, 17). As well as keeping their reserves in sterling, Malaya and other sterling area countries formed a discriminatory block against dollar imports by purchasing British manufactured goods and services to prevent capital outflow from the sterling area (Cripps and Bevin 1949). Additionally, the European Payment Fund for recovery programs in Western Europe allowed Britain to borrow on the basis of the economic performance of the sterling area, which meant mainly the performance of Malaya (Strange 1971, 89). In contrast, other European countries borrowed on the basis of their own country's economic performance. The former governor of Singapore, Sir Shenton Thomas (1948), pointed out that Malaya's export/import ratio with the US was sometimes as great as a factor of 25. Between 1946 and 1953, Britain had a negative BOP with the US but a positive BOP with the sterling area including Malaya. At its peak in 1951 the movement of sterling from Malaya to Britain was as high as £343 million even as Britain's deficit with the US ran to £431 million (Polk 1956, 112). Malaya's dollar earnings, which amounted to around a third of Britain's deficit to the dollar area in 1951, were then exchanged on the London market for sterling (Polk 1956, 190–191). Hence, the need to minimize Malayan withdrawals to maintain confidence in sterling's stability. It is important to note that since the balance was colonial, there was no electorate to challenge the policies on sterling. Moreover, loans to colonies had to be completely covered by their reserves, once again ensuring that sterling reserves were kept high if a colony was to qualify for a loan. In addition to repaying the US, Britain was aiming for full currency convertibility eventually so the idea was to minimize withdrawals until its economy had recovered and could maintain the value of sterling on its own. The Colonial Office took the view that what was good for Britain was good for the colonies so economic austerity in the colonies was worth it. But currency controls could not be applied without the informal agreement of the US.

So far, I have argued that Malayan tin and rubber were important factors in Britain's imperial economy. However, when Britain reoccupied Malaya at the close of World War Two, they returned to a world that, from the perspective of non-Europeans, had changed fundamentally. A psychological barrier had been breached, and the British would henceforth rule on borrowed time. The colonial prewar strategy for managing the Malayan population capitalized on, and exaggerated, stereotyped racial differences, precisely because the social environment had destabilized so precipitately. Colonial appropriation of material resources artificially induced scarcity locally (see Chapter 3). Conveniently, exaggerating racial differences, especially negative traits, deflected attention from colonial over-appropriation while maintaining the perceived colonial position of neutral arbitrators. But Britain's desire to retain control of Malaya's wealth ran into two obstacles in postwar Malaya: the military resistance of the MCP and the growing skepticism of even the Malayan elite that colonialism was good for them. The British would use the first to intimidate and negotiate with the latter. The colonial strategy weaponized racial anxieties by tapping into Orientalist stereotypes of native brutality while playing up the positive Western stereotype of the just, neutral colonial ruler (Spurr 1993, 109–124). As we shall see later in the chapter, the British first played up Malay fears of subjugation by the mainly Chinese MCP. Later, when even the Malay elite began to consider an alliance with the MCP as preferable to continued colonialism, the British amplified racial anxieties by exaggerating the threat of racial annihilation to persuade the largely Malay elite that they needed the protection of the British for which, of course, they had to pay.

The racial schisms encouraged by the British over the last 100 years meant that at the close of World War Two, despite the rise of Asian nationalism all around them, Britain did not expect to relinquish Malaya in the near future. The reoccupying British Military Administration (BMA) countered the numerous class-based strikes by stoking racial anxieties. The public discourse at the time essentialized geography and race for all non-whites in the local newspaper coverage of demonstrations (*The Malayan*

Post 1946). While English language papers had little influence over the general non-English speaking population, the Malayan elite took note. Any challenge to British control was framed as the work of the "alien Chinese" while simultaneously reminding the US of its commitment to the Truman Doctrine (*The Times*, 11 September 1948). The battle was depicted as one in which the MCP was "... meeting with stubborn resistance from the Malays and the Indians who know the threat that Chinese domination would produce" (*The Times*, 23 September 1948). In short, "There is no future for Malaya without the British" (*Truth*, 7 December1951). Malcolm Muggeridge (19 February 1952) described the Emergency as a "Chinese conspiracy" and argued that the Chinese goal was to be the "residual legatees" once the British were thrown out of Malaya (21 February 1952). They were represented as an "elemental force" who intended to breed "babies and wealth" with whom Malays could not compete (*British Survey* 1952, 19). Still, the Emergency dragged on. But the British recognized that while racial anxieties were successful in keeping the Malays from cooperating with the Communists, neither were they actively hindering the Communists.

By the time of the killing of Henry Gurney, the High Commissioner of Malaya, on 6 October 1951, Whitehall was galvanized into thinking that they had to get the Malayan population onside if they were to defeat the MCP (Stockwell 1995b). But as late as 1955, Anthony Eden and the Colonial Office were congratulating themselves on the fact that Malayan politicians understood the need to delay self-government until the end of the Emergency (Lennox-Boyd 1955a). In June 1955, the MCP changed the terms of reference dramatically by offering a ceasefire. They sent the letter to the United Planters of Malaya Association (UPAM), senior members of the Malayan Chinese Association, a pro-British association of businessmen and the Malay newspaper, *Utusan Melayu* (Malayan Communist Party 1955). The decision to send the letter to the UPAM as the representative of the colonial government highlighted the capital-state collaboration that was so much at the heart of the Emergency. Here it is useful to recall Roitman's (2003) insights on negotiation being predicated on a consensus of the just social order. In this case, the MCP were suborning the colonial order by directly approaching the Malayan elite and signaling that the two sides were equals and leaders of their peoples. Their first offer was rejected. But after the Alliance, a coalition of local politicians, won the elections on 27 July 1955 to represent Malayan interests, Tunku Abdul Rahman, the Chief Minister, made two significant moves. He wrote to the Secretary of State to inform him that Malaya wanted an early date set for independence (Rahman 1955). And he offered an amnesty to the MCP on 8 September 1955 (MacGillivray 1955a). Thus, while the MCP attempted to suborn the existing order, the Alliance, while fearing the MCP more than the British, attempted to steer a course that improved their standing in the social order by implicitly threatening the British rulers with a potential settlement with their enemies.

A perusal of key documents from the period October through to December 1955 shows the British watching with consternation as Tunku appeared determined to end the Emergency, if that was what it took to obtain independence from Britain (I have the listed the main documents here: United Kingdom, Cabinet Colonial Policy Committee 1955; Colonial Office Far Eastern Department 1955; Lennox-Boyd 1955a,c; MacGillivray 1955a,b,c; MacGillivray's Senior Officials 1955; Reading 1955; Scott 1955a,b; United Kingdom, Colonial Office 1955; a key document is Watherston 1955). The High Commissioner, Sir Donald MacGillivray, worried that in the negotiations Chin Peng, the Secretary General of the MCP, would insist that Britain provide a fixed date for independence (MacGillivray 1955a). Even the appearance of negotiations between Chin Peng and Tunku horrified the British, who did not want Tunku to gain in prestige by negotiating with such an important foe. Finally, to prevent Tunku from opening negotiations for independence with the MCP, one month before the start of the Baling Talks with the MCP, Britain announced that the end of the Emergency was no longer a pre-requisite to self-government, thus opening the way to setting a date for independence (MacGillivray 1955b). The importance of the Communist threat in obtaining concessions from the British can be seen in a secret inward telegram from Sir Don MacGillivray, the High Commissioner, to the Secretary of State for the Colonies:

> [I]f the Alliance should be dissatisfied with the outcome of the London Conference they will not return to Malaya with the determination to rally the country in an all out effort against Communist terrorism and are more likely to seek a settlement with the MCP on terms which might in the end constitute a new and greater threat to internal security.
>
> During the 24 hours before leaving Kuala Lumpur, Abdul Rahman [future Prime Minister] twice stated publicly that her Majesty's Government had already agreed in principle that the elected Ministers should be responsible for internal security and that the Alliance was going to London merely to work out the details. He must be aware that this advance was not being achieved on account of Chin Peng's conditional offer but had been obtained by the Alliance before the Chin Peng meeting took place. He would not wish it to appear that he was *beholden* [emphasis mine] to the MCP for this achievement or to allow them to get a measure of credit for it (MacGillivray 1956).

Note that the term "beholden" signals the anxiety of the British at the possibility of the Malayan elite's sense of obligation reversing toward the MCP, and the British losing the moral upper hand implicit in being the recipient of the colonized's gratitude and, thus, deserving of its tributes of wealth. But the justification for *legitimate* tribute rests on introjection of a discourse of a just social order (Memmi 1967, 84–89; Said 1978, 3–6, 41–45; Spurr 1992, 62–75). In his reply to the Secretary of State for the Colonies, the High Commissioner MacGillivray (1956) wrote that the Alliance would argue:

> that a self-governing Malaya could deal more successfully with the communists than a Colonial regime running a country anxious to be rid of it. Acceptance of the Alliance view on this [self-government] might help to secure satisfactory agreements on *defence and other important issues* [emphasis mine] while refusal to go far enough with them on the question of self-government would not only seriously prejudice the chance of getting such agreements but also probably lead to refusal to cooperate in the administration of the government and to a serious deterioration in internal security. The sympathies of nearly all local members of the public service and police, the great majority of whom are Malays, would lie with the Chief Minister and his colleagues. Faced with a hostile public, we should soon have to concede in the most unhappy circumstances what we could earlier have *granted with an air of generosity* [emphasis mine], the support of world opinion and the promise of loyal co-operation.

The above passages show the importance of the MCP as a bargaining device by both the Malayan elite and the colonial authorities. The Malayan elite could threaten to throw their support behind the MCP, while the colonial authorities had to hope that the fear of yielding the advantage to the MCP would prevent the local elites from abandoning their alliance with the British. In essence, the MCP purchased Malaya's independence. It should be noted that only a secure power could afford true generosity; Britain's recognition that it was a waning power meant that the Malayan elite would pay a high price and they did. Almost 50 years after the Baling talks, Chin Peng (Ong 2003) revealed in his memoir that the British later unsuccessfully tried to cut another deal with him in order to regain the upper hand with the Alliance politicians.

Having been promised independence as payment for not siding with the MCP, the future Malayan government had to tread a fine line between the MCP and the British while attempting to appear to the electorate to be the natural heirs to British rule. This was no easy feat if one of the "natural" features of a legitimate ruler was martial prowess. But in Malaya, since the war was being fought between the British and the MCP, preventing a Communist victory meant that the British would have to continue to defend the new government. The Colonial Secretary, addressing the Federal Executive Council, K.L. on 1 September 1955, argued against the transfer of responsibility for defense to the independent government, saying that Malaya was "a key point in the free world's defense against the spread of Communism"(Lennox-Boyd 1955c). Accordingly, defense would stay under British control, so the real issue became how to designate a Cabinet Minister for non-defense in a way that he (sic) would not "lose face" by having to admit to a lack of control (Malaya [Colonial Government], Defence Department 1956). The future Prime Minister Tunku Abdul Rahman faced the dilemma of privately protesting to the British that internal defense arrangements should be determined mainly by the elected Government while publicly defending the fledgling government's defense agreement with Britain. In articulating his introjection of colonialists as natural defenders, he said, "It must be appreciated that with the geographical and strategical position of this country, Malaya offers herself as an easy target and will always be open to aggression if she is not properly guarded" (Rahman 1956).

The Price Tag

By handing over the governance of Malaya to a sympathetic local elite, Britain retained control of 70 percent of the import-export trade, 60 percent of the mining industry and 83 percent of the plantation sector (Gomez and Jomo 1997, 11–12). Yet both the British and the newly independent government, which included Chinese businessmen, found it convenient to blame the Chinese for dominating the economy (Jomo 1988). Given the proportion of sector control shown above, Britain was eager to obtain assurances that there were no nationalization programs in the offing after independence. Gomez and Jomo (1997, 14) suggest that the Malay-led government may have seen cooperation with British interests as a way of preventing the Chinese from expanding their share of the economy. Again, the influence of racial anxieties affected the economic decisions made by the new government. Gomez and Jomo's argument is plausible in light of the problems involved in maintaining Malayan reserves in sterling. Britain's 30 percent devaluation of sterling against the American dollar in 1949 adversely affected all currencies pegged to sterling. Since colonial sterling balances provided a buffer for Britain's reserve position during financial crises as in 1947, 1949 and 1951, discriminatory measures were implemented to prevent withdrawals on sterling balances (Krozewski 1996, 60–62). But for the colonies, the high level of sterling balances meant that they had a hard time borrowing on the London market for development projects. Given these disadvantages for Malaya combined with its healthy economy, Malaya was the one colony that would have been in a position to peg its currency to either gold or dollars, or at least diversify its reserves, after independence. It bears investigating why Malaya did not do so.

To the dismay of the British, in 1955 the International Bank for Reconstruction and Development (IBRD) recommended that Malaya have its own central bank (Schenk 1993, 413). Recall that the central bank acts on behalf of the state as guarantor of its currency's value by setting monetary policy (Harvey 1982, 18, 245). The threat posed to the British by an independent Malayan central bank lay in its capacity to set monetary policy such as currency pegs, interest rates and, hence, credit availability. Both moves would result in a rundown of Malaya's reserves and, in turn, affect the value of sterling. The Treasury Department immediately tried to get the IBRD to soften its recommendations and succeeded in doing so (Schenk 1993, 415). Nevertheless, the topic had been broached and was now taken up by Alliance politicians. Malaya's Chinese finance minister, Tan Siew Sin, argued in favor of taking Malaya out of the sterling orbit but was overridden by the Malay Prime Minister (Rudner 1971, 15). Publicly, Tan hewed to the elite discourse and defended the sterling peg until 1972 (White 2003, 224). Dr. Ismail, the Federation's Minister of Commerce and Industry, also argued that the future central bank should be able to alter the sterling exchange rate and centralize the assets of private (mostly British) banks in Malaya (Schenk 1993, 419). Initially worried that a central bank would issue policies detrimental to Britain's privileged position, the British soon realized that the symbolic value of having a central bank as opposed to actual policy changes was more important to the newly independent government.

However, Britain's argument that Malaya benefitted from remaining in the sterling area because it could continue to borrow on the London market outraged even Currency Board officials in Malaya who noted that since Malaya's dollar earnings were crucial to keeping sterling afloat, it would take a great deal of borrowing before the cash flow reversed itself (Spencer 1951). Malaya's tax on profits for British investment in its resource industry was the lowest of the top three countries for direct investment return (Strange 1971, 112). Malayan resources were additionally a lucrative investment because taxes were low. Yet Malaya did not see much of these profits because much of it was repatriated to the controlling companies in Britain. According to Treasury officials, Malaya surpluses in 1951 and 1952 "... consisted largely of transfers of capital, including funds transferred to London by British-owned companies, where they were used to pay taxes and dividends, or were placed in reserve" (Moorhouse 1952). Recognizing the psychological capital inherent in maintaining the direction of obligations from the Malayan elite to the British, Sir Gerald Templer, the Malayan High Commissioner, asked that the figures on surplus and capital transfers be withheld from the public. He wrote:

> If correct they would invite devastating criticism that British companies in Malaya have in two years taken 282 million pounds sterling out of Malaya on an original capital investment in Malaya, estimated officially by the Bank of England to be, no more than 68 million pounds sterling.
> (Templer 1952a)

Privately, he complained that "Malaya was fighting an internal war ... and has at the same time contributed handsomely to dollar reserves of the sterling area" (ibid). Because of the Emergency, Britain had cut back on development programs and moved the funds into military projects (MacDonald 1952). This decision would come back to haunt the postcolonial government with the May 13 riots in 1969 (see Chapter 6). The colonial government estimated Emergency expenditures to be 50 percent of the government's budget

(MacDonald 1952). A memorandum from the Colonial Office pointed out that Malaya only received £5 million from a pool of £120 million allocated for colonial welfare and development.

Strange (1971, 112) claims that between 1955 and 1961, 60 percent of the GDP or $844 million was moved out of Malaya, while between 1961 and 1970, outflow of profits was $1.8 billion ringgit as opposed to $1.00 billion in investment. In return for British defense, the Malayan government would show preferential treatment toward British firms and continue to maintain the formidable Malayan surplus in sterling reserves (United Kingdom 1956a,b, 1957b). When Britain refused further defense and development aid and started troop withdrawals East of Suez in 1967, the Malaysian government reacted angrily by removing Commonwealth preferences for British goods (White 2003, 230). Perhaps no better illustration of the libidinal basis of colonial financial policies can be found than the passage below. It is a peculiar dimension of the hegemonic relationship between Britain and her ex-colonies that points to the confidence in maintaining the established social relations of colonialism, that no formal agreement was needed to safeguard British economic interests because the relationship was insured by the anxieties of Malaya's elites. During British Cabinet discussions on the subject, Lennox-Boyd, the Colonial Secretary, actually argued against a formal agreement, referring to the example of Britain's relationship with India and Pakistan on the subject of expropriation. Lennox-Boyd (1956b) said:

> The fact is that the sort of assurances we could expect to secure in any formal agreement are not as valuable to us as the recognition of mutual interest and the establishment of understanding and cordial relations between the commercial interests and the local governments.
>
> ... I shall represent to the [Federation] delegation that the repetition of these assurances, which relate to overseas interests, would be to their own advantage in ensuring a prosperous economy for Malaya.

In fact, the simplest of assurances sufficed regarding Malaya's position in the sterling area, past and future borrowings on the UK capital market, and the maintenance of preferential treatment for British commercial interests:

> *Exchange control.* The Federation Government will continue to regulate its dollar expenditure in general conformity with the policy followed by the Sterling Area and in consultation with Her Majesty's Government. (Annex A)
>
> *Overseas investment.* The conference recorded ...that it would remain the policy of the Federation Government to encourage overseas investment, industry and enterprise to look to Malaya with every assurance of fair and considerate treatment and without fear of discrimination.

> This included continuation of the present policy whereby the overseas investor could, after payment of local taxes and obligations, remit to his country, within the framework of ordinary and reasonable exchange control requirements, funds for the payment and repatriation of his capital. (Lennox-Boyd, see Annex B, 1956c).

Conclusion

This chapter examined the negotiations that resulted in the decision to invest Malaya's export earnings in British sterling reserves in the years leading up to independence in 1957 as an entry point to understanding the reasoning and motivations of the different actors in the negotiations. I argued that an introjected social order undergirded the assumptions of who legitimately deserved to control Malaya's wealth. The British colonial government fought to retain the rhetorical high ground by invoking Orientalist stereotypes to flesh out a fearful future for their native allies without them to justify continuing access to Malaya's export income precisely because they had been displaced in the international hierarchy by the US. Strong sterling reserves would allow the British to minimize obligations to the new superpower by paying off wartime debts. Among the Malayan elites, the decision to go along with British plans for Malayan currency reserves reflected a trade-off between an introjection of the manifest colonial order that allowed Britain tribute of Malaya's export income in return for a limited independence rather than a future governed by the mainly Chinese MCP.

Even after independence, Malaya's conservative development program could be said to be a reflection of its agreement with Britain not to use up its reserves too quickly. External assets were kept at 35 percent of its liabilities, banks could not lend more than 12.5 percent of government revenue, while borrowed funds had to be repaid within three months of the end of the fiscal year (United Kingdom 1956b). Britain also continued to set interest rates in Malaya, thus controlling the rate of local borrowing and maintaining reserves for British banks to use for their purposes. I have argued that the negotiations over the fate of Malaya's currency reserves in the period leading up to Malayan independence in 1957 were framed and presented to the different interest groups involved based on the evolving social relations among them. The British needed Malayan reserves to discharge its wartime debt to the Americans. At the same time Britain maintained the appearance that Malaya was obligated to them because of its "natural" role as protector of the weak from the predations of the MCP, a narrative thread that invoked unconscious anxieties of fetishized racial stereotypes of irrational violence on the part of the colonized. The consequences of the Malayan government's decision to accommodate the British position on finance led to low-key development. This was the price that the Malayan elite chose to pay to appease their anxieties. Ironically, while these decisions were based on the racial consideration of maintaining Malay primacy in the political arena under British military shelter, the slow pace of development would ultimately lead to an eruption of discontent on the part of the Malays in 1969.

But Britain's 1961 acceptance of article VIII of International Monetary Fund (IMF) Agreement on full sterling convertibility, agreed upon in principle at Bretton Woods (Oppenheimer 1966, 122), signaled that its days of dependence on colonial balances were waning and it was increasingly looking toward a European destiny. The Malaysian Government continued to keep faith with sterling even when sterling experienced difficulties in 1966. Only after 1972 when Britain opted for a floating currency, did the Malaysian government convert its reserves to a mixture of currencies so that even then there was no immediate running down of sterling balances (https://www.bnm.gov.my/significant-milestones-in-the-malaysian-foreign-exchange-market). The Malaysian elite did not substantively break its economic ties with Britain until the Mahathir era began in the 1980s. I do not want to claim that the underlying social currents of the period described in this chapter survive unchanged into the twenty-first century. Moreover, Mahathir's conflicted relationship with the West is a separate subject beyond the scope of this chapter, but his rhetorical break with Britain signaled practical policy shifts, among the most significant being the decision during the 1997–98 "Asian Flu" crisis to ignore the received wisdom of Western agencies and institute curbs on exchange rates. That the Malaysian economy emerged relatively undamaged from the financial crisis that swept the region is now recognized as a tribute to the Mahathir regime's policy, and a modest indicator that at least on some issues, Malaysia was slowly casting off the legacy of colonialism.

Notes

1 In 2023, the World Bank prefers the term Gross National Income (GNI) to GNP as all income earned by its nationals anywhere that remains in the country of the citizenship of its owners, presumably to account for transfer payments and tax evasion.

2 Unless stated otherwise, much of the remainder of paragraph summarizes Oppenheimer (1966, 100–105).

6 Postcolonial Anxieties and Performing Territorialization

Introduction

In Chapter 4 I described the trauma and loss of safe space in the violence of the Emergency that ultimately resulted in the political independence of Malaya in 1957, which, in 1963, evolved into Malaysia including the Federation of Malaya, the states of Sabah and Sarawak of the former British North Borneo and Singapore. The political union broke down in 1965 and Singapore was expelled to form an independent country. Paradoxically, the moment of political freedom for both countries coincided with the moment of trauma. Chapters 5 and 6 pick up on the major economic decisions that emerged out of the ensuing anxieties of psychic survival. Where Chapter 5 deals with the financial negotiations leading up to political independence, Chapter 6 focuses on the post-independence years particularly the groundbreaking New Economic Policy (NEP) and the Federal Land Development Authority (FELDA) schemes in Malaysia.

This chapter examines the specific configurations that territorialization comprising cultural ownership took in the postcolonial Malaysian state within the context of the crisis of authority that accompanies violent conflicts. I examine the dilemmas of psychic legitimacy that accompany the humiliation of being colonized. I define psychic legitimacy to be the unchallenged acceptance by both participants and observers, in this case, of a state's status as a confluence of group identity with a territorial claim, in other words, its *cultural* ownership of space (Sioh 2010b). Malaysia is an interesting study in the wider geopolitics of state-building and cultural ownership as the postcolonial Malaysian state attempted to legitimize itself after its elites supported the British in the counterinsurgency campaign, known as the Emergency, against the mainly Chinese Malayan Communist Party (MCP) who fought for independence after World War Two. From a military standpoint, the Emergency became the textbook case for successful modern counterinsurgencies (Thompson 1966; Stubbs 1989; Bayly and Harper 2007; Marston and Malkasian 2008). It enjoyed a resurgence of interest because in the Iraq and Afghanistan US-led counterinsurgencies, the strategy of "clear, hold, build" and the language of "winning hearts and minds" were lifted from the Malayan

DOI: 10.4324/9781315440286-7

Emergency. The underlying racial dynamics of the Malayan conflict were an important factor in crafting the optics of the postcolonial reterritorialization strategy. Moreover, between 1963 and 1966, Malaysia also faced the *Konfrontasi*, the simmering military conflict with Indonesia over the creation of the Malaysian nation-state, which was also largely fought in the forests (Ibrahim bin Haji N.d.; Mezerik 1965; Mackie 1974; Dickens 1983; Dennis 1996). In the psychological perception of the *Konfrontasi*, despite being fought with another sovereign nation-state, the conflict, in its location and in challenging the leadership's right to rule, almost seemed a continuation of the Emergency. The subsequent tactics of the Malaysian state to establish cultural ownership, spearheaded by the state-sponsored FELDA agricultural schemes, replaced the displaced forest populations with settlers loyal to the state and inspired admiration in observers such as centrist policy pundit Parag Khanna (2008) and leftwing postcolonial intellectual Mahmood Mamdani (2008). The latter holds it up as a model for the modernization efforts of postcolonial agrarian economies. Perhaps the Emergency's greatest significance lies in how a brutal counterinsurgency and subsequent forcible population displacement translated into a narrative of moral triumph in the public domain even in the Western media usually critical of such practices.

Successful postcolonial nationalisms, as with any discourse, require hiding the sightlines of their inventions to qualify as authentic (Foucault 1972, 14, 227). And just as social hierarchy is depicted as natural so too are nations ranked in progress as a reflection of inherent abilities. Thus, a nation-state's success as a viable identity, particularly for groups attempting to overcome the shame of conquest and domination, requires that it must be recognizable as a modern project. Postcolonial nationalisms sought an identity that combined historic purpose with one that could be inserted positively into the global hierarchy. Territorializing Malaysia required both physical reconfiguration and imaginative recuperation of the landscape. In Malaysian historiography, the masculinist national narrative was configured around the retaking of the land from the Communists and then the British occupiers, a two-step approach that first involved political independence, then signaling their cultural inheritance of the country.

Chapter 6 makes two related arguments. First, the anxieties of the postcolonial state determined the tactics to constitute a moral scopic politics while being simultaneously productive for capital accumulation. These goals resulted in massive deforestation to accommodate the new state-sponsored settler economy, creating a "new nature" that embodied the territory of the nation-state. Second, the postcolonial state's strategy to naturalize its right to exist was realized through the multiple, quotidian performances of its subjects as citations of social conventions, each in themselves moments of "condensed historicity" (Butler 1997, 3). These postcolonial subjects function as Kohut's (1973) selfobjects to the agentic Malaysian state and together create the foundational fantasy (see Chapter 1 for the theoretical review) of postcolonial Malaysia. Chapter 6 tracks how the population as a whole becomes the focus of tactics to render them productive in disciplined spaces to create selfobjects for the new Malaysian state. Working with Judith Butler's concepts of interpellation and performativity, I argue that the state purchases legitimacy through a process in which the practices of its subjects are given meaning by their symbolic, yet economically necessary, performances within a physically reconfigured landscape serving as a stage.

The success of the Malayan counter-insurgency rested on two ambitious spatial policies: the New Villages and the FELDA agricultural schemes, which served as the stages for the essentialized performance of moral theaters based on race. In Chapter 4 I argued that the forest was the key sign of the power struggle during the Malayan Emergency; thus, successfully territorializing the forest became a synecdoche for territorializing Malaya by stamping ownership through violence. In Chapter 5, I argued that the financial policies at independence were the consequence of the anxieties of an elite that had not militarily "earned" their freedom from the colonial occupiers; victory in the forests came through courtesy of the colonial rulers. The forests "cleansed" of the MCP and its supporters now incarcerated in the concentration camps of the "New Villages," formed one aspect of the postcolonial state's own foundational fantasy through providing constrained selfobjects upon whom to inflict the new nation-state's narcissistic rage. Yet the punitive landscapes of the New Villages, while providing a foil for the postcolonial nation in terms of what it was **not**, were insufficient for psychic legitimacy for inheriting the state's territory. Psychic legitimacy demands affirmative theater. May Joseph (1999, 13) offers a particular form of moral theater that she terms "citizenscapes," defined as "socially and politically produced conceptions of participatory democracy that inform the performance of available and imagined vehicles of citizenship." The Malaysian government's response to the second prong of territorialization was the construction of an economically productive postcolonial nature to legitimize its authority. Here, state power would be performed through the positioning and differentiating of its subjects and citizens within an affirmative landscape to construct a new nature upon which to stage the nation. The trauma of material dispossession of land and figurative dispossession of identity through colonization had to be recuperated, and it had to be accomplished without the seal of a military victory, recall that Malaysia was still under British military shelter (Chapter 5). The answer, in scale and provenance, was the FELDA agricultural scheme.

Territory and Scopic Politics

The study of how territorialization succeeds requires first understanding how power is physically deployed through space beyond brute force, and second, how it is psychologically legitimized. Foucault (1995, 2007) argues that while state control can be achieved by discipline, that is, a physical reconfiguration through geometries that promoted visibility and limited mobility of subjects, it also requires a moral scopic politics that establishes what a representation of those geometries mean in themselves and in relation to each other. Foucauldian biopower involves manipulating the population in part through self-regulation, but is based on statistical knowledge to maximize productive behavior while minimizing anti-social behavior and political dissent among the population (Foucault 2007, 11–19). The result was a combination of tactics that constituted modern statecraft. For Foucault, the accent goes from the guarantee of a frontier, a Weberian notion (Weber 1947), to the guarantee of legal identity which accompanies the transition from the emphasis on the state, that is, a political entity, to the emphasis on government, that is a series of practices (Elden 2007, 563). Within the postcolonial Malaysian state, concerns of territory and practices of governmentality coexisted in a continuously shifting dynamic; discipline, punishment and biopower would all be present in the FELDA schemes. But Foucault's attention turned to what he referred to as the ultimate question of "security" in statecraft—how populations are managed productively (2007, 271–273). Instead of the state vengeance described in Chapter 4, Foucauldian security now integrates production with psychology to arrive at the most economical framework for government (Foucault 2007, 5–9, 45–47, 379–381). This incorporates self-regulation by the majority of its population who have come to see their well-being as tied to the fate of the state. The FELDA schemes were both disciplinary and biopolitical in conception converging on a "blueprint" of statecraft for postcolonial Malaysia. But FELDA as biopower had a second purpose: it provided the scopic politics for the nation-state's legitimacy.

Foucault was also interested in how discourse organizes its subjects by categorizing information, establishing relevances and placing all in relation to each other (Foucault 1972, 6, 11). As subjects, our identities are constituted within a symbolic order. This can be applied to territorialization in the sense that where we are allowed to be and what we are allowed to do there is a recognition and acknowledgment of our identity, the "moral theatre" that forms the stage for identity performance. This brings the question of how we arrive at that tacit knowledge of *where* we are placed within that symbolic order. Foucault claims that what we see is less a product of physical sight than a product of the "encoded eye"—a constitution of meaning through our tacit knowledge according to our respective culture and time that trains our eyes to "sightlines," and he referred to these tactics as a "system of feints" (1994, 3–16). But this natural arrival at meaning only works if the effort involved is erased (Foucault 1972, 14, 227). The role of the "encoded eye" raises the question of who the audience is, and how we appeal to those implicit codes.

Walter Benjamin was concerned with how a montage of objects creates meaning through their relationships with each other, while simultaneously erasing all signs of artifice involved in the constitution of the image (Buck-Morss 1989, 68–69, 74). Technology, in the service of state and capital, produces a "wish image"—the image of what is desired rather than the existing material reality. This produces a "new state of nature," but it is one that could only enforce its vision by referencing the lineage of "old" nature (Buck-Morss 1989, 114–115, 143–145; Leslie 2000, 91). Benjamin actually used the term "second nature" to describe environments that were constructed artificially through technology that over time became part of a reformulated consciousness, but Buck-Morss and Leslie prefer the term "new nature" to emphasize that far from being an ecological successor, it comes to be the **only** nature recognized by the majority in society. The FELDA landscapes constructed through the racial divisions entrenched during the Emergency became the "new nature" of Malaysia in more than just replacing the old growth forests ("old" nature); they were literally the stage of the new nation in the sense of staging the "imagined community," to invoke Benedict Anderson's (1991) famous expression. Benjamin's crucial insight was to remind us that when historical referents are naturalized, the political danger is a quiescent population convinced that oppression is predetermined and, therefore, cannot be resisted. Extending Benjamin's insights, scholars have highlighted that while nationalism is a modern project, nationalists legitimate their claims by presenting them as primordial (Hobsbawm and Ranger 1983; Anderson 1991; McClintock 1995, 352–379; Joseph 1999). I argue that newly independent states anxious to forget past humiliations resorted to tactics that referenced nature as a source of legitimacy. Within the postcolonial context, nativism is positively constituted—a convenient strategy to hide the sightlines of nationalist invention to qualify as authentic. But if nations have to be grounded in primordiality to claim authenticity, to claim worthiness in the modern world rests on proving their modernity. Just as social hierarchy is depicted as natural so too are nations ranked in progress as a reflection of inherent abilities. When requiring positive recognition, it helps nationalists to be able to interpellate their identity into existing symbolic orders such as the archaic and the technological. And in the second half of the twentieth century, the development narrative became the economic, technocratic counterpart of the postcolonial nationalist narrative of politically overcoming hardship (Gupta 1998, 42). It is economic achievement that provides the moral justification for claiming equality with the West. In contrast, to be underdeveloped is to be a national community that is inferior, backward, subordinate and inadequate (Ibid, 40). Thus, a nation-state's success as a viable identity capable of progress, particularly for groups attempting to overcome the shame of conquest and domination, requires that it is recognizable as a modern project yet imbued with historic purpose. In Malaysian historiography, the masculinist national narrative was configured around the heroic retaking of land from the British occupiers and the Communists. The tension then is to show the identity of the subject-citizen that appears both timeless yet modern. Here, I want to introduce the dimension of performance as central to statecraft through inferring the right to be.

I argue that a saturation of quotidian stagings, rather than spectacle, was the main tactic of cultural persuasion for legitimacy. These performances both constituted and invoked subjectivities, the latter through the tacit knowledge of the "encoded eye." I link cultural ownership to territorialization through quotidian perfomativity rather than the spectacular because the trick to constructing an aura of psychic legitimacy was to make the performance look organic. Judith Butler's reconceptualizations of interpellation and performativity offer potential interventions. For Butler, identity is not ontological but continually created as an illusion "through language, gesture, and all manner of symbolic social sign" (1990, 270), which she described as a "discursive constitution" (1997, 19). Butler used the Althusserian concept of interpellation to argue that a subject "exists" not only by virtue of being recognized, but by being recognizable (1997, 5, 28). Thus, interpellation as a form of identity requires our tacit acknowledgement of historical hierarchy (Butler 1997, 2). Butler concedes that one need not consciously register identity construction for the construct to work as it succeeds through its embeddedness within a mesh of signification that exceeds self-knowledge (1990, 310, 1997, 28, 34). To sum up, Butler's conception of interpellation is organic: it references existing circuits of signification and each act of recognition reinforces the process. Butler, like Foucault, argues that it is by endlessly citing the conventions and ideologies of the social world that we naturalize artificial conventions (1990, 272). Her dialectic between performer and performance creates a space for intervention and adaptation in identity construction. May Joseph (1999) addresses this issue of citizenship as a performance of acceptable subjectivities interpellated within different symbolic orders—Cold War geopolitics, nativism, Orientalism, development and technological proficiency. She sees power in the staging gestures of mass consent such as parades dramatizing the legitimacy of new states haunted by failures in other contexts (1999, 10,15). But the fastest contemporary route to naturalizing legitimacy is to purchase a place in the hierarchy of nation-states through economic success as we see in the East Asian economies. But at the time of Malayan independence, the trajectory to psychic legitimacy for non-Western countries was unclear—even the Japanese economic miracle was in the future.

In the following pages, I track the convergence of various discourses in the narrative of FELDA as a stage for the performances to appease the anxieties and support the aspirations of postcolonial Malaysia. I show that just as the performance of nationalism and citizenship required a stage (territory), so do the performances constitute their location as territory by virtue of the interpellative subjectivities cited in the performance. The quotidian imagery of the FELDA schemes were stages for the collective performance of identity for its settler-citizens. In terms of national recovery, FELDA performs the second stage of the Emergency and one in which the valorized subject is not the Commonwealth soldier but the male *bumiputera* retaking his place in the land of his fathers. These settler-citizens also fulfilled the second category of selfobjects for the nation-state by providing an approving mirror for its modern identity.

Staging Affirmative Moral Theater: Citizenscapes

Malaya was granted independence in 1957 as continued colonization would come at the potential cost of Britain losing economic control of Malaya if they alienated the local elite to the point of the latter allying themselves with the Communists (see Chapter 5). But the postcolonial government soon recognized that punitive theater as described in Chapter 4 was insufficient statecraft for psychic reterritorialization, more so as economic profits were repatriated to Britain leaving the independent Malayan state little room for economic development. This remained low-key as sterling currency reserves were channeled into propping up the value of British pound sterling (Chapter 5). In the 10 May 1969 elections, the ruling Alliance party[1] lost seats to opposition parties partly due to the desertion of rural Malays. A combination of factors, including rising unemployment which could not fulfill the rising expectations in the wake of independence and volatile racial antagonisms, led to race riots on 13 May (Rahman 1969; Gagliano 1970; Comber 2009). A state of emergency was again declared. Following the riots, the reformist faction of the Alliance party took power under Tun Abdul Razak who replaced the more fiscally cautious Prime Minister Tunku Abdul Rahman. Razak understood that if Malaysia as a nation-state was to survive, the government had to address the racial disparity in incomes. In the Foreward to the Second Malaysia Plan (SMP), he laid out Malaysia's goals thus, "eradicating poverty and eventually eliminating the identification of race with economic function" (Malaysia 1971a, v).

Malaya achieved independence and officially "ended" the Emergency as one of the most racially divided countries in the world. In 1970, in the fraught aftermath of the May 13 riots, as they came to be known, the Malaysian government introduced the NEP, followed a year later with its blueprint for operations, the SMP. The primary objective of the NEP was to achieve national unity through social restructuring to achieve interethnic economic parity. According to the new Prime Minister, the SMP set out to "eliminate the identification of race with economic function," long taken for granted in Malaysia. [Its] "objectives, priorities, and strategies ... have all been shaped by the over-riding need to promote national unity" (Malaysia 1971a, v). National unity was now predicated on a positive discrimination program in education, business and employment opportunities. But these opportunities themselves were dependent on continued economic growth and particularly, export growth (Ibid, 6). The most visible manifestation of the NEP was in the transformation of the landscape through the ambitious FELDA programs. The Malaysian government, as the "owner" of FELDA, became one of the largest plantation owners in the world by 1992 and resettled over a million people on FELDA plantations, mostly between 1971 and 1987. Its current landbank in Malaysia and Indonesia stands at 440,000 hectares (FGV 2019, 2). FELDA was planned as a resettlement program for landless Malays although the Land (Group Settlement Areas) Act of 1960 did not specify race

(Lim 2007). Race rather than poverty was the practical determining factor for eligibility since rural poverty was undeniably the lot of the thousands of Indian estate laborers who were excluded from the FELDA program (Ibid). Agricultural development would duplicate the large scale, standardized monocultural corporate model. For a newly independent country, the simplest solution to raising incomes was to intensify old practices which were well documented through its existing commercial plantation sector. FELDA created a complementary agricultural export system that did not compete with the corporate estates, serendipitous in light of the eventual government control of the largest estate companies. Between 1961 and 1985 FELDA developed three times more land area than the private sector (Shamsul and Lee 1988, 23–26). Much of the statistical information in the following passages, unless stated otherwise, is derived from Shamsul and Lee (1988) who wrote the official history of FELDA.

The target of the SMP was to develop over 400,000 hectares of land. FELDA eventually developed over 850,000 hectares (FGV 2020). An example of the scale of regional development is the Jengka Triangle project which called for the development of 116,500 hectares of virgin forest and the resettlement of 120,000 people in 97 villages serviced by over a thousand miles of roads (*Malaysia* 1971b, 111). Eight industrial centers were planned for the region. The main crop of the scheme would be oil palm followed by rubber. A typical FELDA scheme consisted of an estate of approximately 2,000 hectares dedicated either to oil palm or rubber (Shamsul and Lee 1988, 37–41). To promote the appearance of an organic community, each settler was allocated 3.2–4 hectares as well as an additional hectare for their house and orchard or *dusun* (Ibid, 38). The settlement area or village was grouped around the local management complex and included basic facilities such as a mosque, clinic, food credit shop operated by FELDA, school and recreation field or *padang* (Ibid, 119). The irony of the village layout is that it owed more to an estate living area than a traditional *kampung* (Malay village). The presence of a food credit shop especially echoes the arrangements on private estates and was a source of some resentment (Halim 1992). But this ignores the very significant differences between the lives of the FELDA settlers and the Indian tappers on the private estates. The former were citizens of the new country; the latter were often holders of red identity cards with concomitantly fewer rights. The former were allowed some political participation through the complex patronage system of the United Malays National Organization (UMNO) and the regular monthly *mesyuarat* (meeting) at settlement administrative levels, the latter had none. Both the New Villages and FELDA were "theatres of moral lessons" (Foucault 1995, 113), but where the New Villages were examples of the negative landscape *against* which national identity was constructed in opposition, the FELDA schemes staged affirmations of national identity. They were "citizenscapes," in Joseph's (1999, 13) expression, more powerful for appearing organic through the hundreds of thousands of quotidian performances of FELDA settlers that "sediments" identity to invoke Butler's expression (1997, 34). Conveying the convenience of piped water to readers who take it for granted is difficult, but memories of rubber hoses connected to communal taps snaking their way to households inspired my eventual career in hydrology. The paved roads, electrical and water mains of the FELDA schemes formed the physical networks that connected the libidinal ecosystem of the new nation-state.

Performing the Settler-Citizen

At the core of the FELDA schemes was the icon of the *bumiputera* (son of the soil) settler. The Malaysian government grafted a hybrid identity that cited both the archaic and the modern. As McClintock (1995, 352–379) and Joseph (1999, 5–15) argue, the archaic, and I would add, and nature, were significant dimensions of legitimizing an often incoherent identity wrested from the multiple and sometimes conflicting discourses of patriarchy, nativism, scientific rationalism and modernity. For Malaysia, the FELDA schemes were the postcolonial nature that staged Benjamin's "wish image" (Buck-Morss 1989, 143–145) of the ur-nation performed by *bumiputera* settler-citizens. FELDA also fulfilled the other urgent need of statecraft—capital accumulation. FELDA authorities concentrated on monocultures, mainly rubber and oil palm, conflicting with settlers who wanted to concentrate on food crops (Shamsul and Lee 1988, 33). In its bid to construct a modern narrative of national identity, the Malaysian government distanced FELDA especially from the failed Indonesian *transmigrasi* program which promoted peasant agriculture, instead declaring "peasant psychology" as their main barrier to success (Shamul Bahrin and Lee 1988, 33). Although Halim (1992) recorded conflict situations similar to those that surface on the estates, with each performance of the latest agricultural techniques such as using hybrids, graftings and improvements to the smoking process, all ultimately contributing to state coffers, the FELDA settlers, regardless of their views, using Butler's (1990, 310, 1997, 28, 34) argument, were continuously constituting Malaysian nationalism. Citing Benjamin (Buck-Morss 1989, 143–145), Joseph (1999, 14–15) and Butler (1990, 272), it was the multiple discursive invocations of the archaic in the form of the agrarian, and the modern in the form of the newest scientific techniques, that reinforced the identity of FELDA participants as worthy selfobjects providing an approving mirror to the Malaysian nation-state's modern identity.

Even if we extend Benjamin's concept of "montage" (Buck-Morss 1989, 74) to the dynamic interplay of citizenship that FELDA presented, the FELDA schemes actually transformed the Malay peasantry into a proto-proletariat through the relationships regarding land ownership, labor control and control of production and marketing of crops not dissimilar to estate laborers rather than settler-citizens (Guinness 1992; Halim 1992, 107–132; Gomez and Jomo 1997). In an interplay of Foucaldian disciplinary regimes and biopower, FELDA settlers were trained to support the corporate state in the following ways. Settlers had to transform their working hours from a seasonal routine to a daily routine of eight hours under an overseer, and if settlers did not complete their work either on the plantation or their household compounds on time, the income of the settler was reduced (Shamsul and Lee 1988, 34, 47, 51, 129). Settlers were also paid a salary, reinforcing the image of estate labor (Ibid, 88–92; Guinness 1992, 159). FELDA authorities argued that this departure from the "pioneering" concept was necessary since settlers were unreliable. Because FELDA officials also forced settlers to sell through the state-run agency FELMA at lower than market rates, settlers responded by smuggling rubber out of the estates into the neighboring towns to be sold to the highest bidder (Guinness 1992, 159; Halim 1992, 112, 120). Finally, although the Group Settlers Act of 1960 allowed individual ownership, it had strict clauses on the resale of land, forbidding subdivision and dictating what could be grown on the land (Shamsul and Lee 1988,20). Early settlers may have been grateful for the land, but these clauses later caused some of them to describe their position as *sewa* (renting) or *tumpang* (borrowing) (Halim 1992). Yet, as Butler (1990, 310) reminds us, every response is a performance that becomes part of the interpellative process constituting the overall discourse, regardless of the mindfulness of the performer. And despite the conflicts, the discourse of Malaysian nationalism was being constituted through the cumulative practices of thousands of FELDA settlers working according to their trained aptitudes. Together, they were building the citizenscapes of Malaysia. Even if settlers occasionally rebelled against the FELDA rules, there was no systematic opposition to the state. Growing up next to several FELDA schemes in northern Selangor, I cannot recall any incident beyond day-to-day disagreements. In the larger scheme of statecraft, survival is predicated on more than just small acts of disobedience. If there was any systematic resistance to the state, this came in the form of the ongoing Emergency against the Communists, which, if anything, strengthened the role of the state vis-à-vis the settlers precisely because it gave the Malaysian state a readymade comparison to the alternative fate of not supporting the Malaysian government.

Citizenscapes and Coding Performances

The FELDA program for settlers was described as "bioeconomics" to reinforce the organic aspect of the economic system (Shamsul and Lee 1988, 33). The notion of the FELDA settler itself was constructed through the lens of establishing a permanent population of Malay farmers who worked the soil. The Malay-led government was keen to establish the image and the material reality of Malay settlers working the earth as part of the national conception of *bumiputera*. The forest harboring Chinese Communists would be erased to make way for Malay settlers. And relative racial gains were a significant prop in appeasing Malays who might otherwise have protested at the slow pace of development. Despite the isolated protests, FELDA export income supported the Malay proto-proletariat and funded the economic takeoff of Malaysia. This successful distancing from the inferior, subordinate and backward status is a goal that all developing states aim for (Gupta 1998, 40–42). Through the FELDA programs, the "sons of the soil" would be returned to their place on earth. What more concrete form of territorialization could take place?

In Malaysia the politics of fixing an identity literally came about through territorial appropriation and grounding it in the earth through cultivation. FELDA literature repeatedly used the terms "settlers" and "pioneers," referred to characteristics of fortitude and industry in overcoming travails as criteria for acceptance into the FELDA schemes and referred to the cultural ties with soil (updated as bioeconomics). An important aspect of the success of the internal migration program was the orderliness and institutional environment in which FELDA projects were carried out. It helped establish an air of normalcy and inevitability to the program. Recalling Butler's (1990, 272) insights, interpellating its identity within the mesh of signification of science and technology allowed the Malaysian nation-state to appropriate some of the cultural authority that went with it. Moreover, by invoking a technical vocabulary, the biases of the state were cloaked by the neutral language of science and planning. Instead, the state entered as a neutral arbitrator of resources rather than as an actor throwing in its lot with certain groups, never forgetting that state capital accumulation was one of the paramount twin goals. It also bears remembering that if colonization is conceived as trauma because of losses incurred, the material plenitude of the FELDA plantations went a long way towards creating a sense of national redemption. Opening up the forests to be replaced by planned agriculture using the latest laboratory tested techniques came to symbolize going forward in space to reverse the ravages of colonial time, that is, taking back the land. The decision to use the terms "pioneer" and "settler" also (un)consciously drew connections to the US founding mythology of hardy men and women who won the frontier. This, too, was a case of interpellation within a valorized narrative whose meaning was widely commensurable and acceptable to an international audience. Cutting down the forests was the physical equivalent of the *telos* of national territorialization; this was not the same as pioneers in the US or Canada who took the land, but a *retaking* of the land. The point about *re*taking the land is significant because it signals that moral ownership was always theirs, rather than the morally ambiguous "taking" which implied theft. The FELDA program, by allowing only Malays to participate in the schemes to settle the frontier, perpetuated the idea of the *bumiputera* as the ontological heirs of the nation who were nonetheless progressive participants in modernity.[2] The tension was to create a new "circuit of recognition" from the available discourses (Butler 1990, 310).

McClintock argues that nations have typically been seen through the framework of the family (1995, 357–358). Industrialization may be seen as crucial to the progress of the state, but it is the vocabulary of agriculture and fertility that is made to represent the birth and survival of the nation. The gendered aspect of this relationship between nationalism and agriculture was reinforced in the acceptance criteria for the program that allocated most of the points to the husband. There were no criteria for the acceptance of women alone. Symbolically, the Malay women's political association in Malaysia is known as *Kaum Ibu* (mothers of the family). But the cathexis between territorialization, race and gender can be most openly seen in the favoring of ex servicemen or, in the early years after the Emergency, the favoring of ex Home Guards (Shamsul and Lee 1988, Appendices II and III). This last feature of FELDA is a political counterpoint to the "land for life" campaign in the New Villages scheme. Where that campaign used betrayal and killing of Communists to openly justify while covertly discrediting the awarding of land to the killers, the FELDA schemes invoked the very same acts to valorize and, hence, justify the worthiness of the recipients of FELDA land. It seems fitting that the connections between race, gender and territorialization should be manifested in replacing the militaristic Communists in the forests with their former opponents in the erased forests. I suggest that Malaysian self-identification of rural simplicity could not be identified with the primeval forests in the plans of the government because it was too close to the lack of civilization denigrated by the Western model of progress. In this sense, only highly technological societies such as Canada and the US can afford to assert confidently the relationship between nature and heritage because there is no possibility of being mistaken for backwardness.

Conclusion

I have examined the material and metaphoric transformations the Malaysian postcolonial state believed available to it to control its population and project cultural ownership. Instead of spectacle, I emphasize the quotidian aspects of performed citizenship in the FELDA schemes. The FELDA schemes were the stage for the political theater of postcolonial Malaysia. At the macroscale, moral representations were mapped across the country as FELDA schemes made the Malaysian government owner of one of the largest plantation schemes in the world. The spatial representations reified the identities of the resident population as citizens in the transition to postcoloniality. In the aftermath of the May 13 riots, the FELDA schemes merged contradictory identities—they were at once a modern showcase through the scale of agriculture and technological emphasis while harking back to the archaic identities of *bumiputera* settlers. Without the physicality fetishized in FELDA, the new postcolonial state's mass stagings of citizenship would have remained empty spectacles like the North Korean show villages. Moreover, unlike the New Villages in Chapter 4, FELDA was not a punitive landscape but the multiplication of productive images of the iconic settler-citizen. To the "encoded eye" of participants and observers, FELDA invoked numerous positive discourses of nativism, capitalism and scientific rationality to celebrate the travail and fortitude of the *bumiputera* who not only defeated the Communists but were now making the land fruitful for capitalism—the key lay in a disciplinary landscape that was both imaginatively and materially productive.

Finally, although vastly beyond the scope of this chapter, the second prong of establishing the NEP called for the creation of government-owned private or public limited companies to accord with the SMP objective of creating a Malay entrepreneurial community within one generation (Malaysia 1971a, 31). These companies acted as holding companies and trust agencies when the government embarked on its ambitious program to nationalize parts of the private sector. Although these two prongs, land development and corporate takeovers, have been discussed as different aspects of the political economy of Malaysia, the symbolic aspect of the relationship between the two so far has been overlooked. Together, they carved out that part of the economic space that was most symbolic of returning sovereignty to the Malays—the plantation sector. FELDA's control of the downstream processing of agricultural crops, marketing and investment of profits from sales laid the groundwork for the extension into other corporate sectors such as insurance, transportation and banking. Joint ventures with Japanese firms such as Mitsui and Denka all replicated the way the large estate firms of Boustead, Guthries and Sime Darby had expanded over the years (Shamsul and Lee 1988, 168–198). Sime Darby was acquired by the Treasury Department's holding company Pernas, followed by Guthrie, the largest plantation company, and then Golden Hope, formerly Harrisons and Crosfield, the oldest (Gomez and Jomo 1997, 38). Just as British corporate investment had transformed the scale of spatial reconfiguration of the nineteenth-century Malayan landscape, now indigenous control of the grand plantation companies symbolically signaled the return of sovereignty to the Malays. FELDA Global Ventures (FGV), the global investment arm of FELDA, would eventually create its own extraterritorialization strategy as state capitalism expanded into Indonesia and beyond (FGV 2019). The NEP's two-pronged approach was addressed to different sectors of the Malay population. FELDA was to meet the needs of the Malay peasantry, while the government-controlled companies set out to create a space for a Malay entrepreneurial class. FELDA plantations became the postcolonial nature that was the companion to the corporate stage. Thus, modern innovation is presented as historic restitution as FELDA represented modern science enacted by the embodied archaic of the *bumiputera* settler, while largely containing Malay class resentment for the time. By physically staking territory through FELDA and capturing space in the corporate world, the Malaysian government was constructing the stage to accommodate the Malaysian nation. This is not to say that the narratives of FELDA schemes have stayed fixed but they served their purpose in the physical and metaphoric territorialization of the Malaysian nation-state in the depleted psychic environment after political independence.

Notes

1 The ruling Alliance Party (now known as Barisan Nasional) was made up of three distinct entities representing the main racial groups in Malaya: the United Malays National Organisation or UMNO, representing the Malays, the Malaysian Chinese Association or MCA, representing the Chinese and the Malaysian Indian Congress or MIC, representing the Indians. See essays in Goh et al. (2009) for a description of the racial divisions and their political representation in contemporary Malaysia.

2 I want to note that the government uses the *Orang Asli* as a convenient "primitive" foil to primordial identity. In forests reserves, *Orang Asli* settlements are tourist attractions. These settlements existed beside the FELDA schemes so that the different communities were part of the same allochronistic performance that gives force to FELDA's claim to modernity.

7 The Logic of Trauma in Financial Crisis

Introduction

This chapter focuses on the Western response to the Malaysian government's controversial decision to defy the international financial community by implementing currency controls during the 1997–98 East Asian financial crisis. Financial crises, far from being watershed moments of extraordinary financial danger, are now a common part of life in the era of globalization. The coverage of the 2009 Greek financial crisis was notable, among other things, for the widespread recognition that humiliation factored in the negotiations between the Troika, comprising the European Central Bank, the European Commission and the International Monetary Fund (IMF), and Greece on the Greek repayment schedule (Matteo Renzi quoted in Halimi 2015, 2; Nougayréde 2015; Smith 2015). Former Greek finance minister Yanis Varoufakis described the €86 billion bailout deal agreed to by Prime Minister Alexis Tsipras as "a new Versailles Treaty" and as "the politics of humiliation" (McClintock 2015). Perhaps the overdue recognition was a function of Greece being a European country. For East Asian observers, the coverage of the Greek crisis must have seemed like "dreaming a never-ending nightmare over again" (Shin 2015, 76). Paul Krugman (2015) describes global governing institutions such as the Troika as "learning nothing from experience" (para. 7) implying repetitive neurotic behavior that does not succeed in achieving its stated aims. As Joseph Stiglitz (2001, xiv, 2006, 2015) noted, the Asian financial crisis was the forerunner of the modern financial crisis particularly in the concerted international attempts to roll back the sovereignty of the state.

I revisit the 1997–98 East Asian financial crisis to examine the psychoanalytic mechanisms underpinning the externally imposed punitive political and economic restructuring in the affected countries. The East Asian crisis saw national currencies lose 75 percent of their value and stock markets wiped out, as well as becoming a vitriolic and racialized referendum on "Asian values" between certain Asian governments and their Western critics. Asian values is a concept vaunted by several East Asian governments referring to Asian societies prioritizing the role of community and family over

DOI: 10.4324/9781315440286-8

the individual, order and harmony over personal freedom, while also upholding such social values as thriftiness, hard work and respect for authority (Mahbubani 2002, 31). I argue that the debate over Asian values can be understood as contests over the changing place of the East Asian economies within the global hierarchy. These contests reflected the psychoanalytic challenge and defense of the conventional hierarchy of international relations that followed its symbolic disruption due to the success of regional Asian economies prior to the crisis. Until the crisis, East Asian countries were the poster children for globalization whose success the World Bank (1993) attributed to their embrace of free-market export-oriented production. East Asian governments equally attributed their success to state intervention in the form of the developmental state and Asian values. The developmental state is one in which the political elites influence the direction and pace of economic development by directly intervening in the development process through policy activism (Beeson 2004, 30). The difference between a developmental and activist state is vague other than the former carried cultural implications. The developmental state was already considered a challenge to free-market economic principles, but even more controversially, it came to be associated with Asian values by both its proponents and critics. While the East Asian governments invoked Asian values as the cultural basis of their success (Mahathir and Shintaro 1995; Mahbubani 2002), their critics invoked Asian values as a linguistic code to conjure images of corruption, greed and general dishonesty (see essays in Goodman et al. 1998; Bell 2000; Barr 2002).

My point is not whether a discernible set of Asian values exists but rather about the geopolitical significance of the deployment of the concept by its proponents and critics. During the crisis, the IMF-imposed financial restructuring (more commonly known as austerity and deregulation programs) occurred in tandem with a humiliating, racially pejorative commentary. Economic choices are seen as belonging to the domain of rationality, yet in the case of the East Asian financial crisis, the public discourse consistently transformed economic decisions into cultural and, more significantly, emotional battlegrounds. I argue that the emotional force surrounding these decisions on the side of their proponents and detractors can only be explained by examining the contests and negotiations that take place in the parallel narratives that foreground issues of race and identity. Group conceptions such as race may be cultural constructs, but they are important because development has come to be viewed as the potential of a group or region to progress (Kasese-Hara 2004, 545). And development is still commonly equated with economic growth. Finance, race and human worth are yoked together in a relationship of logical equivalence (Chapter 5), which raises the stakes for economic growth.

Using the libidinal economy framework, I examine the unofficial discourses that parallel the economic debates on the region's monetary policy to elicit the real, politically charged responses. I work with Heinz Kohut's

(1973) framework of narcissistic injury and anger and Bollas' (2011) framework of psychopathology to analyze financial crises as displacements of the libidinal economy in globalization. When I began this research, I set out to argue that humiliation, even more than material austerity, is the key factor in inducing the psychic regression that leaves the targeted countries open to an identity compliant with the neoliberal aims of economic restructuring. But this opens up the question of who was supposed to be implementing the strategy? And did Western pundits and representatives of global governance institutions have anything in common to allow them to coordinate such a strategy? After all, there is a distinction between official IMF figures (e.g., Michel Camdessus and Stanley Fischer) and Western media pundits. Yet the surprising issue was how much the discourse of humiliation was repeated and deployed among all these figures. Perhaps what is often overlooked is that these figures have a cultural and geopolitical location as much as a professional location. Moreover, coordination implies a conscious effort, which presupposes a mastery of a situation. Instead, as we shall see, every attribute of narcissistic injury and anger appeared present in the behavior of the perpetrators of the humiliation. This is not to say that the humiliation did not anger the East Asian governments, or for that matter the broader general population, but that the desire to humiliate was an act of aggression by the West that needed explaining. I argue that the strategy to humiliate was not a covertly conscious attempt at economic discipline but rather an unconscious acting out of anxieties by the West, a reaction to the perception of economically and geopolitically ceding its premier international position. These anxieties resulted from the changes that began the move to a post-industrial economy in the 1970s in the West as part of what Harvey calls the "the spatial fix" of globalization to ensure continuing profits for Western capital (Harvey 1989). Harvey (1982) uses the term "spatial fix" to describe the tendency of Western capital, when confronted with declining profits in the West, to seek a solution through expanding their operations geographically to exploit new resources and investment opportunities. But as Teresa Brennan (1993, 9) reminds us, conscious or unconscious acknowledgment of exploitation invites anxieties of retaliation. Western anxieties of retaliation by their former colonial subjects and now erstwhile competitors in globalization erupted in the very aggressive public discourse that followed in the wake of the Asian financial crisis highlighting the long denied racialized dimension of the global economic order.

Humiliation and the Logic of Trauma

Identity

Development theory highlights the material dimension of inequality while postcolonial theory highlights the links among issues of identity/culture, representation and agency (Kapoor 2008). What has never been explained is why

East Asian economic decisions have turned into such vitriolic cultural battlegrounds internationally. During the East Asian financial crisis, the Asian values discourse included both criticism and defense of monetary policy in the region at large, but especially of currency controls in Malaysia. This section provides a theoretical framework for analyzing how economic success becomes a means of identity construction so that economic challenges, in turn, become threats to identity. In Chapter 1, I reviewed Freud's conceptualization of how individuals come to identify with a larger entity. For a group to exist, the fate of the group must become part of the individual's fate. But for this to happen, its members must understand what the group stands for and who qualifies for membership (Freud 1959a, 24–25, 72, 86). Hence the appeal of race and ethnicity, where members are easily identifiable. The libido attaches itself to the people who have a common share in its needs; therefore, the libidinal tie is narcissistic (Freud 1959a, 44). The tie that binds is the experience of being loved in compensation for group loyalty.

Freud (1959a, 1962) proposed that ideas bind individuals into a common identity. But if, in identifying as part of a group, the individual becomes less vulnerable, they also take on other anxieties from their group identity. Still, while individuals experience perceived injuries against their group personally, paradoxically, the competition with other groups actually consolidates group identity (Freud 2004, 23, 48). Moreover, we enjoy the competition (Freud 1962, 23–27). Hence, emerging as winners in economic competitions becomes a means of satisfying this impulse for contrast and exerting superiority. But since identifying with a group requires sublimation of individual instincts, that aggression must now be projected elsewhere (Rose 2004, xii). Paradoxically, if groups need competitors to fashion their identity, they also require their competitors to recognize, acknowledge and desire them to maintain their ideal self-image. Capitalism is a way of servicing an ideal version of the self. East Asian countries' adoption of the export-oriented manufacturing model of development made them the ideal junior participants in a racialized capitalist narrative that featured the West as the dominant subject. But the slow decline of Western manufacturing from the 1970s and the rise of its capitalist protégés as competitors trampled on the self-image of the omnipotent West. The latter's approval of East Asian countries, an expedient relationship contingent on an anti-communist alliance during the Cold War, was unlikely to survive the challenge to the West's self-image. And when a people's self-love is threatened, they resort to narcissistic self-defense (Freud 1959a, 37).

Aggression

Freud (1962, 39) suggests that people will repress their aggression and anxiety as the price of group belonging as long as there is an outlet for their aggression. Just as fear of others binds a group, complicity in inflicting aggression onto an external scapegoat binds the perpetrators together. He (23) also suggests that the oppression of others is a precondition of a group's identity, an idea echoed in Teresa Brennan's (1993) foundational fantasy. Peter Gay (1994, 4–5) describes aggression as ranging from confident self-advertisement to sadistic torture. Verbal aggression is less fatal but still unmistakably aggressive. Gay (1994, 6) notes that the kind of aggressiveness a culture rewards depends on the times and circumstances, but the point is everyone recognizes aggression for what it is. The acceptable form of aggression is through mastery of others in competition and ranking. In our time, the obvious acceptable arena for aggression and the ultimate assertion of superiority lies in the financial arena. Here, the criteria for winning and the registration of the effect are recognizable to everyone because economic globalization has meant that signals of economic contests are now culturally commensurable.

Gay (1994) suggests that the "capacity to be aggressive which works itself out in a wide variety of circumstances ...[is] mobilized by whatever is experienced as unpleasurable" (536). For my purposes, I argue that earlier historical manifestations of colonial/imperial aggression are now acceptably channeled into finance. Ironically, postcolonial states in globalization attempt to create safe space through economic practice. And when Freud (1959a, 18, 27) suggests that prestige is a sort of domination exercised over us by an individual but is lost in the event of failure or by a competitor's success, it is easy to understand why the proposition of Asian values as a cultural basis for their economic success came to be experienced as a narcissistic injury by the West. Within the hegemonic framework of global capitalism and its antecedents in colonialism, the East Asian assertion of an indigenous basis for success was culturally commensurable as a challenge to the old order.

Narcissistic Injury and Rage

Understanding the Asian values discourse in the wake of the financial crisis requires an understanding of why it evoked such an emotional response. Much of the contemporary scholarly work applying psychoanalysis to the role of group identity in international aggression focuses solely on nationalism and military conflicts (see essays in Rajchman 1995; Rose 2005). Yet, the international financial sector is probably the most common site of everyday aggression with the possibility of catastrophic consequences. Old patterns of hegemonic identity are being superseded by those that are finance-oriented because that is where the stakes are highest. I argue that because the prestige of a group's identity is so closely associated with its economic status, a change in that status is experienced as a narcissistic injury. This section expands on the related concepts of narcissistic injury and rage developed by Heinz Kohut (1973) to explain how the antagonistic Asian values debate was played out.

Recall that Kohut (1973) reconceptualizes narcissism using the term "selfobject" to refer to any narcissistic experience in which the other is in the service of the self, the latter being defined as a structure that is required for an individual's sense of psychic coherence and well-being. He (1973, 637–638) sees a selfobject as inseparable from the self so that the other person's functions are related to the self. The selfobject offers support for the vulnerable self through an approving mirroring response, which Kohut (1973, 628) envisions as forming the basis for realistic self-esteem. But he argues that if the subject's prior experience has not allowed for transformation of the narcissistic cathexis with the grandiose self into a healthy self-esteem, then deprived of an "approving mirroring response" (628) from the selfobject, the self will experience a narcissistic injury and respond with extreme rage. Earl Gammon (2017) uses Kohut's concept of narcissistic rage to argue that neoliberalism both encourages and reinforces an unhealthy narcissism by impeding the attainment of a stable sense of self. The ensuing lack of self-esteem then finds a compensatory outlet in a lack of empathy and aggression against others. I extend the concepts of self and selfobjects to encompass groups to explore the role of racial dynamics in capitalist aggression.

Bollas (2011, 81) suggests that under intense emotional pressure such as envy or anxiety, an individual's or group's negative traits will be projected externally to coalesce into allegories or stereotypes of other groups. Likewise, Kohut (1973, 644) proposes that defensive responses, of which narcissistic rage is an extreme version, are activated because the recalcitrant selfobject is not seen as an autonomous source but as a *flaw in a narcissistically perceived reality* [his emphasis], over which the narcissistically vulnerable self had expected to exercise control. Thus, the selfobject's independence or difference is experienced as offensive. This is the crux of Western behavior to challenges, real or perceived, to its authority under globalization. Given that Kohut (1973, 643–645) posits that a narcissist must exert absolute control over their environment and demand unconditional availability of the approving mirroring for the maintenance of self-esteem, the narcissist will grind down the opponent who dares to outshine them because this contradicts the self-image of the grandiose self. Global economic competitions create intense anxiety even among the winners, and envy among those who perceive themselves as losers, even if this loss is only relative. When the premier form of identification is economic and is coupled with a sense of historically based racial entitlement, then by the above logic, the success of rivals becomes a defeat of the self and is experienced as narcissistic injury. The success of the East Asian emerging economies destroyed the sense of unconditional approval of Western social organization, especially when the East Asian states put forth a cultural and racial basis (Asian values) for their economic success. Their subsequent stumbling and weakness during the financial crisis then seemed to invite the moralistic punitiveness of the IMF and Western commentators. It is in this context that I argue that the vaunting of Asian values as the cultural/racial basis of East Asian economic success became a flashpoint for the economically punitive austerity programs that were imposed upon East Asian countries, as well as for gloating by Western pundits in the wake of the financial crisis.

Humiliation

Kohut (1973, 642) argues that we can recognize that narcissistic rage is involved when an individual is excessively preoccupied with a situation involving other people, which he attributes to the narcissistic indivdual's inability to recognize others as independent subjects. We see this in the West's response to the Asian financial crisis, which focused on denigrating the cultural basis for East Asian success. Kohut (1973, 637–638) suggests that narcissistic rage occupies a very specific position in the spectrum defined by an obsession for revenge because of an archaic fixation. In the case of the Asian values discourse, the rage was a function of a historic sense of Western entitlement, while racism and colonialism conveniently provided the historic substance to the language used in the Asian values discourse because the stereotypes invoked were commensurable to commentators as a colonial legacy. Bollas (2011, 176) goes on to hypothesize that extreme reactions occur as part of an unconscious restructuring of past trauma in which the subject puts others through an equivalent, if different, trauma. In this logic, aggressive narcissists identify only with those aspects of their identity that provide them with admiration and a sense of superiority (Bollas 2011, 82). Western contempt and ridicule of Asian values reflects its narcissistic rage at the economic challenge, but it could also be a function of the West projecting its own anxieties of the social dislocation inherent in the rising inequality in their home countries that accompanied the transition from a manufacturing to a service economy from the 1970s onward. Humiliation of East Asian countries then is not just as an outlet for narcissistic rage but also a way of Western countries working through their own trauma of lost status. Thus both Western and East Asian responses during the crisis originate in defensiveness, but the West is defensive and outraged at the perception that its culturally privileged position has been assailed, whereas East Asian outrage is driven by anxiety at their relative lack of power in economic globalization. In any case, the East Asian response to the humiliating economic policies imposed on them in the aftermath of the financial crisis was tempered by their inability to retaliate.

For Bollas (2011, 83–87), if the shame of narcissistic injury must be projected elsewhere in the "circuit of depersonalization" (87), traumatizing their victims must also be justified in the name of a militant ideology. Instead of the "White Man's Burden," now the ideology of neoliberalism asserts its higher purpose to create a prosperous world through its proponents' intellectual superiority which requires the sacrifice of its victims in realizing neoliberal policies. Bollas (2011, 168–171) describes a militant ideology as an active process involving seduction, the promise of a false safe space and the development of a dependent relationship so that the subsequent shock of betrayal becomes even more traumatic. The goal is to induce a traumatic experience which will cause the victim to lose perspective and leave the victim open to compliance (Bollas 2011, 171–173). This process makes sense when applied to the promises of financial deregulation in globalization. In globalization, Western financial institutions present freedom for capital to developing countries as the solution to their poverty. In the event of asset bubbles, and subsequent unsustainable debt leading to capital flight and a liquidity crisis, the false hope of prosperity is replaced by the imposition of shock therapy in the form of austerity by the very institutions that once promoted the asset bubbles. In tandem with the material betrayal, the trauma is reinforced through a parallel humiliating discourse that dehumanizes the victims. This form of the narcissistic injury is inflicted through the following commitive practices: stereotyping through aggregate group identity; distorting the victims' views so that they appear less intelligent; and belittling and caricaturing the victims, which can include character assassination of specific individuals (Bollas 2011, 88–89). All of these practices were present in the Asian values discourse during the financial crisis in 1997–98.

Insurgent East Asia

Anxiety about the West, as represented by the US being superseded by an economically insurgent East Asia, is on display in the current US-China tech war. Western anxieties about the East Asian challenge pivoted around economic gains even before the advent of the tech war (Jacques 2009). In the contemporary world the ultimate assertion of superiority lies in the financial arena. Financial prestige, long the privilege of the West was now threatened by its competitor's success. If initial East Asian success could be considered an approving mirror of the West, their later assertions of a cultural basis for their success shattered the mirror. Recalling Kohut's description (1973, 637–638) of the selfobject as inseparable from the self, we can say that East Asia is perceived as the selfobject of the West. While much of contemporary Western anxieties have to do with the rise of China, they have their roots in the fears of Japanese competition in the 1980s and the block of Asian countries—South Korea, Taiwan, Singapore and Hong Kong; and to a lesser extent Malaysia, Indonesia and Thailand—in the 1990s. For excellent reviews of Malaysia's modern political economy rather than the psychoanalytical approach that this book takes, please refer to Jomo (1988), Gomez and Jomo (1997) and Gomez et al. (2017). The significance of East Asian economic success lay in two factors: their success proved that Japan was not a racial aberration in economic development; and they represented an indigenous development model that was initially acceptable to the West as opposed to the socialist-inflected Latin American import-substitution model.

In the early 1990s, the World Bank (1993) described the East Asian economies as a "miracle." Until the 1997–98 financial crisis, they were poster children, to invoke Bollas (2011, 168), for the "militant ideology" of the neoliberal policies promoted by the IMF and World Bank.

So why was a financial crisis tacitly reframed in the international, and largely Western, media within the cultural and psychological parameters of a debate on Asian values? While Western opprobrium targeted all the governments affected by the crisis, Malaysia was especially singled out for its defiance of the IMF in imposing currency controls. Originally a controversial decision, it is now accepted that the move stabilized the Malaysian economy (Kaplan and Rodrik 2001; IMF 2012). But even in 1998, it was accepted that Malaysia's ability to defy the international financial community rested on its healthy reserve-to-external debt ratio (Jomo 2001, 41).[1] This would have long-term consequences in the buildup of foreign reserves by all East Asian states. As of June 2023, the figure for the affected East Asian states, as well as Japan, Taiwan and China (Hong Kong included as a separate figure), came up to over $6.6 trillion dollars (https://tradingeconomics.com/search.aspx?q=foreign%20exchange). In the immediate aftermath of the crisis, an IMF-led Western intervention forced countries that appealed for external help to restructure their economies, resulting in massive local social unrest. Instead, overlooking the material hardship and social upheaval, Western media focused on the financial crisis as a referendum on Asian values. Finance, race and human worth became yoked together in a relationship of logical equivalence once again (also see Chapter 5).

Prior to the financial crisis in 1997, poverty in Malaysia was down to 8 percent from 60 percent in 1970 (Jayasankaran and Hiebert 1997). By the mid-1990s Gross Domestic Product (GDP) growth was averaging nine percent a year (Fox 1998, 100). The *Financial Post* described the Malaysian model of privatization as one of the most successful in the world (Wheeler 1995, 29). On the left of the political spectrum, Mahmood Mamdani (2008) later held up Malaysian development to African countries as a model of the material benefits and dignity that development could deliver. Globalization as the savior of the developing world was primarily a trope referring to East Asian countries. Their success offered hope to the rest of world that exiting poverty was possible through their own agency (Sheridan 1997, xiii; Ghesquire 2007). Malaysia, like the other East Asian economies, was admired for its pro-capital, pro-West policies (Khanna 2008, 267). But even before the crisis, Malaysia and the other East Asian economies were rebelling against the model student image of one who has succeeded by simply copying the West (Inoue 1999, 39). This rebellion manifested itself in the promotion of the developmental state, itself implying a socialistic turn toward state intervention. More subtly, the conflation of race and nation-state, a legacy of colonialism, meant that the promotion of the role of the state set the stage for arguing that culture and race played a role in their success. This indirect appeal became overt through the promotion of Asian values. Freud (1959a, 1962, 2004, 23, 48) would have noted the significance of race as the libidinal tie which was strengthened through competition with the West in globalization.

Malaysia became a focal point for Western critics because of its combative Prime Minister at the time, Mahathir Mohammad. Brummer (1997, 19) noted that: "Nobody has symbolized East Asia's confidence in itself and its ability to take on the world single-handedly more than the [now former] Malaysian Prime Minister, Mahathir Mohammad." What exactly was Mahathir taking on? Development, after all, as Kasese-Hara (2004, 547) notes, is construed as an indicator of racial potential for progress. In asserting that the economic improvement of their national economies was a product of the controversial Asian values, its proponents implicitly argued that race and culture, the traits that condemned them to colonization, were now the basis of Asian success. A number of Asian commentators observed that Western unease over Asian success was rooted in Western anxiety over the region's rise from former colonies to competitors (Lim et al. 1998; Inoue 1999; Sen 1999, 96–97; Mahbubani 2002). Admittedly, the position of East Asia in the colony role extends beyond official colonized status but colony is used here to indicate a differential power relationship. If, in Kohut's (1973, 637–638, 644) framework, former colonies are selfobjects meant to provide an approving mirror to the West, then the success of the East Asians was now construed as an offense to the West. Mahathir's pronouncements convey the new confidence that emerged in the region at the time of record-breaking economic growth. The Asian values controversy signaled a psychic shift that got underway in the 1980s with Japan, followed by the other East Asian countries and now China.

The Asian Financial Crisis

The 1997–98 financial crisis began with the slide of the Thai baht in May 1997 (Lee 1998; Jomo 2001). By July 1997, currency traders were short-selling other Asian currencies resulting in currency depreciation, lowered share prices and a trade deficit in those countries. The spillover effects of market uncertainty in the region frightened off potential investors while existing investors began to sell their securities. In August 1997, Thailand abandoned its currency peg and defaulted on its debts, turning to the IMF for help, followed by Indonesia in October and South Korea in November. In return for IMF aid, those countries had to abide by IMF conditions to raise domestic interest rates, lower social spending, open domestic markets and deregulate to allow foreign ownership of local assets, policies that would have long-term consequences in terms of opening up these countries to foreign control (Berthier 2000). Give that only a short time ago they were held up by the IMF and the World Bank (1997) as examples of what market freedom could deliver, this was a sharp reversal of fortune; it reminds us of Bollas' point (2011, 168- 173) that it is the shock of the sudden betrayal of a former mentor that disorients the victim and causes it to lose perspective beyond that of its victimizer. But while Singapore, Taiwan and Hong Kong all suffered currency depreciations, they were spared the worst because they had no external debt and healthy reserves. All three also successfully managed exchange rates, which reduced the threat of currency speculation. And Malaysia avoided IMF intervention as its debts were held by the private sector and the government possessed a positive reserves-to-external debt ratio avoiding a liquidity shortfall (Jomo 2001).

Nevertheless, by July 1997 the Malaysian ringgit was depreciating steadily, followed by falling share prices, and in turn causing the debt-holding banks to experience liquidity difficulties. The Malaysian government then also faced revenue shortfalls as businesses were unable to pay taxes and purchasing power fell by about 50 percent (Jomo 2001). Initially, Malaysia voluntarily adopted IMF-type policies to cut government spending, increase reserves and defer government projects, but it soon found these austerity measures exacerbated the financial crisis (Jayasankaran 1997). The ringgit continued to depreciate, at one time almost reaching five ringgit to one US dollar, increasing the costs of debt servicing.[2] As the crisis worsened, Prime Minister Mahathir took the controversial decision to suspend currency trading and place a one-year moratorium on the outflow of foreign portfolio capital in October 1998, reduce reserve requirement to increase liquidity, and lower interest rates to stimulate investment and consumption (Hiebert 1999). The ringgit was fixed at 3.80 to the US dollar thus ending ringgit speculation. The government announced it would guarantee bank deposits and a special agency would restructure corporate debt and recapitalize financial institutions. State-owned firms also bought shares to halt the slide on the bourse. Finally, also in defiance of IMF wisdom, the government maintained price controls on essential consumer items and boosted government spending to trigger a Keynesian reflation of the economy (Bank Negara Malaysia 2001; also see Chapter 8 for further government policies).

Humiliation and Financial Crisis

Unfortunately, Mahathir's judicious policy activism was overshadowed by his antisemitic comments blaming George Soros for the Asian financial crisis (Soros 1997). This served to deflect attention from the Western commentators who interpreted the economic crisis as the death of the Asian values debate (Milner 2000). I am indebted to Milner (2000) for pointing me to examples of language used in the Asian values debate. I followed up on those examples but framing these examples and others that I have added psychoanalytically is my interpretation alone. But in the "us" against "them" pressure of economic globalization, we also see the truth of Bollas' assertion (2011, 81) that a group's negative traits projected externally coalesce into allegories of Asian versus Western values. The economic crisis was a manifestation of Freud's point (1959a, 18, 27) that the failure of a competitor can reestablish the prestige of the narcissistic subject, in this case, the West. The role of the economy in the real contest over racial and cultural superiority was important because the parameters of economic success were commensurable to both sides. As Gay (1994, 6–7) reminds us, because aggression is transactive, the aggressive act must be culturally commensurable. East Asia's economic challenge transformed its role from the provider of the "approving mirroring response" (Kohut 1973, 628) to competitor, which Western commentators experienced as a narcissistic injury and to which they responded with rage. This took the form of commitive practices of erasure through humiliation (Bollas 2011, 82, 88–89, 176) and the imposition of austerity programs. The humiliating discourse included aggregating Asians into derogatory stereotypes quoted below so that Asian leaders were at best "amoral" and "opportunist" and at worst "drug traffickers and gangsters" (Mallet 1999, 16). Wealth was given the gloss of vulgarity so that the Thais and the Singaporeans were "nouveaux riches"[3] and Indonesians "witless," while Mahathir was singled out as a "blackmailer" of the West and a "menace to his country" (Hoagland 1997a, C09). The same commentator would go on to boast that "American values ... have much to offer for the financial stability of the global economy" (Hoagland 1997b, C07) ... at least until 2008.

I have argued that finance, race and human worth became yoked together in a relationship of logical equivalence. The *US News and World Report* claimed that "Asian values have become Asian liabilities" (Zuckerman 1998, 77). The *Washington Post*'s Jim Hoagland (1997a, C09) similarly equated ringgit and baht depreciations with racial devaluation: "Just as sharply devalued are the political hubris and racial conceit [of] 'Asian values.'" Elsewhere, Francis Fukuyama (1998, 27) stated that the crisis would "puncture the idea of Asian exceptionalism." For his part, Walter Russell Mead (1998) claimed Asia itself as "devalued" confirming the link between human worth and financial success. And Victor Mallet (1999, 45) claimed that Westerners had been too "diffident" in criticizing Asian governments. The gloating over the Asian crisis appeared to span the ideological spectrum in the Western media. *The Independent*'s Diane Coyle (1997) concluded that the crisis will "finally lay to rest this unquestioning worship of Asian values." The *New Statesman*'s Jonathan Mirsky (1998, 26) sarcastically labeled Asian values "a fabulous notion" only good for "crushing dissent and fending off criticism from democrats" and, oddly, for crashing planes. However, perhaps Sebastian Mallaby (1998, 2) got to the heart of the matter: "Asia is vulnerable ... the IMF's progress through Asia over the past year recalls the long-ago voyage of Commodore Perry." Highly critical of the concept of Asian values himself, Amartya Sen (1999, 96–97) questioned whether underlying Western criticism was an anxiety about the threat posed to the West by the combination of economic success and nationalist confidence. Sen's views echo Kohut's (1973), so that while Western elites play on racial and cultural anxieties to perpetuate the global political and economic status quo, the appropriation of the same tools by others provokes narcissistic rage among Western politicians and media commentators.

Conclusion

Malaysia survived the crisis, although credit for its survival remains contested, variously attributed to its policies, selective reflation, the worldwide electronics boom or inevitable regional recovery (Khor 2008). But the acrimonious rhetoric, not to mention the punitive measures imposed upon indebted countries by the IMF led to much farther-reaching financial policymaking. In the late 1990s, Malaysia was able to defy the IMF because its foreign debt did not exceed reserves and, moreover, was concentrated in three partly privatized companies, as opposed to government held debt (Jomo 2001). Its example triggered the subsequent regional trend of high reserves, which today continues to finance the American deficit as East Asian currency devaluations in the aftermath of the crisis created an export boom and facilitated the US trade deficit. Subsequently, other East Asian countries took note of what had saved Malaysia. As of June 2023, the East Asian countries, including China, held $6.6 trillion in reserves (http://www.tradingeconomics.com/country-list/foreign-exchange-reserves).

Malaysia's danger was always that it would be seen as an example of a recalcitrant selfobject by other Asian states in its defiance of international financial institutions. The other significant lesson noted by the East Asian countries concerned the US and IMF's objection to Japan's proposal during the crisis for an Asian Monetary Fund which would tide members over future financial emergencies (Golub 2016, 99). Recognizing that access to credit during the Asian crisis was firmly in Western control, in 2015, China created the New Development Bank and the Asian infrastructure Investment Bank as a source of investment and as lender of last resort to provide an alternative to the World Bank (Chapter 8). I have argued that the debate over Asian values can be understood as contests over the changing place of the East Asian emerging economies within the global hierarchy. These contests reflect the psychic challenge to, and defense of, the conventional hierarchy of international relations, in the wake of the East Asian Miracle, followed by the crisis in 1997–98. The emotional force underpinning the economic policy decisions during the crisis can only be explained by examining the parallel narrative on Asian values, in which Western commentators sought to humiliate East Asian states through their public rhetoric. But using the psychoanalytic framework of narcissistic injury and rage, I have tried to show that public humiliation may have been an unconscious acting out of anxieties by the West, a reaction to its perception of a slow economic and geopolitical decline. In my argument, Western anxieties are projected onto its perceived competitors and erstwhile protégés in East Asia, resulting in the very aggressive public discourse which brought out the long denied racialized dimension of the global economic order. Writing at the start of World War One, Sigmund Freud (1915, 5) noted that war "cuts all common bonds between the contending peoples and threatens to leave a legacy of embitterment that will make any renewal of those bonds impossible for a long time to come." He was writing about the long-term psychic consequences of a military conflict, but his words could just as easily be applied to our contemporary economic conflicts.

Notes

1 Although Malaysian debt as of 2023 runs to 61 percent of its GDP, 77 percent of that debt is owed domestically (Ho 2023). Malaysia also consistently ran a debt to GDP ratio of 50 percent until the pandemic.
2 The exchange rate on 7 July 2023 was $4.67 Ringgit to US $1.00. The adverse exchange rate is an issue of serious political concern for the federal government as state elections loom in August 2023.
3 Unfairly maligned in the case of the Singaporeans who were only affected through regional contagion rather than due to poor policies or sovereign debt.

8 Anxiety and Economic Policy in Resurgent East Asia

Introduction

There are many narrative threads to the story of globalization but few commentators, even when critical, would deny that one of the most powerful in capturing public imagination has been the economic rise of East Asian countries. This narrative trope is so powerful that, as I point out in the Introduction, countries hitherto categorized as Southeast Asia became figuratively relocated into East Asia as their economies grew. The West, hitherto accustomed to perceiving East Asia as its approving mirror, were instead confronted with potential rivals. But the Asian financial crisis unraveled this narrative. Western anxiety found a perfect opportunity in the Asian financial crisis to reinscribe East Asia in the passified position of the colonial/imperial foundational fantasy. This chapter examines the consequences of the traumatic Asian financial crisis on Malaysian and, more broadly, regional financial policy in the wake of the crisis to circumvent Western financial "blockades." As Mahathir Mohammad (Lim et al. 1998, 97), the Malaysian Prime Minister during the financial crisis, noted, "Gunboats are no longer necessary ... it is really much cheaper ... to use [economic] pressure in order to achieve the effect of colonization."[1] The way forward, then, is to construct alternative financial ecosystems.

This chapter focuses on how the Malaysian state and other East Asian state actors responded to the crisis building on the possibilities of and limits to their perceived agency. Referencing Teresa Brennan's foundational fantasy, Judith Butler's performativity and Bruno Latour's network theory, I argue that the economic narrative of the East Asian response to the financial crisis not only refuses the interpellated identity of a constrained passified identity in the global hierarchy but by reversing the factors that define how trauma is experienced, the response constructs a modern capitalist subjectivity through the performance of active state agency. Where Chapter 7 analyzed the cultural discourse of Asian values and its geopolitical repercussions on Malaysia, I now analyze the motivations behind the policies of state intervention. Although it seems to reverse the chronology, I have chosen to cover theories of the activist state here rather than in the previous chapter. Given the

DOI: 10.4324/9781315440286-9

organization of the book that tracks a cycle of repeated trauma and anxious reaction, this chapter covers the role of activist states in disrupting the cycle. I focus on Malaysian but more broadly on a Southeast Asian strategy linking national financial policy to *transnational* policy to circumvent Western institutions' restrictions on credit. Here, the state is the active agent, and its economic policies constitute the strategy through which it breaks the repeated trauma of racial humiliation. I use the term "agency" in Brennan's (1993, 80–81) sense as a directed, motivated will with the means for actualizing itself. A brief note on terminology; some readers may take exception to the use of the term victim when used in the context of states but while I use the term "victim" reservedly, in the psychoanalytical context of the introjection of a value system that works in the long run against one's own interest, I feel this use is justified.

Beginning with a brief overview of orthodox models of the state's role in economic development, I move on to a discussion of psychoanalytic approaches to studying the nation-state. The latter studies have almost entirely focused on a critique of essentialized national identities, but I offer an alternative perspective by focusing on the state as the entity that combines the sovereign territory comprising a country and its government. The second half of the chapter applies the psychoanalytic framework to state agency to make sense of how financial policy can break the cycle of racial trauma. In explaining how an understanding of the libidinal economy, even if it is partial and not named as such, can guide policy activism, I reference Brennan's (1993) foundational fantasy to explain how Malaysia perceived externally imposed obstacles to its development as repeated trauma. Then, conceptualizing the state as a collective ego that performs the agentic subject, I analyze Malaysian and Singaporean strategies to defend against externally imposed financial trauma. I use Butler's theory of performativity to explain how Malaysia and other East Asian states attempted to transform the narrative about their place in the international hierarchy. Finally, I use Latour's network theory to argue how applying a network strategy to credit liquidity can dismantle the foundational fantasy.

The Activist State

One of the most pressing problems for non-Western countries, many newly decolonized in the 1950s and 1960s, was how to grow their economies. Post-Bretton Woods, the dominant strain of Keynesian-influenced welfare economics in their former colonial rulers and, crucially, in the context of the Cold War, meant that governments of non-Western countries were granted some autonomy in implementing economic development, albeit under the guidance of Western experts. These counselled external financing and access to some technology. The dependent dynamic and enduring trade and exchange rate inequalities carried over from the colonial era inevitably obstructed economic growth (McMichael and Weber 2021, 27–92).

Marxist-influenced political economists, several from South America, diagnosing the problem as one of unequal trade relations between the rich industrialized core countries and the poor commodity exporting peripheral advised economic decoupling in tandem with state-fostered domestic production, a process known as import substitution industrialization (Sheppard et al. 2009). But it was not until the rise of the Japanese economy in the 1960s–1970s that a non-Western country appeared to have found the formula for rapid economic development (Johnson 1982). Still, Japan seemed a racial outlier until the economic success of South Korea, Taiwan and Singapore in the 1980s and 1990s (Amsden 1989; Castells 1992; Studwell 2013; Golub 2016; Chua 2017). The Commission on Growth and Development (2008, 19) would go on to note that 9 of the 13 countries that achieved sustained high growth of seven percent over 25 years were located in East Asia. However, the basis of that growth was a source of contention. The World Bank (1993), referring to the phenomenon as "the East Asian miracle," attributed success to an unfettered market. In contrast, many scholars (Johnson 1982; Amsden 1989; Castells 1992; Studwell 2013; Golub 2016; Chua 2017) saw the state as central to the successful industrial policies of what became known as "the developmental state." This was controversial because there was little consensus on how to define the developmental state (Beeson 2004). Even those who give it credence argue that its policy prescriptions were too historically specific (Beeson 2009; Lin 2012; Wade 2017; Takagi, Kanchoochat, and Sonobe 2019).[2]

Although development spawned an industry of public, private and nonprofit sector consultants, for developing countries, it is still largely the responsibility of the nation-state. For late comer economies, there are few alternative viable alternatives to the state when it comes to coordinating policy and marshalling resources. For the purposes of this study, the real significance is what role the state plays, and if so, what forms the basis of its policy activism (Acemoglu and Robinson 2012; Ang 2016; Dercon 2022). Ang (2016) and Dercon (2022), while focused on pragmatic policy activism, call out the universalist assumptions of a one size fits all model in development economics because the discourse of the activist state in East Asia has always been fraught with undertones of cultural essentialism from its association with the concept of "Asian values" (see Chapter 7). Taking a psychoanalytic perspective, Kapoor (2014) notes that a prominent "blind spot" in development discourse is ignoring the significance of colonialism, thus denying the complicity of the West in development failures, while Kapoor et al. (2023) highlight the role of fantasy in capitalist models of economic growth. Kapoor (2020) turns the perspective around by also asking what psychoanalytic elements "drive" development. This chapter examines the drive behind the policy activism of East Asian nation-states.

Most political psychoanalytic-inflected scholarship focuses on the nation because of the interest in essentialized identities and their impact on political dysfunction (Chowdhry and Rai 2009; Garner 2017; Mercer

2017; Gniazdowski 2018). I want to turn the focus to the *state* as the site of policy activism even if we acknowledge the nation as the site of affects that drive state actions. Gallagher (2018) applies psychoanalytic concepts to theorize the state, rather than only the nation. The focus on the state is valuable because of its potential to function as a vehicle to realize the agency of the nation, which in Gallagher's (2018, 883) words offers "state-subjectivity as analogous to self-consciousness." In Freudian terms then, the state functions as the ego to the nation's id. Since the state is the embodiment of both identity and aspirations of its, albeit, most powerful citizens, its policies are a manifestation of the state's agency with "sovereignty" as the code for agentic subjectivity. Fridell (2014, 1180) astutely notes that development agencies in embracing the fantasy of market solutions, dismiss the very real agency of the state to mobilize resources and deliver higher standards of living. East Asian states all recognize that the state acts as an agent whose policy activism is driven by a libidinal economy. And they openly acknowledge that identity anxieties drive their policy activism and draw attention to the racialized discourse invoked to justify global governance policies.

Much of this book so far elaborates how collectives such as states "experience" trauma through the colonial foundational fantasy. For if a political subject experiences trauma because of its perceived cultural identity, the practices to impose the trauma are realized through the interstate system, and increasingly, through economic practices. Referencing Teresa Brennan's foundational fantasy, I argue that for developing countries/emerging economies, constraints to development are a major avenue through which trauma is experienced. While Kapoor et al. (2023) have analyzed China's attempts to circumvent a US-led strategy to constrain China's economic development, here I focus on small states. I show how financial strategies can function as an active response to trauma by reviewing a selection of East Asian responses to the financial crisis. Malaysia's strategy to circumvent potential Western financial institution intervention after the Asian financial crisis was to pivot from an exogenously driven economy to one driven by domestic consumption. Singapore ramped up its financial extraterritorialization strategy through its government-linked corporations (GLCs) as a defense against financial predation. And regionally, East Asian countries attempted to construct a libidinal ecosystem of networked allies linked by their anxieties to circumvent the economic and political constraints imposed upon them by Western institutions such as the International Monetary Fund (IMF) and Western-influenced institutions such as the Asian Development Bank.[3] But Latour's network theory (1987) reminds us that the successful construction of an alternative network requires not just alliances but also widespread acceptance of a different narrative to support the networks' existence. Here I use Judith Butler's theory of performativity to offer an interpretation of financial strategy as a script for the interpellated performance of masculinity in globalization. And if state actors enable the state to resist economic trauma, then they function as the defenders of the realm.

Recall, in Chapter 1, that Teresa Brennan's (1993, 11–22) conception of the era of the dominant ego is associated with the active masculine subject who relies on scientific rationality manifested through the use of technology to control the subject's environment. Brennan argues that the ego's era is composed of active, self-contained and invulnerable subjects who arrive at their identity through the psychical fantasy of controlling the passive object as a fixed reference point in the psychical "Foundational Fantasy." Brennan's (52–53) central thesis is that an objectifying projection is a condition of subjectivity because it is only through creating the fantasy of a fixed inferior that the subject can overcome the anxiety of its own unstable identity. The "other," as with the Kohutian selfobject, could be the racial other or nature as I have argued so far in this book. Brennan's (5–11) foundational fantasy manifests itself in a territorialization imperative for the active subject, and conversely, constraint (literal or figurative) is the fate of the passified object. Freudian castration manifests itself as constraint most effectively in contemporary geopolitics through financial measures. Extending Brennan's thesis to analyzing the economic rise of East Asian countries, I argue that the West, especially the United States, conceives itself as the superior active geopolitical and economic subject of modernity. But that identity is contingent on constraining those that the West sees as its inferiors. This relational identity was destabilized by East Asian economic growth in the 1990s but reinscribed during the Asian financial crisis (Chapter 7). East Asian states responded to this reinscription by taking on the task of dismantling the externally imposed foundational fantasy by creating an alternative financial ecosystem.

However, dismantling the foundational fantasy through policy works through both material practice and narrative. Successful identity constitution requires a mutual acknowledgment of the same social structures (Butler 1997, 36). Butler's (1990, 310) conception of interpellation refers simultaneously to existing networks of signification while reinforcing the process through each successful act of recognition. I argue that in striving for positive recognition, some emerging economies inserted their identity into the existing symbolic orders of capitalism and technology through their mastery of both. Certainly, the key defensive strategy by Singapore rests on maintaining exchange rates, but of equal significance is the sophistication of the techniques used to maintain the exchange rates, which contributed to transforming perceptions of the country's place in the global hierarchy.

Finally, I use Bruno Latour's (1987) network theory to expand on Butlerian performativity to explain how alternative networks gain credence through the acquisition of allies and control of the narrative. Latour notes that certain statements and practices become accepted as standards only if they become embedded within a *network* of statements and practices. The recruitment process of allies that will link strongholds or nodal points to create a network involves multiple small translations so that potential allies see themselves as having common goals (Latour 1987, 108–111, 180). My application of network theory to the East Asian policy response to the regional financial crisis departs from Latour's conceptualization of a network controlled by a single actor in that it is a decentered network of allies who have in common the libidinal experience of being humiliated. In the last five years, the alliance has been both invigorated by China's growing economic power while simultaneously engendering tensions within a group already attempting to escape the dominating dynamic with the West but now facing a new potential dominant. Notwithstanding East Asian anxieties regarding China, the very powerful drive of anxiety that links these countries has laid the basis of a libidinal ecosystem. In this sense, they are attempting to create an alliance that is connected organically to the past and continuing experience of humiliation.

Finance and Sovereign Borders

Small countries have not done well under the Westphalian definition of sovereignty, nor have their fates improved under globalization. As the Asian financial crisis showed, the fastest way to compromise a country's sovereignty is to attack its exchange rate; hence, defending its exchange rate becomes the synecdoche for an inviolable national sovereignty. For small countries the policy focus on exchange rates dates back to the Asian financial crisis of 1997–98 that saw some Asian currencies lose as much as 35 percent of their value (Sioh 2010a). Even Singapore, known for its prudent macroeconomic policies, lost 15 percent on the value of its currency (Clark et al. 2014, 94). The significance of exchange rates lies in how they affect the costs of servicing external debt and the price of imports (Low 2006, 186–199). And because exchange rates are relationally linked to interest rates, which affect employment rates, maintaining stable exchange rates is crucial if the goal is high employment and growth and, in turn, social and political stability. In the final analysis, if a country can't pay its debts and cannot print unlimited amounts of its own currency, it will be forced to turn to the IMF or an external power and be held hostage to its demands. This was a critical point for Malaysia and other East Asian countries during the Asian financial crisis as Western control of lenders of last resort would reinscribe the active subject-passified object relationship of the neocolonial foundational fantasy that East Asian economic growth had only recently begun dismantling.

If capital flows are in the form of debt and that debt is short term and denominated in a foreign currency, then the state becomes vulnerable to a financial crisis if creditors demand repayment. The key policy issue then is what can be done to avert a crisis. Continuing on from the Malaysian survival strategies described in Chapter 7, I analyze the post-crisis policies that Malaysia and other affected East Asian economies took to avert future financial crises. The policy goal in the event of a run on a country's currency must be to access sufficient liquidity, the lack of which constitutes a key constraint and makes a country vulnerable to foreign intervention. Malaysia's strategy took the form of rebalancing its economy so that growth was driven by domestic consumption rather than foreign credit. Singapore, through the vehicle of its GLCs, particularly its sovereign wealth funds (SWFs), used derivatives' hedging and profitable foreign investments to keep reserves high. In the event of speculation or currency runs, these reserves could be used to prop up exchange rates. And more intriguingly, East Asian countries turned to bilateral swaps and attempted to create a regional pool of credit. While the latter strategy did not succeed in its original goal, that is, the creation of a regional lender of last resort, the swap mechanism created a template for future institutions that would mount the first serious challenge to the economic and geopolitical status quo of the last two centuries.

The Return of Trauma: The Liquidity Crisis and Financial Blockade

Keynesian macroeconomic theory asserts that national prosperity rests on control over money supply to set domestic interest rates. Under those terms, capital control is essential (Bryan and Rafferty 2006, 145–147). But Keynesian assumptions only work if institutions exist that can guarantee the value of a national currency. Instead, the Asian financial crisis of 1997–98 forced non-Western countries to acknowledge that the value of their currencies was defined exogenously. Small states are especially vulnerable to economic shocks in market liberalization because of the high costs of service provision, yet neoliberal orthodoxy holds that their solution is to be open to the global market with the attendant retreat of the state from welfare provision. However, even mainstream economic opinion changed with the advent of the mainly US 2008 financial crisis: "[Government] should not be written out of the script; rather, they should use industrial policy to promote investment in new sectors and manage their exchange rates through select capital controls and reserve accumulation" (Commission on Growth and Development 2008, 4–5, 7). Instead, the key factor becomes how governments counteract financial volatility when crisis has become routine and predicting market behavior all but impossible (Clark et al. 2014, 2).

The Asian Financial Crisis of 1997–98 was a watershed moment in international finance for more than just the Asian countries affected. For scholars of globalization, it highlighted a reality long known by the countries themselves, that for small countries, even macroeconomic prudence, such as manifested by Hong Kong and Singapore, might still find them powerless while simultaneously highlighting the importance of investor perception in dictating capital flows (Stiglitz 2001, 1; Krugman 2009, 91–97).

There was an unsurprising acceptance domestically and internationally that, although an economic crisis, investor perceptions rested as much on racial parameters as on economic ones (Sioh 2010a). Addressing investors at the JP Morgan Investors Conference, Singapore's current Prime Minister Lee Hsien Loong's (1998b) response to the crisis was racially freighted:

> The crisis started last year as an Asian problem. This engendered much soul searching and criticism: Was the Asian miracle a mirage? Was the Asian model of economic growth fatally flawed? What about Asian values? Did this crisis prove the correctness, even the supremacy, of the American and European versions of free market economics and democratic transparency?

Recall that for Freud (1965, 118), anxiety has a twofold origin—as a direct consequence of the traumatic moment and as a signal anticipating the danger repeating itself. The financial crisis brought underlying anxieties to the surface. Lee's father, the first Prime Minister of Singapore, Lee Kuan Yew described the prevailing sentiment as "a sense of anguish at the sudden loss of prosperity and status" (McCarthy 1998).

Resurgam I: Malaysia

Malaysia, having weathered the sudden anguish of loss of prosperity due to the Asian financial crisis, set about rebalancing its economy to be less dependent on oil exports and foreign infusions of credit. Much of this section, unless stated otherwise, is taken from an interview with Tan Sri Zeti (Lo 2016), the Governor of Bank Negara Malaysia, who oversaw the Malaysian strategy for ending the financial crisis. In addition to stock buyback and bailouts (Chapter 7), the post-crisis strategy focused on creating a domestic consumption-driven economy through sectoral diversification in manufacturing and services. From 42 percent of Gross Domestic Product (GDP) at the time of the crisis, FDI's share of Malaysia's GDP as of 2022 was estimated to be around 18 percent (Akhbar 2023).[4] Zeti also noted that while a domestic consumption-driven economy meant lower and slower growth of five to six percent a year compared to eight to nine percent pre-crisis, the benefits of a more diversified economic structure outweighed the costs. Needless to say, a major benefit of the pivot to an economy driven by domestic consumption was maintaining economic autonomy. Zeti described the negative global market reaction to Malaysia's much criticized capital control measures as "overreaction" arguing that "the objective of the measures was to restore stability in the financial markets" by preventing speculation on the ringgit, which it did. Moreover, capital controls only lasted a year to provide the government with breathing room to begin the longer term restructuring of the economy through building up manufacturing and services for domestic consumption instead of relying on commodity exports. Malaysia also began implementing a goods and services tax, which generated a revenue stream for the state and rationalized subsidies on goods, which cushioned the cost of living for the population during the crisis.[5] And as business reporter Bernie Lo (2016) noted, despite the "horror of the IMF and other international agencies [] years later, the administration got kudos for actually doing the right thing." The restructuring also saw Malaysian dependence on oil revenue drop from a crisis high of 40 percent of GDP to 12 percent of GDP by 2022 comprising five percent crude oil exports and seven percent refined oil exports.[6]

Resurgam II: Singapore's "Lifeline in a Crisis"

Paradoxically, financial markets, the greatest source of risk for small countries, have also become the most significant source of revenue for some countries with no obvious means of generating foreign exchange (Clark et al. 2014, 2). For governments trying to survive a financial crisis prone world, one coping mechanism is the accumulation of financial assets through their SWFs (see Hassan 2009; Balding 2014; Clark et al. 2014 for historical background on SWFs). Lee Kuan Yew described Singapore's foreign reserves as a "lifeline in a crisis" (quoted in Orchard 2021, 132). In this scenario, the technocrats who are government fund managers are cast as entrepreneurs and the new defenders of the realm. The rise of SWFs as GLCs are referred to in the popular media, although around since the 1950s, coincides with the first decade of the twenty-first century. They are recognized as the last hope of state power assertion over the hegemonic forces of global capitalism in the context of the need for the diversification of assets and reserves (Balding 2014; Clark et al. 2014). Reserves, the proceeds of SWFs' efforts, are used as a buffer against potential capital outflows, thus allowing governments to stabilize exchange rates and, in turn, their domestic economies. A key function of the reserves is the ability to resist the encroachment of multilateral institutions on state sovereignty. Invoking the developmental state, Clark et al. (2014, 92) declare the legitimacy of a state to be dependent upon the extent to which its government (i) meets the basic needs of its citizens and (ii) claims autonomy in relation to other nation-states and multilateral interests. The first reflects the expectations of the relationship between a state and its citizens. But the East Asian countries during the 1997–98 financial crisis showed that the two criteria are related because GLCs including SWFs sustain state legitimacy by underwriting social welfare through maintaining the state's autonomy from externally imposed austerity programs. As early as 1965, Singapore's finance minister Lim Kim San described the issue of controlling reserves as "a matter of national survival" (Orchard 2021, 28). In 2001, Singapore's Prime Minister Lee Kuan Yew attributed the reason for founding its Government Investment Corporation (GIC) was "so we could better control our long-term destiny" (quoted in Orchard 2021, 125).

In the context of floating exchange rates, derivatives allow governments to hedge currency values through SWF investments. Acting as a network of anchors for the currency, derivatives fulfill the role that gold used to play by "allowing one unit of capital to be converted into another unit of capital through a logic of equivalence in value" (Bryan and Rafferty, 2006, 104–106, 131, 141). In terms of currencies, hedging derivatives keep the value within an acceptable band while allowing for easy liquidation and conversion as needed—this is an important insurance policy in an age of financial volatility. Today, those who play the derivatives market successfully command social power because a significant factor in the current financial climate is that derivatives allow states to address anxieties about sovereignty by reducing dependence on Western-controlled institutions of global governance such as the IMF and World Bank. But there is another, unremarked aspect that favors the use of derivatives by emerging economies. For countries with no obvious resource other than their brains, the emphasis on, and pride in, having the dominant resource be their intellectual abilities after 250 years of being derided for their intellectual inferiority is a signal of their arrival on the global stage. Success is not only the evidence of material gain but *how* that gain has been achieved. The following section opens up the discussion to examining the psychocultural mechanisms underpinning sovereignty as a focus for anxiety and the psychic investment in finance as the arena for national success.

Singapore has long conceptualized its place in the world in terms of its vulnerability, and it has sought to alleviate its anxieties through financially defensive tactics. The tropes of vulnerability, defense and safety are threaded throughout its official economic narrative. Lee Kuan Yew, its founding father, even challenged the likelihood of its existence; "[Y]ou've got to start off with the fact that it's not supposed to exist and cannot exist" (Mydans and Arnold 2007). But its economic success, given the unlikeliness of its existence due to a total lack of natural resources, becomes the basis of a valorized national narrative where intellectual acumen generating revenue from investments is on the frontline defending a vulnerable sovereignty. The significance of its exchange rate as a line of defense is such that the government does not disclose the target band it uses to manage the rate with respect to a basket of currencies (https://www.bis.org/mc/currency_areas/sg.htm). But if Singapore's leaders are justifiably proud of their achievements, they nonetheless have acknowledged their powerlessness. Its current prime minister Lee Hsien Loong (2001) noted shortly after the Asian financial crisis that "[we] could not afford to assume that speculators ... would automatically be punished." Its response has been to create an army of financial defenders of the realm.

Between 2011 and 2013, I conducted 14 interviews with candidates who at some point in their careers had worked for or advised GLCs in **both** Malaysia and Singapore. In selecting the candidates for the interview, the only criterion (other than their willingness to speak to me) was that they had to have had a major role in a GLC or its subsidiary's decisions. I define a major role as having a direct say or having an advisory role in projects worth from tens of millions to billions of dollars. Each interview lasted from a minimum of two hours to seven and a half hours. Although my interviewees, as in public pronouncements, generally valorized capitalist modernity and accepted claims that meritocracy would win the day in global capitalism, the concept of race, used interchangeably with culture, permeated the interviews. Race was sometimes the focal point but usually inserted in casual asides when discussing very considerable sums of money. The interviewees' narrative structure can be understood as the desire for and internalization of the ego ideal of the Western capitalist. Referring to the hiring process, one interviewee noted that "white males predominated in the most senior management positions." And should an Asian be hired, there was an over-reliance on certain kinds of "formal qualifications – Oxbridge or Harvard or a bias towards mathematics/science degrees rather than actual field-specific experience." The most striking example offered was the case of a Chinese bank's initial public offering (IPO). As a gesture of mutual respect, the GLC was offered shares in the IPO, which it purchased. But as the Western financial press and investors began to voice concerns about the Chinese bank, the GLC's senior management began to doubt its investment culminating in the sale of the shares. This decision not only had the material repercussion of driving down the share value but, more significantly, in East Asian societies the gesture was also interpreted as disrespectful and questioning the viability of the Chinese IPO causing the Chinese government to "lose face." The behind-the-scenes diplomatic tension was eventually resolved when the GLC reinvested in the bank's shares but tensions continued to simmer and the situation was criticized by my interviewees as an example of an unnecessary difficulty caused by an unwarranted faith in Western judgment. While decision-makers could interpret the original decision as a defensive measure to protect the country's investments, the divestment action was also interpreted as a simultaneous lack of confidence and passive acceptance of the ego ideal of Western judgment. More than one interviewee also brought up the conundrum, in Singapore's case, of its desire to expand into the 700 million strong market that is Indonesia with only one cabinet minister capable of speaking the language. The point is not the shortage of interpreters but, potentially, a signal of disrespect displayed by the lack of interest in a major trade partner. Indonesia, after all, was brought up in my interviews as the future "hinterland" providing the resources and market that would be coupled with Singaporean capital and know-how.

The different conditions of social disempowerment that link anxiety to defensive responses can be conceptualized through the psychoanalytic term of castration because if race is a precondition of social disempowerment/humiliation, then the raced subject is a castrated object, while white subjects remain discursively unracialized. The anxious subtext to the category of race/culture came up in a group interview that at first seemed unrelated to the topic of investments. When I arrived at the designated location for the interview, two of my interviewees were already present. Including me in their conversation, one of them remarked that the country was "a cultural desert. No one speaks any language with any degree of nuance." Intrigued,

I pursued the line of the conversation asking why it mattered so much to them. The response was that material survival was predicated on cultural interrogation and renewal. One interviewee recounted the experience of accompanying a prominent politician on a foreign visit and being embarrassed when the politician could not recognize the literary allusions in their host's official welcome. Material success, often seen by Western commentators as the only criterion for respect in newly rich Asian nation-states, is not shared among its elites in my experience of fieldwork; interviewees often expected a recognition of local culture, idiom and convention. In refusing to separate culture from race, they were simply insisting on the truth of Slavoj Žižek's (1997, 168) statement that "any account of cultural identity that does any cultural work requires a racial component."

Performing Global Masculinity

Psychoanalytic race scholars note that marginal populations bear the brunt of the shocks of modernity insofar as privations and humiliations traumatize those at the lower end of any social hierarchy (Eng 2001, 178–179). But even as they become wealthier, the emerging economies may still be relatively powerless in the international hierarchy. Thus, if nationalism by default is coded male, relatively powerless, non-white nation-states are interpellated as castrated within the fantasy of globalization. The ability to act as guarantor of economic growth then goes some way to recovering the traditional masculine roles of provider and defender of realm.

To return to Singapore, establishing the Asian Currency Units (ACUs) that were key to paving the way for the creation of the Asian Dollar Market, pioneering a financial futures exchange in Asia and establishing itself as a major foreign exchange (FOREX) center, particularly in the renminbi (RMB) derivatives trade, constructs its global identity. In Judith Butler's (1997, 34) schema social reality tenuously constructs identity through language and a stylized repetition of acts. Her conception of interpellation refers simultaneously to existing networks of signification while reinforcing the process through each successful act of recognition (Butler 1990, 310). But she also reminds us that the success of the interpellative process rests on certain conventions invoked at the moment of utterance such as whether the person has the authority or the staging is right (Butler 1997, 3). I argue that in striving for positive recognition emerging economies attempted to insert their identity into the existing symbolic orders of capitalism and technology through their mastery of both. In my study, while the key defensive strategy rested on maintaining exchange rates, of equal significance to the defensive strategy was the sophistication of the techniques used to maintain the exchange rates and the setting of Singapore as a financial center that gave credibility to the naming and performance of this new identity of a successful global capitalist. In Singapore, this status is anchored by its GLCs, especially the SWFs. That they succeeded in this arena is without doubt to which every commentary attests by unfailingly praising the spectacular economic success of the country despite Western criticism of its government as authoritarian. Such is its economic example that during an interview with an economic advisor in a neighboring country, my interviewee bemoaned the lack of success in his government's attempt at creating an SWF and attributed it to a lack of intellectual capability. The ownership and success of an SWF has become such a signal of national economic prowess that the economist Christopher Balding (2014, 18–19) describes the phenomenon of vanity SWFs established simply to convey status.

However, a successful identity transformation has two requirements: the country needs to find a common language if it wants to change how it is seen by the desired other, the rich and powerful West; and the change has to seem essentialized and predetermined. One interviewee said; "The coming century is Asian because we are geared towards mathematical thinking. Technology will close the gap." The point about the scale of transformation through the financial sector is important for transforming assumptions because it is a mundane and ritualized form that legitimizes subjectivity through the thousands of keystrokes involving the sale of securities on a quotidian basis. Each keystroke "sediments" the new identity, as Butler (1997, 34) would claim. And for all the Western criticism that the East Asian elite's nationalism is opportunistic, the men I interviewed were as proud of the state's achievements in which they had no part. For they were clear that certain actions by the state reflected on their own identities and, equally, that their success came from their national identity, which in the contemporary world had risen in estimation. In another example, a GLC's purchase of shares of a beleaguered state-owned enterprise, much derided by the Western financial press, was described as a justifiable "message to foreigners" by an interviewee. Two other interviewees made the same argument even if they agreed with the foreign financial press that the deal made little sense from a business perspective. Another interviewee had recently overseen the multibillion dollar sale of technology to a BRICS country and admitted that the deal was sealed because his country was seen as more trustworthy than its Western competitor that was likely to short-change non-white countries. In this sense, my interviewees were tacitly acknowledging a power asymmetry that made the above actions perfectly justifiable as defensive gestures.

Resurgam III: The Libidinal Ecosystem of Currency Swaps

Perhaps the most ambitious defensive measure is one that integrates a new economic and geopolitical narrative for Asian societies that came out of the financial crisis. East Asian countries understood that the crisis was caused by temporal mismatch between liabilities and foreign exchange reserves exacerbated by the absence of a lender of last resort; therefore, there was an urgent need to address both problems. The Chiang Mai Initiative Multilateralization (CMIM) was signed between ASEAN nations, Japan, South Korea and

China, known as ASEAN+3 in 2000, itself building on the original agreement between five ASEAN countries as a cooperative response to the Asian financial crisis (Sussangkorn 2010). The CMIM comprised two components: a multilateral withdrawal agreement based on double its contribution and linked to an IMF designed conditionality program (and therefore not much better than the IMF arrangement) and a more useful network of bilateral swap and repurchase agreements, generally on a three-month basis subject to renewal. Initially, the CMIM attracted little international attention because of the small sum involved—US $1 billion dollars in 2000 increasing to US $2 billion by 2005 (Sussangkorn 2010, 5), but later bilateral mechanisms drawing upon Japan's and Singapore's larger reserves gave access to US $64 billion (Nakao 2010, 13). By 2014, the CMIM had increased capitalization to $240 billion and extended the bilateral swaps to swaps with the common pool, the CMIM Precautionary Line (CMIM-PL) which raised the amount that could be swapped without IMF conditionality (Pitakdumrongkit 2015). But its real significance lay in the creation of a template for a regional mechanism that could potentially bypass the authority of the IMF and the World Bank.

Emerging markets' central banks have used swaps before CMIM (see Asian Development Bank 2017 for a review of how swaps work). Swaps on the commercial market can be used to protect from hot money flows or depreciating currencies instead of resorting to interest rate hikes or sales of foreign reserves. While swaps can make reserves go further, the dangers of commercial swaps lie in a mismatch between the movement of the exchange rate and the due date in the forward market, in which case central banks will be forced to sell their foreign exchange. The swaps under the bilateral and multilateral geopolitical arrangements provide foreign exchange, usually dollars, in the short term. The libidinal significance lies in the defensive benefit of a political incentive to protect allies unlike the situation with commercial swaps. However, in raising the issue of the independence of the executive decision-making body of the CMIM, Pitakdumrongkit (2015) questions whether East Asians can avoid "the old game of sovereign politics" falling back on the trope of Asians as unable to cooperate without commenting on the traumatic historical context, as Herman (2015, 80) may have done to elaborate on why trust upon which cooperation rests would have been difficult to achieve.

The true significance of the CMIM, in terms of its financial clout and geopolitical ramifications, has been the creation of two new sources of liquidity, one of which is also designed to be an alternative lender of last resort. These are the Beijing-based Asian Infrastructure and Investment Bank (AIIB) launched in January 2016, and the Shanghai-based New Development Bank (NDB), formerly the BRICS Bank, launched in 2014, with the latter particularly stepping in as a lender of last resort. The European Political Strategy Center (2015), the in-house EU thinktank, described the AIIB as a "potential game changer" and asked if it was a "prelude to a new world order?" The source of two new lenders of last resort is of geopolitical magnitude because at that time (1997–98), the main source of financial liquidity outside the West was Japan which caved in to American pressure to withhold economic aid to distressed East Asian countries (Golub 2016, 100). Singaporean banks too shorted regional currencies adding to the hardship while both Malaysian and Singaporean GLCs purchased regional businesses at fire sale prices (anonymous, personal communication during an interview). Herman notes that the final step in total psychic conquest is forcing victims to violate their own moral principles by betraying each other (Herman 1992, 83). This is the most important step because it creates suspicion and prevents solidarity. Recall her point (80) that disempowerment relies on the ability to disconnect the victim from others, especially potential allies. In the absence of any outside connection, the victim will come *to see the world through the eyes of the perpetrator*, in this case Western financial institutions which controlled access to credit. Powerful perpetrators get to create social norms at the very least, if not define reality. Victims come to introject the victimizer's values and, in the process, shame themselves or project onto weaker others, such as immigrants, minorities, LGBTQ people, the working class or weaker neighboring countries, the blame for their misfortune oftentimes absolving the actual perpetrators of blame. Thus, the selfobjects of the global economic order will seek to construct their own selfobjects upon which to project their rage or provide an approving mirror. And financial institutions have the capacity to inflict trauma repeatedly. Prolonged contact in such asymmetrical power situations means the victim's worldview is shaped by perpetrator. In my interviews what stood out were two comments from the interviewees when the conversation turned, at their instigation, to what they perceived as dangers to future economic development, which in their perception included geopolitical considerations as opposed to mere growth. In response, they cited US control of the internet and the concern that China and Japan could not overcome historical hostilities to provide the building block of Asian cooperation. For resistance hinges on creating alternative narratives and a future which preserves connection with another reality (Herman 2015, 80–81). The CMIM and eventually, far more powerfully, the NDB, the AIIB and the People's Bank of China (PBOC) created that alternative reality by providing liquidity.

Conclusion

In this chapter I argued that East Asian countries' post-Asian financial crisis policies can best be understood as strategies to address the anxieties of survival and dignity in globalization. Using a psychoanalytical framework grafted to a political and economic analysis of the role of exchange rates, I analyzed a combination of publicly available documents and interviews with decision-makers, to show that securitizing the state today is defined financially. In that context, foreign exchange reserves and currency exchange rates have become the new sovereign borders. This concern has dominated political discourse in Malaysia and other East Asian countries. The ability to defend the exchange rate and, through it, to prevent external encroachment on a country's sovereignty, reverses the trope of a disempowered postcolonial identity whereby emerging economies, many of them postcolonial nation-states, have been interpellated as castrated objects in the international hierarchy. This trope has been amplified by the constraints on their national capacities when emerging economies are forced to turn to external agents such as the IMF for help in the case of financial crises.

The policy response has turned on breaking dependence on Western-led financial institutions in various ways. Malaysia focused on reorienting from an export-led FDI-driven economy to a domestically driven one. Singapore boosted its outward-bound investment through its GLCs. Regionally, building on ASEAN, the Southeast countries, later joined by Japan, South Korea and China, created a liquidity pool accessible by member countries in the case of a financial crisis. But it bears remembering that the above policy moves were driven not only by anxieties of liquidity constraints in the case of a crisis but, crucially, the countries' lack of policy autonomy from Western-led financial governance. Finally, successful alternative economic ecosystems also require tandem alternative imaginaries. This is not to say that either Malaysia or the other East Asian countries have chosen to repudiate capitalism. Far from that choice, they have instead adopted capitalism and financial technology as a way of interpellating their identities into hegemonic narratives. These identities are characterized by participation in high stakes financial transactions made possible by new technologies which if successful, will give the processes of lactification and remasculinization a logical equivalence with that success.

Emerging market liquidity in times of crisis today will hinge on the willingness of the PBOC, AIIB or the NDB to provide liquidity in terms of central bank swaps. This arrangement is different from the US model, whereby US banks provided liquidity through loans or floating bonds of emerging market sovereign governments. Between June 2010 and 2014, the PBOC signed over US$426 billion worth of bilateral currency swaps with 21 central banks worldwide, and its PBOC's bilateral RMB swap line was already larger than the Fed's swap lines with the Select Five of US$333 billion (Sheng 2016). The European Commission's think tank, the EPSC (2015), noted that China-led financial institutions, including the AIIB, the New Development Bank (BRICS Bank) through the Contingent Reserve Arrangement, have a combined capital base of $250 billion on par with the World Bank, and together with the swap arrangements, accounted for financing availability close to $589 billion. The AIIB, which began with 57 founding members, had, as of June 2023, 106 members (https://www.aiib.org/en/about-aiib/governance/members-of-bank/index.html). The expansion of RMB use through swap agreements and AIIB loans has paved the way for its gradual internationalization, although it is still a minor player as a reserve currency. For emerging economies hopeful for a new lender of last resort, it must be hoped that trade facilitation will function as a natural extension of the path for RMB to go global, in the same way that Japan paved the way for Yen internationalization through lending and providing aid in the 1990s, only with more autonomy from the US this time.

Notes

1 Mahathir appeared to accuse China of similar tactics in the case of debt incurred through the Belt and Road Initiative, although he claimed the criticism was misunderstood (Jaipragas 2018).

2 China, of course, has produced its homegrown models of economic development, most notably Mao Zedong's Marxist model and Deng Xiaoping's pragmatic mixed economy—the starting point of China's successful growth trajectory (Schell and Delury 2013, 197–323).

3 Although Japan is not a Western country, in caving in to US pressure to refuse extending credit to beleaguered East Asian countries, it effectively "behaved" as a Western institution (Golub 2016, 99–102).

4 This figure was almost half in 2021, reflecting the growth surge as pandemic restrictions were lifted.

5 These subsidies have largely returned as Malaysia attempts to mitigate the effects of inflation in 2023.

6 The statistic for crude oil was calculated from https://www.ceicdata.com/en/indicator/malaysia/crude-oil-exports, while the refined oil statistic came from https://oec.world/en/profile/country/mys. Statista estimates export value for crude oil to be closer to four percent https://www.statista.com/statistics/794687/export-value-of-crude-oil-malaysia/

Conclusion

I began this book by asking what we know about economic growth. This is the premier question in economic development as the concern is how to go about accumulating wealth to uplift a population from poverty, a condition in which decolonizing countries found themselves at independence. The objective then is to identify policies that result in economic gains. But many of those policies, when actually implemented, have been derided from the perspective of rational economics whether of the neoclassical orthodoxy or political economy schools because the decisions resulted in economic losses. For most part, these poor decisions are attributed to ignorance or cupidity. This book set out to turn the perspective to that of the affected countries themselves to ask what they had as the goals of their decision-making. This is not by any means an attempt to absolve developing countries/emerging economies of culpability in their own choices but to understand their calculus of costs and benefits in making those choices. The terms of this calculus, I have argued, are libidinal rather than rational. Or put another way, if the rationality is libidinal rather than monetary, then monetary losses may translate into libidinal gains. Malaysia is interesting example because it was the focus of extreme derision due to its economic policy choices during the Asian financial crisis of 1997–98. This is not to say that the state's decisions never reflect ignorance or individual greed; witness the trial and jailing of former prime minister Najib for corruption in the 1MDB (1Malaysia Development Berhad) scandal (Wright and Hope 2018). Notwithstanding the caveats of individual politicians making poor national decisions for personal gain, I am interested in how key economic decisions in the last 70 years traced back to preceding events of collective trauma. I have argued that economic decisions reflected the unconscious anxieties about survival and dignity experienced as a cycle of repeat trauma originating in the first trauma of loss in colonialism. Malaysia's economic choices are haunted by the trauma of colonialism which constructed race as an embodied wound, and this cycle of trauma continues in contemporary economic relationships. Each new experience of collective trauma triggers anxiety in the state as collective ego because it recalls the previous experience.

When I began writing this book, my idea for the organization of the chapters had a very different form. It was only after completing almost 70 percent

DOI: 10.4324/9781315440286-10

of the manuscript that I realized the chapters had organized themselves into a sequence that mimicked the book's argument that Malaysia's experience of colonialism, development and globalization are different iterations of trauma, what clinical psychology would describe as repeat or complex trauma (Chapter 1). Referring back to the Shostakovich fugue described in Chapter 1, each chapter responds to "undergound" themes in preceding ones where those themes operate below and haunt the official themes only exposing themselves in shocking expressions of violence or verbal aggression. The basic logic of stimuli (trauma) and response (anxiety and attendant defensive mechanism) is derived from Freudian psychoanalysis onto which I grafted Teresa Brennan's (1993) foundational fantasy and Heinz Kohut's (1973) self-selfobject model to explain why and how trauma wends its way through collective decision-making in Malaysia's history. The two theoretical frameworks overlap to a certain extent. First, the foundational fantasy sets up the opposing but relative roles of superior active subject versus the inferior passified object as a condition of the former's identity. Next, the dynamics of the foundational fantasy are elaborated using Heinz Kohut's self-selfobject relationship in which the latter provides an approving mirror, willing or not, as a precondition of the former's psychic well-being. But Kohut was at pains to point out that a healthy self should evolve beyond the constant need of an approving selfobject (Chapter 1). Instead, if we accept Brennan's contention that we live in an age of psychosis, then the logical conclusion is that the grandiose colonial/imperial self never did evolve beyond the need for a constant approving mirror. Confronted by the resisting/recalcitrant selfobject, the enraged grandiose self will attempt to reinscribe the foundational fantasy and, in the process, inflict trauma (Chapters 4 and 7) as a response to each moment of resistance. In turn, the traumatized selfobject will seek to escape the bounds of the foundational fantasy that is the animating condition of its trauma and, in doing so, will seek its own selfobject upon which to project its aggression. In the case of the postcolonial Malaysian nation-state, each experience of trauma calls forth the state's defensive responses which was to construct its own selfobjects in the form of the inhabitants of the New Villagers upon which to project its rage (Chapter 4) and the Federal Land Development Authority (FELDA) schemes to provide an approving mirror (Chapter 6).

British encroachment and eventual colonization of Malaya in the nineteenth century resulted in material losses for the local population as land alienation and formal changes in land tenure induced scarcity of arable land. In doing so, the British set up the colonial foundational fantasy upon which a stable, self-satisfied colonial identity was based (Chapter 2). Cultivated land was now dedicated to surplus production in monocultural plantations rather than to fulfilling basic needs. The scale of cultivation expanded and accelerated with the introduction of rubber plantations as the demand for rubber in the modern economy grew. The needs of the plantation economy also transformed Malaya's demography through immigration. This was not just due to the need for more workers but because capitalist demands required a certain kind of worker socialized for plantation work from lack of options due to their impoverished circumstances. Participation in a monetized economy was essential for plantation labor who had to purchase food but even the Malay peasantry who refused to work in plantations found that participation was no longer discretionary as they needed to pay taxes. Concurrently, high capital investment for new plantations shut out non-Europeans because of the difficulty in accessing financing. Lastly, the input of colonial science was crucial in advancing the expansion of European-owned plantations by reducing risk and wastage in cultivation, thereby improving profit margins. By the 1930s, Malaya had transformed from a plantation economy into a plantation society with a complex set of rules both manifest and latent that structured the psychic function of the colonized selfobject as a support for the colonial self through "approving mirroring responses" (Kohut 1973, 629). The reconfiguration of space and the demographic changes necessitated by the plantation economy can also be understood as a psychic loss for the local population in terms of the rupture from and loss of traditional ways of life. But this experience pertained to immigrant laborers as well who had to contend with an unfamiliar environment and harsh working conditions. Yet because the losses from colonization happened over time and violence was sporadic and limited, it was normalized and not conceived as trauma at the moment of occurrence. If we accept Freud's (1959b) analysis of trauma that only becomes recognizable as such through retrospection, Malaya's non-European population recognized and responded to colonization as traumatic only through the Emergency (Chapters 3 and 4). But first, the advent of World War Two and the Japanese defeat of the British would begin the process of shattering the illusion of the invulnerable colonialist.

Malaya fell to the Japanese in 1942. The Japanese Occupation of Malaya lasted only three years, but it was critical in terms of framing future political contests through its effect on the prewar organization of Malayan society. It demolished the idea of Europeans' invincibility and entitlement. In doing so, the war triggered the recalcitrance of many non-Europeans. This, after all, was the generation suspicious of European claims to entitlement having witnessed the British defeat by the Japanese. The new generation of anti-colonialists ranged from the mainstream members who sought to replicate capitalist structures only with a different racial ownership to radicals who embraced communism. The Japanese policy of centralizing administration of the country and training Malays and Indians in administration also formed the basis of a psychological challenge to colonial rule. Most troubling for the returning colonial rulers, their erstwhile allies, the Malayan Communist Party (MCP) now trained in guerilla warfare, shifted their resistance toward them. Postwar racial score settling, widespread labor strikes and material shortages under the newly reoccupying British Military Administration (BMA) were early indicators that a reassessment of the colonial right to rule was underway. In 1948, colonial authorities declared a state of emergency. Confronted with the recalcitrance of their previously relatively quiescent colonized population, they responded with narcissistic rage. The brutal conduct of the Emergency saw vast areas of Malaya declared under curfew, civil rights suspended, mass incarceration of 20 percent of the population in barbed wire enclosed camps referred to as New Villages, shelling and aerial bombardment and finally, public executions and exhibitions of corpses (Chapters 3 and 4). In Freudian terms (1959b, 65) the Emergency was the second traumatic experience through which the first, the colonial encounter, was assimilated and understood as trauma. The experience of colonization now took on its real significance as trauma—the return of the "outlaw" repressed (Freud 1959b, 86). Its traumatic legacy continues to haunt Malaysia's domestic political and economic interactions.

Britain granted Malaya independence on 31 August 1957 reversing their previous policy of delaying independence until the defeat of the MCP. But the fear that the Malayan elite and the MCP would form an alliance against the British finally galvanized them into a settlement. The MCP later claimed that the colonial authorities tried to negotiate with them as way of cutting out the Malayan elite but the negotiations fell apart (Chapter 5). Malaysia was created in 1963 from the Federation of Malaya, the states of Sabah and Sarawak of the former British North Borneo and Singapore. The political union broke down in 1965 and Singapore was expelled to form an independent country. The lead-up to independence and the post-Emergency years were significant for the role of anxiety in policy formulations whether by colonial authorities or the Malayan elite before and after the independence (Chapters 5 and 6). Britain ended World War Two indebted to the US. For Britain, this was an anxious time as the superpower torch passed on to their main creditors, the US. Henceforth, Britain's status vis-à-vis the US would depend greatly on its financial reserves. Within a libidinal economy framework, Britain would now be one of the selfobjects to the new imperial power, the US. For the Malayan elite, inheritance of the country came as a consequence of an independence war fought by the MCP, and maintaining Malayan export income in sterling was the price of the political handover. This was the price that the Malayan elite chose to pay to appease their anxieties of inheriting a country without winning it militarily. These anxieties would lead the new nation-state to construct its own foundational fantasy in the search for its own selfobjects to shore up its anxious identity. The search in part was fulfilled by the New Villages but that was only half of the equation of cultural ownership. The other half would come courtesy of the FELDA schemes.

The anxious newly decolonized Malaysian nation-state had to confront two issues urgently. Maintaining a high sterling balance and low expenditure on development was the price the Malayan elite paid for independence under a British military shelter. The lack of investment and the slow pace of development would ultimately lead to an eruption of discontent on the part of the Malays on 13 May 1969. Hence, for the Malaysian government, finding a path to economic growth that would allow capital accumulation and welfare redistribution among its Malay constituency became a priority and led to the New Economic Policy (NEP) and the Second Malaysia Plan (SMP). The second more subtle dilemma concerned the issue of stamping psychic legitimacy regarding the state's cultural ownership of the territory. The New Villages (Chapter 4) were part of the new nation-state's foundational fantasy of constructing its own immobilized selfobjects in a punitive landscape against which the identity of the citizens of the new nation would be defined. But more urgently, the moral theater of nationalism demanded a valorized subject operating in an affirmative theater. Accordingly, in 1970 the Malaysian government introduced the NEP followed by the SMP, its blueprint for operations in 1971 to address dilemmas of poverty alleviation and psychic legitimacy. The NEP and SMP resulted in a huge investment in, and an expansion of, the existing FELDA schemes which would create a population of settlers from landless Malay peasants (Chapter 6). Similarly organized after the corporate plantation sector, although with the crucial difference of state and cooperative ownership (settlers owned their own plots of land), FELDA required massive deforestation to provide land for the scheme. These, over time, would come to represent the "new nature" of the country providing a stage for its settler citizens. The FELDA scheme achieved three key objectives. First, it created a revenue stream for the state. Second it provided income for the settlers, thus appeasing a major political constituency. Third, the quotidian performances of thousands of settlers on the stage of the new nature for the nation-state created a positive moral scopic politics that naturalized the state's cultural ownership of territory. Moreover, the decision to use the terms "pioneer" and "settler" unconsciously drew connections to US founding mythology, a case of interpellation within a valorized narrative that was widely commensurable in meaning to most onlookers. Finally, through the creation of government-linked companies, the second prong of the NEP was realized through the creation of a Malay entrepreneurial class (Malaysia 1971, 31).[1] These companies acted as holding companies and trust agencies when the government embarked on its ambitious program to nationalize parts of the private sector. Together, land development and corporate takeovers carved out that part of the economic space that was most symbolic of returning sovereignty to the Malays, the retaking of the plantation sector.

Development in Malaysia through the 1970s was still largely a domestic affair despite some join ventures with Japanese companies. And it continued to depend on traditional commodity exports. Beginning in the 1980s, with the election of Dr. Mahathir Mohamad coinciding with the relocation of Western manufacturing to developing countries, Malaysia's economy took off. There are many narrative threads to the story of globalization but few commentators would gainsay that one of the most powerful imaginative themes has been the economic rise of East Asian countries (Chapters 7 and 8). This narrative trope is so powerful that, as I point out in in the Introduction, countries hitherto categorized as Southeast Asia became figuratively relocated into East Asia as their economies grew. *The Financial Post* described the Malaysian model of privatization as one of the most successful in the world (Wheeler 1995, 29). East Asian countries were the poster children for globalization whose success the World Bank (1993) attributed to their embrace of free-market export-oriented production. East Asian success made them the perfect approving mirror to Western countries since it was assumed that their success was a tribute to adopting Western economic models, which incidentally are also cultural. But East Asian governments equally attributed their success to state intervention, in the form of the culturally based activist state known as the developmental state. And Malaysia's prime minister was one of the most vocal in promoting the cultural dimension for the country's success. This trope transformed the approving mirror of capitalist protégés to competitors who trampled on the self-image of the grandiose West. The West, hitherto accustomed to perceiving East Asia as its approving mirror, were instead confronted with potential rivals who appeared to deny their cultural debt to their former colonial rulers.

The Asian financial crisis in 1997–98 unraveled the narrative of ascendant East Asia. Western anxiety found a perfect opportunity in the Asian financial crisis to reinscribe East Asia in the passified position of the colonial/imperial foundational fantasy. The crisis also provided the opportunity for the West to vent its narcissistic rage at East Asian hubris. Criticism of economic policy rapidly transformed into a vitriolic and racialized referendum on culture in the form of Asian values. I am not defending culturally essentialized value systems but rather I focused on the psychological significance and geopolitical implications of the above discourse. Malaysia became a flashpoint for the criticism because contravening all orthodox economic advice, it instituted currency controls. For international financial institutions, this policy was probably an extreme incidence of recalcitrance. In hindsight, the humiliation of the affected countries in the crisis is easy to understand if we recall that Freud (1959a, 18,27) noted that prestige is lost in the event of failure or by a competitor's success. The proposition of Asian values as a cultural basis for their economic success came to be experienced as a narcissistic injury by the West and the crisis presented an opportunity to reassert the self-selfobject dynamic of the traditional global order.

The Asian financial crisis was a moment of trauma in the region's recent history. In the anxious aftermath, regional self-searching diagnosed the problem less as to whether a global financial crisis could be avoided in the future as to what could be done to survive future crises. The policy goal pinpointed access to liquidity in the event of a run on a country's currency to avoid vulnerability to foreign interference. But the underlying issue was less the availability of credit than that access was controlled by Western-led financial institutions (Chapters 7 and 8). The overall strategy pivoted on reducing the need for a Western-controlled lender of last resort. Malaysia's strategy took the form of rebalancing its economy so that growth was driven by domestic consumption rather than foreign credit to lessen exposure to speculation. Singapore, through the vehicle of its government-linked corporations (GLCs), particularly its sovereign wealth funds (SWFs), used derivatives' hedging and profitable foreign investments to keep reserves high which could be used to prop up exchange rates. More intriguingly, East Asian countries turned to bilateral swaps and attempted to create a regional pool of credit. While the latter originally was unsuccessful in their original goal, that is, the creation of a regional lender of last resort, the swap mechanism created a template for future institutions that would mount the first serious challenge to the economic and geopolitical status quo of the last two centuries. These policies, while driven by anxiety and manifesting the introjection of capitalist values, are a very different defensive approach to that in Chapter 5. Malaysia, now as with its regional cohort, openly acknowledges anxiety as the driver for its policies but seeks to respond in manner that interpellates itself in global capitalism in a less openly challenging manner to the current global order. This is by no means a satisfactory solution but Malaysia's survival in a global order, where the rules are devised elsewhere, requires compromise, adaptation and, most of all, self-awareness of its possibilities and limitations.

As I write this conclusion, Malaysia is facing state elections on 12 August 2023. Its remarkably resilient prime minister, Anwar Ibrahim, has fought to unite the country under a multiracial consensus regarding its economic future. His longtime nemesis, the equally remarkable Dr. Mahathir Mohamad, the architect of Malaysia's modern economy, who at 97 years of age is still politically active, is warning against the dismantling of Malaysia's sectarian-based economic policies, which he argues is the only workable model for the survival of the Malays. Meanwhile, the Malay youth vote appears to be flocking to Malaysian Islamic Party or *Parti Islam Se-Malaysia* (PAS), the Islamist party. These divisions are a legacy of Malaysia's past trauma which continue to haunt its policymaking. As with trauma victims, the Malaysian nation-state itself is a fragmented subject and cannot construct a unified response. The different constituencies, e.g., youth vote, racial groups, labor, etc. represent its fractured subjectivities. These may overlap in their aims, but they also contradict each other as each acts on their partial knowledge while searching for their own selfobjects to shore up unstable identities. Thus, if Malaysian state actors acknowledge introjection of a racialized capitalist value system to interpellate the country within the global capitalist order to break the cycle of racial trauma, these defenses are undermined by Malaysia's fractured subjectivities that make an illusion of its actors' objectives of a coherent response to racialized capitalism. These then are the illusions that determine Malaysia's economic decisions such as whether to preserve its sectarian-based economic policies or not. But as Nikolas Rose (1996, 3) has claimed, illusions are the truth by which we live. Prime Minister Anwar Ibrahim, perhaps because of his own traumatic path to power, appears to understand that to move forward, Malaysians must accept and reconcile as best they can with the country's history and its fractured and contradictory subjectivities. This book has been my attempt to unearth the "truth" of the last 70 years of Malaysia's underground history in the hope that greater exposure can contribute to creating a different future.

Note

1 Today most of FELDA's investment in Malaysia is in the corporate sector rather than land development although it owns plantations in Indonesia.

Bibliography

Abraham, S. 1952. Minute [Re: Trial of Lee Meng], 11 October, CO 1022/3.

Acemoglu, D., and J. R. Robinson. 2012. *Why Nations Fail: The Origins of Power, Prosperity, and Poverty*. New York: Crown Publishing.

Adamson, J., and H. Clark. 1999. "Introduction: Shame, Affect, Writing." In *Scenes of Shame: Psychoanalysis, Shame and Writing*, edited by J. Adamson and H. Clark, 1–34. Albany: SUNY Press.

Agricultural Bulletin of the Straits Settlement and Federated Malay States. 1910. "The Abolition of the Botanic Gardens of Penang, March," 100–5.

Aiken, S. R. 1994. *Imperial Belvederes: The Hill Stations of Malaya*. Kuala Lumpur: Oxford University Press.

Akhbar, S. 2023. "Prestasi Ekonomi Suku Keempat Tahun 2022." Bank Negara Press Conference Slides, 10 February.

Amsden, A. 1989. *Asia's Next Giant: South Korea and Late Industrialization*. Oxford: Oxford University Press.

Anderson, B. 1991. *Imagined Communities: Reflections on the Origin and Spread of Nationalism*. New York: Verso.

Ang, Y. Y. 2016. *How China Escaped the Poverty Trap*. Ithaca: Cornell University Press.

Arnold, D. 1998. "India's Place in the Tropical World, 1770–1930." *Journal of Imperial and Commonwealth History* 26: 1–21.

Arasaratnam, S. 1970. *Indians in Malaysia and Singapore*. Bombay: Institute of Race Relations; London: Oxford University Press.

Asian Development Bank. 2017. *The Asian Bond Markets Initiative: Policy Maker Achievements and Challenges*. Manila: ADB.

Atlee, C. 1944. "Constitutional Policy in Malaya." War Cabinet Memorandum, 22 December, CAB 66/60, WP(44)76.

Balding, C. 2014. *Sovereign Wealth Funds: The New Intersection of Money and Politics*. Oxford: OUP.

Balachandran, G. 1996. *John Bullion's Empire: Britain's Gold Problem and India Between the Wars*. Richmond, Surrey: Curzon.

Bank Negara Malaysia. 2001. *The Malaysian Economy in 2001*. Kuala Lumpur: Bank Negara Malaysia. https://www.bnm.gov.my/documents/20124/830764/ch01.pdf

Barber, N. 1971. *The War of the Running Dogs: How Malaya Defeated the Communist Guerrillas, 1948–60*. London: Collins.

Barr, M. 2002. *Cultural Politics and Asian Values: The Tepid War*. London: Routledge.

Barton, C. J. J. T. 1953. "Situation on the Thai-Malayan Frontier." Minute. June or July (?), CO1022/205.

Bayly, C., and T. Harper. 2007. *Forgotten Wars: The End of Britain's Asian Empire.* Cambridge: Belknap Press of Harvard University Press.

Beeson, M. 2004. "The Rise And Fall (?) of The Developmental State: The Vicissitudes and Implications of East Asian Interventionism." In *Developmental States: Relevancy, Redundancy or Reconfiguration?*, edited by L. Low, 29–40. New York: Nova Science Publishers.

———. 2009. "Developmental States in East Asia: A Comparison of the Japanese and Chinese Experiences." *Asian Perspective* 33 (2): 5–39.

Bhabha, H. 1994. *The Location of Culture.* London: Routledge.

Bhargava, M. L. 1982. *Netaji Subhas Chandra Bose in South-East Asia and India's Liberation War, 1943–45.* Malayattor, Kerala: Vishwavidya Publishers.

Bell, D. 2000. *East Meets West: Human Rights and Democracy in East Asia.* Princeton: Princeton University Press.

Berthier, S. 2000. Interview with Dr. Mahathir: The True Significance of the Financial Crisis of 1998. *Asian Affairs on Global Issues*, Spring. http://www.asian-affairs.com/Frameleft/crisis.html

Bird, I. 1967. *The Golden Chersonese and the Way Thither.* Kuala Lumpur: Oxford University Press.

Bishop, D. 1951. "Re: Use of Chemicals to Clear Vegetation." Minute, 16 November, CO1022/26.

Blades, A. E. G. 1952. "Translation of *Freedom News* no. 29 (15 September 1952)." Memorandum from the Director of Special Branch to Commissioner, Police Headquarters, Singapore, internal file ref. SSB 4019/19-17, 20 November, CO 1022/46.

———. 1953a. "Translation of *Freedom News*, issue nos. 30 and 31 (15 October 1952 and 15 November 1952)." Memorandum from Director, Special Branch Singapore to Commissioner, Police Headquarters, Singapore, internal file ref. SSB 4019/19-17. 17 January, CO 1022/46.

———.1953b. "Translation of *Freedom News*, no. 34 (15 February 1953)." Memorandum from Director, Special Branch Singapore to Commissioner, Police Headquarters, Singapore, internal file ref. SSB 4019/19-17, 1 April, CO 1022/46.

———. 1953c. "Translation of *Freedom News*, no. 33 (15 January 1953)." Memorandum from Director, Special Branch Singapore to Commissioner, Police Headquarters, Singapore, internal file ref. SSB 4019/19-17, 23 April, CO 1022/46.

———. 1953d. "Translation of 'Are They Couriers or Comrades?'" Memorandum from Director of Special Branch Singapore to Commissioner of Police, Singapore, File ref. SSB. 4019/19, 3 December, CO1022/46.

———. 1953e. "Translation of 'An Outline of Studies of the International Problem' no. 3 (15 July 1954)." Memorandum from Director of Special Branch, Singapore to Commissioner of Police, Singapore, 3 December, CO1022/46.

Blythe, W. L. 1970. Letter to Hugh Bryson, 2 September, BAM XII/Addenda.

Bollas, C. 2011. *The Christopher Bollas Reader.* London: Routledge.

Breckenridge, C. A., and P. van der Veer. 1993. "Orientalism and the Postcolonial Predicament." In *Orientalism and the Postcolonial Predicament*, edited by C. A. Breckenridge and P. van der Veer, 1–19. Philadelphia: University of Pennsylvania Press.

Brennan, T. 1993. *History after Lacan.* London: Routledge.

British Military Administration. 1945. "Daily Report." 12 December, G/3/60 by H.Q. 571 F.S. Section, No. 2 Area, S.E.A.C., BAM II.

British Survey. 1952. "War in Malaya." 39 (June): 1–23.

Brockway, L. H. 1979. *Science and Colonial Expansion: The Role of the British Royal Botanic Garden*. New York: Academic Press.

Brookfield, H., S. H. Abdul, and Z. Mahmud. 1991. *The City and the Village: The In-Situ Urbanization of Villagers and Their Land Around Kuala Lumpur, Malaysia*. Kuala Lumpur: Oxford University Press.

Brummer, A. 1997. "Malaysian Tiger Takes a Mauling." *Guardian Weekly*, 7 September, 19.

Bryan, D., and M. Rafferty. 2006. *A Political Economy of Financial Derivatives, Capital and Class*. Basingstoke: Palgrave.

Bryson, H. 1967. Letter to Lt. Gen. Sir Brian Horrocks. 14 June, BAM Addenda.

Buck-Morss, S. 1989. *The Dialectics of Seeing: Walter Benjamin and the Arcades Project*. Cambridge: MIT Press.

Burgess, P. J. 1955. "Henry Nicholas Ridley – An Appreciation." *Proceedings of the Institution of the Rubber Industry* 24: 112–3.

Burrows, B. A. B. 1952. Circular letter, British Embassy in Washington. March, CO1022/84.

Butler, J. 1997. *Excitable Speech: A Politics of the Performative*. New York: Routledge.

———. 1990. "Performative Acts and Gender Constitution: An Essay in Phenomenology and Feminist Theory." In *Performing Feminisms: Feminist Critical Theory and Theatre*, edited by S. Case, 270–82. Baltimore: Johns Hopkins Press.

Cahill, M. L. 1955. Memorandum to R. W. Newsam, 3 August, CO1030/1.

Campbell, A. 1953. *Jungle Green*. Boston: Little, Brown and Company.

Chilver, E. M. 1952. "Re: Absentee Landlordism." Minute. 28 February, CO1022/398.

Castells, M. 1992. "Four Asian Tigers with a Dragon Head: A Comparative Analysis of the State, Economy and Society." In *States and Development in the Asia Pacific Rim*, edited by R. Appelbaum and J. Henderson, 33–70. Newbury Park: Sage Publications.

Chapman, F. S. 1949. *The Jungle Is Neutral*. London: Chatto and Windus.

Cheah, B. K. 1983. *Red Star Over Malaya: Resistance and Social Conflict during and after the Japanese Occupation, 1941–1946*. Singapore: Singapore University Press.

Chowdhry, G., and S. Rai. 2009. "The Geographies of Exclusion and the Politics of Inclusion: Race-Based Exclusions in the Teaching of International Relations." *International Studies Perspectives* 2009 (10): 84–91.

Chua, B. C. 2017. *Liberalism Disavowed: Communitarianism and State Capitalism in Singapore*. Ithaca: Cornell University Press.

Churchill, W. F. N. N.d.; circa 1950–51. A Brief and Quite Unofficial Account of the Emergency from the Angle of Kelantan. Unpublished manuscript. BAM IV/33-34.

Clark, G. L., A. D. Dixon, and A. H. B. Monk. 2014. *Sovereign Wealth Funds: Legitimacy Governance and Global Power*. Princeton: PUP.

Clifford, H. 1929. *Bush Whacking and Other Tales from Malaya*. Kingswood, Surrey: The Windmill Press.

Collinge, C.E. 1944. Sime Road Camp, Notice No.3 from the Men's Representative, 22 September, BAM XII/19.

Colonial Office. 1942. "Record of Discussion between the Secretary of State, Viscount Cranborne, and the Dutch Colonial Minister, Dr. Van Mook, at the Colonial Office." 12 June, CO 825/35/4.

———. 1955. "Talks between Chief Ministers of the Federation of Malaya and Singapore and Chin Peng." Draft Memorandum, December, CO1030/27, no. 13.
Colonial Office and Foreign Office. 1953. "A Post-War Settlement in the Far East: Need for a Definitive Policy." Joint Memorandum, 14 May, CO 825/35/4, no. 52.
Colonial Office Far Eastern Department. 1955. Memorandum on "Federation of Malaya and Constitutional Conference," 22 December, CO1030/75, nos. 2.
"Colonies Notes from the Meeting." 1948. Internal file ref. SSB. 4019/19, 3 December, Royal Commonwealth Archives, University of Cambridge.
Comber, L. 2009. *13 May 1969: The Darkest Day in Malaysian History*. Singapore: Marshall Cavendish.
Combined Intelligence Staff. 1953a. "Review of Security Situation in Malaya." 19 August, CO 1022/205.
———. 1953b. "Review of the Emergency on the Thai-Malaya Frontier." 19 August, CO 1022/205.
———. 1953c. "Malay Participation in the Present Emergency." 19 August, CO1022/205.
———. 1955. "The 'White Area' Policy and the Areas to Which it has been Extended." 2 June, CO 1030/1.
Commercial Interests. 1950a. "Record of Meeting between A. Creech Jones, Secretary of State for the Colonies, and Commercial Interests." 19 February, BAM II/6.
———. 1950b. "Record of Meeting between Commercial Interests and Secretary of State for the Colonies." 10 May, BAM II/6.
———. 1950c. "Record of Meeting between the Commercial Interests with the Secretary of State." 19 December, BAM II/6.
———. 1951a. "Record of Meeting between Commercial Interests and High Commissioner at King's House, Kuala Lumpur." 1 January, BAM II/6.
———. 1951b. "Record of Meeting with Representatives of URAM, FMS, Chamber of Mines, Chamber of Commerce, All Malaya Chinese Mining Association, MEOA." 11 January, BAM II/6.
———. 1951c. "Record of Meeting between General Briggs and Commercial Interests." 17 January, BAM II/6.
———. 1951d. "Notes from Meeting between Planters and Miners [Re: Planned Legislation]." 7 November, BAM II/6.
———. 1951e. "Notes from the Meeting between Planters and the Secretary of State for the Colonies." 3 December, BAM II/6.
———. 1951f. "Record of Meeting with Hugh Fraser." 8 December, BAM II/6.
Commission on Growth and Development. 2008. *The Growth Report: Strategies for Sustained Growth and Inclusive Development*. Washington: The World Bank.
Commissioner General for South-East Asia. 1948. "Commissioner General's Meeting at Bukit Serene." Minutes, 12 September, CO 717/167.
Commissioner General's Office. 1957. "The Outlook for Malaya up to 1960." May, FO 371/129342.
Cooper, B., and M. Murphy. 1999. "'Libidinal Economics': Lyotard and Accounting for the Unaccountable." In *The New Economic Criticism: Studies at the Intersection of Literature and Economics*, edited by M. Woodmansee and M. Osteen, 229–41. London and New York: Routledge.
Cross, J. P. 1971. "Jungle Warfare." *Army Quarterly* 101 (3): 323–9.

Coyle, D. 1997. "Why the Asian Model Has Gone Off the Road." *The Independent*, 25 November. http://www.independent.co.uk/opinion/why-the-asian-model-has-gone-off-the-road-1296185.html

Cranbourne, Lord. 1942. Minute. 14 July, CO 825/35/4, f227.

Creech Jones, A. 1950. "Re: Response to Letter on Seditious Propaganda." Letter, Secretary of State for the Colonies, to ABM, 3 March, BAM II/6.

Cripps, S. and E. Bevin. 1949. "Washington Talks, US." Memorandum, September PREM 8/1407/1 EPC(49)152.

Croly, H. G. 1957. "Letter to Chiefs of Staff Planning Committee." 9 October, CO 1033/655.

Daily Telegraph. 1952. "20,000 Punished in Malaya for 'Cowardly Silence': Rations Cut; 22-hr." *Daily Telegraph* 28 November. CO 1022/7.

Daud, L. 1977. "The British Military Administration, September 1945 to April 1946." In *Malaya: The Making of a Neo-Colony*, edited by M. Amin and M. Caldwell, 120–49. Nottingham: Spokesman Books.

de Silva, S. B. D. 1982. *The Political Economy of Underdevelopment*. London, Boston: Routledge & K. Paul.

Dening, M. E. 1945a. "On Need to Publicize British Policy on Malaya." Telegram to Foreign Office, 3 March, WO 203/5642.

———. 1945b. "Political Co-ordination in South-East Asia." Memorandum no. 5, 26 June CO 273/677/3.

———. 1945c. Telegram to Foreign Office. 3 September, WO 203/5642.

———. 1946. "Review of Political Events in South-East Asia 1945 to March 1946." Despatch to Ernest Bevin, 25 March, CAB 21/1954, F 5093/87/61.

Dennis, P. 1996. *Emergency and Confrontation: Australian Military Operations in Malaya & Borneo 1950–1966*. The Official History of Australia's Involvement in Southeast Asian Conflicts, 1948–1975. St. Leonards, NSW, Australia: Allen & Unwin in association with the Australian War Memorial.

Dercon, S. 2022. *Gambling on Development: Why Some Countries Win and Others Lose*. London: Hurst Publishers.

Dickens, P. 1983. *SAS the Jungle Frontier: 22 Special Air Service Regiment in the Borneo Campaign, 1963–1966*. London: Arms and Armour.

Director of Operations Staff for Templer. 1952. "Action Taken Against Village under ER 17D in August." CO 1022/56.

Donald, E. 1997. *The Malayan Emergency, 1948–1960: The Domino that Stood*. Washington: Brassey's.

Drabble, J. 1991. *Malayan Rubber: The Interwar Years*. Houndmills, Basingstoke, Hampshire: Macmillan Academic and Professional.

Eastwood, C. G. 1951. "Re: Use of Chemicals to Clear Vegetation." Minute, 17 January, CO 1022/26.

Edmunds, W. R. 1949. "Malaya: Tin." Minute, 23 September, T 220/134 no. 74.

Elden, S. 2007. "Governmentality, Calculation, Territory." *Environment and Planning D: Society and Space* 25(3): 562–80.

Endicott, K., ed. 2015. *Malaysia's Original People: Past, Present and Future of the Orang Asli*. Singapore: National University of Singapore Press.

Eng, D. 2001. *Racial Castration: Managing Masculinity in Asian America*. Durham: Duke University Press.

European Political Strategy Center. 2015. *The Asian Infrastructure Investment Bank: A New Multilateral Financial Institution or a Vehicle for China's Geostrategic Goals*. EPSC Strategic Notes, 24 April Issue 1.

Fanon, F. 1967. *Black Skin, White Masks*. Translated by C. L. Markmann. New York: Grove Press.
———. 1963. *The Wretched of the Earth*. Translated by C. Farrington. New York: Grove Press.
FGV (Felda Global Ventures). 2019. *About FGV*. Kuala Lumpur: FGV Holdings Berhad.
———. 2020. "FGV's Clarification on the Land Lease Agreement with FELDA." Press release, 27 October. https://www.fgvholdings.com/press_release/fgvs-clarification-on-the-land-lease-agreement-with-felda/
Foucault, M. 1972. *The Archaeology of Knowledge and the Discourse on Language*. Translated by A. M. Sheridan Smith. New York: Pantheon Books.
———. 1980. *Power/Knowledge: Selected Interviews and Other Writings 1972–1977*. Translated by C. Gordon, L. Marshall, J. Mepham, and K. Soper. New York: Pantheon Books.
———. 1994. *The Order of Things: An Archaeology of the Human Sciences*. Translated by A. Sheridan. New York: Vintage Books.
———. 1995. *Discipline and Punish: The Birth of the Prison*. Translated by A. Sheridan. New York: Vintage Books.
———. 2007. *Security, Territory, Population: Lectures at the Collège de France, 1977–78*, edited by M. Senellart. Translated by G. Burchell. Basingstoke: Palgrave.
Fox, J. 1998. "The Great Emerging Markets Rip-Off." *Fortune*, 11 May, 100.
Freud, S. 1915. *Thoughts for the Times on War and Death: The Disillusionment of War* Part *I*. https://www.sas.upenn.edu/~cavitch/pdf-library/Freud_War_and_Death.pdf
———. 1959a. *Group Psychology and the Analysis of the Ego*. Translated by The Institute of Psycho-Analysis and A. Richards. New York; London: W.W. Norton.
———. 1959b. *Inhibitions, Symptoms and Anxiety*. Translated by The Institute of Psycho-Analysis and A. Richards. New York: W.W. Norton.
———. 1962. *Civilization and Its Discontents*. Translated by J. Strachey. New York; London: W.W. Norton.
———. 1965. *New Introductory Lectures on Psycho-Analysis*. Translated by J. Strachey. The Standard Edition. New York: W. W. Norton.
———. 1966 (1920). *Introductory Lectures on Psycho-Analysis*. Translated by J. Strachey. The Standard Edition. New York: W. W. Norton.
———. 2004. "Mass Psychology and the Analysis of the 'I'." In *Mass Psychology and Other Writings*, edited by A. Phillips. Translated by J. Underwood, 15–106. London: Penguin Books.
Fridell, G. 2014. "Fair Trade Slippages and Vietnam Gaps: The Ideological Fantasies of Fair Trade Coffee." *Third World Quarterly* 35 (7): 1179–93.
Fukuyama, F. 1998. "Asian Values and the Asian Crisis." *Commentary*, 27 February. https://www.commentarymagazine.com/articles/asian-values-and-the-asian-crisis/
Gagliano, F. V. 1970. *Communal Violence in Malaysia 1969: The Political Aftermath*. Athens: Ohio University Center for International Studies.
Gallagher, J. 2018. "Misrecognition in the Making of a State: Ghana's International Relations under Kwame Nkrumah." *Review of International Studies* 44 (5): 882–901. https://doi.org/10.1017/S0260210518000335
Gamba, C. 1962. *The National Union of Plantation Workers: The History of the Plantation Workers of Malaya 1946–1958*. Singapore: Eastern Universities Press.

Gammon, E. 2017. "Narcissistic Rage and Neoliberal Reproduction." *Global Society* 31 (4): 510–30. https://doi.org/10.1080/13600826.2017.1280775

Gandhi, L. 1998. *Postcolonial Theory: A Critical Introduction*. New York: Columbia University Press.

Gann. A. S. 1951. "Malayan Rubber Re-planting Cess." Minute, 8 November, CO 1022/70.

Gardner, R. N. 1969. *Sterling-Dollar Diplomacy: The Origins and Prospects of Our International Order*. New York: McGraw–Hill.

Garner, S. 2017. *Racisms: An Introduction*. London: Sage Publications.

Gater, G. 1945. Letter to Sir Henry Wilson Smith, 31 August, T 220/52, IF 23/01.

Gay, P. 1994. *The Cultivation of Hatred*. New York: W.W Norton.

Gent, G. E. J. 1942a. "Forthcoming Talks at the Foreign Office on Malaya's Post-war Policy." Minute, 29 March, CO 825/35/4, f8.

———. 1942b. Minute, 1 July, CO 825/35/4, f10.

———. 1948a. Inward telegram to Creech Jones, 13 June.

———. 1948b. "Re: Declaration of Emergency." Inward telegram to A. Creech-Jones, 17 June, CO 717/167/52849/2/1949.

Gent, G. E. J., and D. M. MacDougall. 1942. "Note on Future Policy in the Far East." July, CO 825/35/4, f227.

Gerber, J.-F. 2022. "The Psychoanalytic Critique of Capitalism: Elements for an Overview." *Psychotherapy and Politics International* 20 (1&2): 1–23.

Ghesquire, H. 2007. *Singapore's Success: Engineering Economic Growth*. Singapore: Thomson Learning.

Ghosh, A. 1997. "India's Untold War of Independence." *New Yorker* 23 and 30 June, 104–21.

Gidden, B. 1950. "RGA Letter to Colonial Office." Ref. 52849/9, 10 February, BAM II/6.

Glynos, J., R. Klimecki, and H. Willmott. 2012. "Cooling Out the Marks: The Ideology and Politics of the Financial Crisis." *Journal of Cultural Economy* 5 (3): 297–320.

———. 2015. "Logics in Policy and Practice: A Critical Nodal Analysis of the UK Banking Reform Process." *Critical Policy Studies* 9 (4): 393–415.

Gniazdowski, A. 2018. "The Politics of Regression: The Idea of the Nation State in the Thought of Ernst Cassirer and Aurel Kolnai." *Eidos* 3 (5): 27–41. https://doi.org/10.26319/5813

Godfrey, F. A. 1978. *The Malayan Emergency 1948–1960*. Catalogue written to accompany the exhibition at the Royal Military Academy at Sandhurst.

Goh, D. P. S., M. Gabrielpillai, P. Holden, and G. C. Khoo, eds. 2009. *Race and Multiculturalism in Malaysia and Singapore*. Abingdon: Routledge.

Golub, P. 2016. *East Asia's Reemergence*. Cambridge: Polity Press.

Gomez, E. T. 1999. "Tracing the Ethnic Divide: Race, Rights and Redistribution in Malaysia." In *Ethnic Futures: The State and Identity Politics in Asia*, edited by J. Pfaff-Czarnecka, D. Rajasingham-Senanayake, A. Nandy and E. Gomez, 167–202. New Delhi: Sage Publications.

Gomez, E. T., and K. S. Jomo. 1997. *Malaysia's Political Economy: Politics, Patronage and Profits*. Cambridge and New York: Cambridge University Press.

Gomez, E. T., T. Padmanbhan, N. Kamaruddin, S. Bhalla, and F. Fisal. 2017. *Minister of Finance Incorporated: Control of Corporate Malaysia*. Singapore: Palgrave Macmillan.

Goodman, R., H. J. Kwon, and H. G. White, eds. 1998. *The East Asian Welfare Model: Welfare Orientalism and the State*. London: Routledge.
Gordon, L. A. 1990. *Brothers Against the Raj: A Biography of Indian Nationalists Sarat and Subhas Chandra Bose*. New York: Columbia University Press.
Gow, Wilson Stanton Ltd. 1906. *Rubber Producing Companies (Capitalised in Sterling) Having Properties in the Malay Peninsula And Ceylon Showing Their History* and *Results*. London: A. Southey & Co.
Grove, R. H. 1990. "Colonial Conservation, Ecological Hegemony and Popular Resistance: Towards a Global Synthesis." In *Imperialism and the Natural World*, edited by J. Mackenzie, 15–51. Manchester: Manchester University Press.
Guinness, P. 1992. *On the Margin of Capitalism: People and Development in Mukim Plentong, Johor, Malaysia*. Singapore: Oxford University Press.
Gupta, A. 1998. *Postcolonial Developments: Agriculture in the Making of Modern India Durham*. Durham: Duke University Press.
Gurney, H. 1948. H. Inward telegram to A. Creech Jones, Secretary of State for the Colonies, 25 January, CO 717/167.
Gutteridge, G. C. 1957. "The Preventive Service, North Region." Assistant Comptroller of Customs, BAM I/15.
Halim, S. 1992. "Peasants, Proletarianization and The State: FELDA Settlers in Pahang." In *Fragmented Visions*, edited by J. Kahn and F. Low, 107–32. Honolulu: University of Hawaii Press.
Halimi, S. 2015. "The Europe We Don't Want." *Le Monde Diplomatique*, English edition 1508 (August): 1–3.
Han, S. 1956. *And the Rain My Drink*. London: Jonathan Cape.
———. 1980. *My House Has Two Doors*. London: Jonathan Cape.
Handbook to Malaya (Federation of Malaya and the Colony of Singapore) and the Emergency. 1952 Singapore: Regional Information Office for the United Kingdom in South East Asia.
Harper, T. 1999. *The End of Empire and the Making of Malaya*. Cambridge: Cambridge University Press.
Harvey, D. 1982. *The Limits to Capital*. Oxford: Blackwell.
———. 1989. *The Condition of Postmodernity*. Cambridge: Blackwell.
Hassan, A. 2009. *A Practical Guide to Sovereign Wealth Funds*. London: Eurobanking Books.
Hayes, G. 2004. "Marxism and Critical Psychology." In *Critical Psychology*, edited by D. Hook, 162–86. Landsdowne, South Africa: UCT Press.
Haynes, A. S. 1950a. Interview with Clement Attlee, 19 April, BAM IV/34.
———. 1950b. Letter to James Griffiths,13 May, BAM IV/34.
———. 1951a. Letter to Oliver Lyttelton, 7 November, BAM IV/34.
———. 1951b. Letter to Anthony Eden, 21 November, BAM IV/34.
Headrick, D. 1988. *The Tentacles of Progress: Technology Transfer in the Age of Imperialism 1850–1940*. New York: Oxford University Press.
Hecht, S., and A. Cockburn. 1990. *The Fate of the Forest: Developers, Destroyers and Defenders of the Amazon*. London: Verso.
Herman, J. L. 2015. *Trauma and Recovery: The Aftermath of Violence–from Domestic Abuse to Political Terror*. New York: Basic Books.
Hiddleston, J. 2009. *Understanding Postcolonialism*. Stocksfield: Acumen.
Hiebert, M. 1999. "Under Control." *Far Eastern Economic Review*, 28 January, 42–4.

Hitler, A. 1953. *Secret Conversations*. New York: Farrar, Strauss and Young.
Ho, S. W. 2023. "6 Interesting Facts about Our Government Debt." *Free Malaysia Today*, 21 May. https://www.freemalaysiatoday.com/category/leisure/money/2021/05/21/6-interesting-facts-about-malaysias-government-debt/
Hoagland, J. 1997a. "From Boom to Bust." *The Washington Post*, 12 October, CO 9.
———. 1997b. "Tinkering with an Economic Mess." *The Washington Post*, 30 November, C07.
Hobsbawm, E., and T. Ranger, eds. 1983. *The Invention of Tradition*. Cambridge: Cambridge University Press.
Hook, D. 2004a. "Frantz Fanon, Steve Biko, 'Psychopolitics' and Critical Psychology." In *Critical Psychology*, edited by D. Hook, 85–114. Lansdowne, South Africa: UCT Press.
———. 2004b. "Foucault, Disciplinary Power and The Critical Pre-History of Psychology." In *Critical Psychology*, edited by D. Hook, 210–38. Lansdowne, South Africa: UCT Press.
———. 2004c. "Governmentality and Technologies of Subjectivity." In *Critical Psychology*, edited by D. Hook, 239–72. Lansdowne: UCT Press.
Howe, C. E. N.d. "Memories of Jelebu District under Emergency 1948–1950." BAM III/14.
Ibrahim bin Haji, Y. N.d. *Sedjarah Dan Perjuangan Di-Malaya*. Jogjakarta: Nusantara Press.
Ingrams, W. H. 1953. "Re: Islamist Nationalism." Minute, 16 July, CO 1022/205.
Inoue, T. 1999. "Liberal Democracy and Asian Orientalism." In *The East Asian Challenge for Human Rights*, edited by J. Bauer and D. Bell, 27–59. Cambridge: Cambridge University Press.
International Bank for Reconstruction and Development. 1955. *The Economic Development of Malaya*. Baltimore: Johns Hopkins Press.
IMF. 2012. "IMF Adopts Institutional View on Capital Flows." *IMF News*, December 3. http://www.imf.org/external/pubs/ft/survey/so/2012/pol120312a.htm.
Jackson, J. 1968. *Planters and Speculators: Chinese and European Agricultural Enterprise in Malaya, 1786–1921*. Kuala Lumpur: University of Malaya Press.
Jackson, R. 1991. *The Malayan Emergency: The Commonwealth's Wars 1948–1966*. New York: Routledge.
Jacques, M. 2009. *When China Rules the World: The End of The Western World and the Birth of the New Global Order*. New York: Penguin Press.
Jain, R. K. 1970. *South Indians on the Plantation Frontier in Malaya*. New Haven and. London: Yale University Press.
Jaipragas, B. 2018. "Is China's Belt and Road Colonialism? Mahathir: Not at All." *South China Morning Post*, 2 October. https://www.scmp.com/week-asia/politics/article/2166693/chinas-belt-and-road-colonialism-mahathir-not-all
Jasanoff, M. 2005. *Edge of Empire: Lives, Culture, and Conquest in the East, 1750–1850*. New York: Knopf.
Jayasankaran, S. 1997. "Hit the Brakes." *Far Eastern Economic Review*, 18 December, 14–5.
Jayasankaran, S., and M. Hiebert. 1997. "Malaysian Dilemmas." *Far Eastern Economic Review*, 4 September, 18–21.
Jerrom, T. C. 1951. "Re: Crop Destruction." Minute, 12 May, CO 1022/26.
———. 1952a. "Re: Dean Acheson's Press Conference." Minute, February, CO 1022/84.

———. 1952b. "Re: Decapitation of Dead Communists by Government Troops." South East Asia Department, Colonial Office Memorandum, 29 April, CO 1022/45.

———. 1952c. "Re: Decapitation of Dead Communists by Government Troops." South East Asia Department, Colonial Office Memorandum, 30 April, CO 1022/45.

———. 1952d. "Re: Decapitation of Dead Communists by Government Troops." South East Asia Department, Colonial Office Memorandum, 5 May, CO 1022/45.

———. 1952e. "Re: Decapitation of Dead Communists by Government Troops." South East Asia Department Colonial Office Memorandum to J.D. Higham, 19 May, CO 1022/45.

———. 1952f. "Re: Decapitation of Dead Communists by Government Troops." South East Asia Department, Colonial Office Memorandum to J. Paskins, 12 December, CO 1022/45.

Johnson, C. 1982. *MITI and the Japanese Miracle: The Growth of Industrial Policy, 1925–1975*. Stanford: Stanford University Press.

Jomo, K. S. 1988. *A Question of Class: Capital, the State, and Uneven Development in Malaya*. New York: Monthly Review Press.

———. 2001. "From Currency Crisis to Recession." In *Malaysian Eclipse: Economic Crisis and Recovery*, edited by K. S. Jomo, 1–46. London: Zed Books.

Jones, E. Ll. 1939. "The Rural Lecture Caravan." *The Malayan Agricultural Journal* 27: 399–402.

Joseph, M. 1999. *Nomadic Identities: The Performance of Citizenship*. Minneapolis: University of Minnesota Press.

Kahn, M. 2002. *Basic Freud: Psychoanalytic Thought for the 21st Century*. New York: Basic Books.

Kaplan, E. and D. Rodrik. 2001. *Did the Malaysian Capital Controls Work?* NBER Working Papers Series, no. 8142. Cambridge, Mass MA: National Bureau of Economic Research. http://www.nber.org/papers/w8142.

Kapoor, I. 2008. *The Postcolonial Politics of Development*. London: Routledge.

———. 2014. "Psychoanalysis and Development: Contributions, Examples, Limits." *Third World Quarterly* 35 (7): 1120–43.

———, ed. 2018. *Psychoanalysis and the Global*. Lincoln: University of Nebraska Press.

———. 2020. *Confronting Desire: Pyschoanalysis and International Development*. Ithaca, New York: Cornell University Press.

Kapoor, I., G. Fridell, M. Sioh, and P. de Vries. 2023. *Global Libidinal Economy*. Albany: SUNY Press.

Kasese-Hara, M. 2004. "Human Development in 'Underdeveloped' Contexts." In *Critical Psychology*, edited by D. Hook, 540–58. Landsdowne, South Africa: UCT Press.

Kasim, S. 2022. "Siti Kasim Gets the 'Last Laugh' about Religion and State." *Free Malaysia Today*, 20 November. https://www.freemalaysiatoday.com/category/nation/2022/11/20/siti-kassim-gets-the-last-laugh-about-religion-and-state/

Kearns, H. G., and E. K. Woodford. 1952. "The Chemical Control of Roadside Vegetation: Report of a Visit to the Federation of Malaya, 4–23 December, 1952." CO 1022/26.

Keynes, J. M. 1945. "Overseas Financial Policy in Stage III." 3 April, CAB 66/65, WP(45)301.

Khanna, P. 2008. *The Second World: Empires and Influence in the New Global Order*. New York: Random House.

Khor, M. 2008. "The Malaysian Experience in Financial-Economic Management: An Alternative to the IMF-Style Approach." In *Capital Market Liberalization and Development*, edited by J. Ocampo and J. Stiglitz, 205–61. Oxford: Oxford University Press.

Killearn, Lord. 1947. "South-East Asia: Work of the Special Commission During 1946." Despatch to Ernest Bevin, 12 April, CAB 21/1955, F6151/6151/61.

Koerner, L. 1996. "Purposes of Linnaean Travel: A Preliminary Research Report." In *Visions of Empire: Voyages, Botany and Representations of Nature*, edited by D. P. Miller and P. Reill, 117–52. Cambridge: Cambridge University Press.

Kohut, H. 1973. *The Search for the Self Selected Writings of Heinz Kohut: 1950–1978, Volume 2*, edited by P. H. Ornstein. New York: International Universities Press.

Krozewski, G. 1996. "Finance and Empire; The Dilemma Facing Great Britain in the 1950's." *The International History Review* 18: 48–69.

Krugman, P. 2009. *The Return of Depression Economics and the Crisis of 2008*. New York: W. Norton and Co.

———. 2015. "The Asian Crisis Versus the Euro Crisis." *The New York Times*, 28 August. http://krugman.blogs.nytimes.com/2013/08/28/the-asian-crisis-versus-the-euro-crisis/?_r=0

Kumar, D. K. 1990. "The Evolution of Colonial Science in India: A Natural History and the East India Company." In *Imperialism and the Natural World*, edited by J. MacKenzie, 51–66. Manchester: Manchester University Press.

Kunz, D. B. 1991. *The Economic Diplomacy of the Suez Crisis*. Chapel Hill: The University of North Carolina Press.

Larkin, P. 1977. *Aubade*. Poetry Foundation. https://www.poetryfoundation.org/poems/48422/aubade-56d229a6e2f07

Latour, B. 1987. *Science in Action: How to Follow Scientists and Engineers Through Society*. Cambridge: Harvard University Press

Lee, E. 1998a. *The Asian Financial Crisis: The Challenge for Social Policy*. Geneva: International Labour Office.

Lee, H. L. 1998b. "Asian Economic Crisis: The Long View." Speech by Lee Hsien Loong Singapore Deputy Prime Minister. JP Morgan Investor Conference 'Investment Opportunities in New Asia.' 14 September.

———. 2001. Keynote Address by DPM Lee Hsien Loong, Chairman MAS, at MAS 30th Anniversary Conference, 20 July. https://www.nas.gov.sg/archivesonline/data/pdfdoc/2001072005.htm).

Lee, K. Y. 2000. *From Third World to First: The Singapore Story, 1965–2000, Volume 2*. New York: HarperCollins.

Lennox-Boyd, A. 1955a. Letter to A. Head, 9 February, CO 1030/67.

———. 1955b. "Re: New Villages." Letter to S. Awberry, MP, 20 June, CO 1030/277.

———. 1955c. "Defence Aspects of Constitutional Development in Federation of Malaya." Address to the Federal Executive Council, K.L., 1 September, orig.FED 36/1/07, CO 1030/71.

———. 1955d. "Re: Amnesty Talks with Communists." Telegram to D. MacGillivray, 22 October, FO371/116941 no. 69.

———. 1956a. "Re: Conference on Constitutional Advance in the Federation of Malaya." Memorandum for Cabinet Colonial Policy Committee, 7 January, CAB 134/1202 CA(56)3.

———. 1956b. "Advising Against a Formal Agreement." Draft Memorandum, February, CO 1030/72, no. 29.

———. 1956c. "Re: Constitutional Conference and Annex." Memorandum to Cabinet, 21 February, CAB 129/79 CP(56)47.

Leslie, E. 2000. *Walter Benjamin: Overpowering Conformism*. London: Pluto Press.

Lesser, W. 2011. *Music for Silenced Voices*. New Haven: Yale University Press.

Leys, R. 2000. *Trauma: A Genealogy*. Chicago: University of Chicago Press.

Lim, K. W., R. Ho, and M. F. Yee. 1998. *Hidden Agenda*. Kuala Lumpur: Limkokwing Integrated Sdn Bhd.

Lim, T. G. 2007. "Felda's Lost Opportunity for Indians." *Malaysiakini*, 9 May. https://www.malaysiakini.com/letters/66993

Livingstone, D. N. 1994. "Climate's Moral Economy: Science, Race and Place in Post-Darwinian British and American Geographies." In *Geography and Empire*, edited by A. Godlewska and N. Smith, 132–154. Oxford: Basil Blackwell.

Lin, Y. 2012. *New Structural Economics: A Framework for Rethinking Development and Policy*. Washington: World Bank.

Lo, B. 2016. "Zeti Akhtar Aziz, Governor of Bank Negara Malaysia Exclusive Interview with Bernie Lo, CNBC." CNBC Transcript, 22 January. https://www.cnbc.com/2016/01/22/cnbc-transcript-zeti-akhtar-aziz-governor-of-bank-negara-malaysia.html

Low, L. 2006. *The Political Economy of a City-State Revisited*. Singapore: Marshall Cavendish.

Lyttelton, O. 1953. "Future Arrangements for Development Finance." Circular letter 601/531, July, CO 1022/331.

———. 1954a. "Re: Alliance Delegation to London." Telegram to Sir Gerald Templer, High Commissioner, 15 May, CO 1030/309, no. 53.

———. 1954b. Letter to Tunku Abdul Rahman, 18 May, CO 1030/310 no. 56.

———. 1954c. Letter to Baron Ogmore, Labour MP, 22 May, CO 1030/310 no. 65.

———. 1954d. Letter to Tunku Abdul Rahman, 11 June, CO 1030/310 no. 91.

MacDonald, M. 1947. "Re: Chinese Demand for Constitutional Review." Telegram to A.Creech Jones, the Secretary of State for the Colonies, 8 November, CO 537/2144, no. 264.

———. 1952. Letter to Secretary of State for the Colonies, 29 February, CO 1022/141.

———. 1953. "Re: Pan-Malayan Scientific Advisory Council." Letter to G. Templer, High Commissioner Federation of Malaya; J. Nicholl, Governor of Singapore, and Vice-Chancellor, University of Malaya, 8 April, CO 1022/215.

MacGillivray, D. 1954a. "Re: Alliance Threat to Boycott Elections." Telegram to O. Lyttelton, 2 June, CO 1030/310 no. 80.

———. 1954b. "Re: Alliance Boycott." Telegram to O. Lyttelton, 23 June, CO 1030/310 no. 109.

———. 1954c. "Re: Alliance Boycott." Letter to J. Martin, 25 June, CO 1030/311 no. 123.

———. 1954d. Telegram [Re: Concessions to Alliance] to O. Lyttelton, 3 July, CO 1030/311 no. 125.

———. 1954e. Telegram [Re: Appointment of Members after Consultation with Majority Leaders] to O. Lyttelton, 7 July, CO 1030/311 no. 130.

———. 1955a. "Re. Communists' Amnesty." Telegram to A. Lennox-Boyd, Secretary of State for the Colonies, 20 October, FO371/116941, no. 67/9.

———. 1955b. "Statement to the Federal Legislative Council that the Continuation of The War [Emergency] Would not Stand in the Way of Self-Government," 30 November, CAB 134/1201, CA 6(55)2.
———. 1955c. "Re: Alliance Demands." Letter to A.M. Mackintosh, 29 December, CO 1030/75, no. 7.
———. 1955d. "Constitutional Problems." Letter to Sir John Martin, CO 1030/65 no. 3.
———. 1956. "Re. Amnesty Talks with Communists." Telegram to the Secretary of State for the Colonies A. Lennox-Boyd, 9 January, CO 1030/73.
MacGillivray's Senior Officials. 1955. "Consequences of a Break with the Alliance." December, Memorandum, CO 1030/27, no. 21.
MacKay, D. 1996. "Agents of Empire: The Banksian Collectors and Evaluation of New Lands." In *Visions of Empire: Voyages, Botany and Representations of Nature*, edited by D. P. Miller and P. H. Reill, 38–57. Cambridge: Cambridge University Press.
MacKenzie, J. 1990. "Introduction." In *Imperialism and the Natural World*, edited by J. MacKenzie, 1–14. Manchester: Manchester University Press.
Mackie, J. A. C. 1974. *Konfrontasi: The Indonesia-Malaysia Dispute 1963–1966*. Kuala Lumpur: Oxford University Press.
Mahathir M. 1990. "Opening speech for the Eighth ASEAN-EC Meeting in Kuching, Sarawak, 16 February." Office of the High Commissioner for Malaysia in the United Kingdom, Information Division.
Mahathir, M, and I. Shintaro. 1995. *The Voice of Asia: Two Leaders Discuss the Coming Century*. Translated by F. Baldwin. Tokyo: Kodansha International.
Mahbubani, K. 2002. *Can Asians Think? Understanding the Divide Between East and West*. South Royalton, Vermont: Steerforth Press.
Malaya. 1960. "Re White Areas" Chapter 4 ftnote 214 (April), pp. 20.
Malaya (Colonial Government). 1946. Summary of Constitution proposals for Malaya. Kuala Lumpur: Malayan Union Government Press, 19 December.
———. 1948a. *Federation of Malaya Gazette*, No. 10, CO 717/167.
———. 1948b. Emergency Regulation Ordinance No. 2033, 13 July, CO 717/167.
———. 1948c. Emergency Regulation Ordinance No. 746, 30 September, CO 717/167.
———. 1952. Minutes of the Legislative Council meeting, 21 November, CO 1022/53.
———. 1953a. "Crop Destruction by Chemicals." Technical Note 1/53 Operational Research Section (Malaya), 21 January, AIR20/8735.
———. 1953b. "Secret Memorandum from Advanced Headquarters Malaya to AHQ Rep for Airborne Chemicals Trial." 23 February, AIR20/8735.
———. 1954. "Punishment of the Town of Tanjong Malim in Malaya – Non-Cooperation with Authorities." CO 1022/54.
———. 1955. "Punishment of the Town of Sungei-Pelak (sic) in Malaya for Non-Cooperation with Authorities." CO 1022/55.
———. Defence Department. 1956. "Transfer of Responsibility for the Federation Armed Forces to an Elected Minister." January, CO 1030/71.
———. N.d. "Communism – Malaya Rehabilitation of Detainees," CO 1022/151.
Malayan Communist Party. 1955. Letter to the United Planters of Malaya Association (UPAM), the Malayan Chinese Association (MCA), *Utusan Melayu*, 1 May, CO 1030/319.

Malayan Union Government. 1947. *Summary of the Report of the Working Committee Appointed by a Conference of His Excellency the Governor of the Malayan Union, Their Highnesses the Rulers of the Malay States and the Representatives of the United Malays National Organization, 19 December 1946*. Kuala Lumpur: Malayan Union Government Press, Royal Commonwealth Society Archives, Cambridge University.

Malaysia. 1971a. *Second Malaysia Plan*. Kuala Lumpur: Government Printing Press.

Malaysia. 1971b. "Pahang's Massive Land Development." July: 111.

Mallaby, S. 1998. "In Asia's Mirror." *The National Interest* 52: 13–22.

Mallet, V. 1999. *The Trouble with Tigers: The Rise and Fall of South-East Asia*. London: Harper Collins.

Mamdani, M, 2008, "Lessons of Zimbabwe." *London Review of Books*, 4 December, 17–21.

Manchester Guardian. 1952. "Corpses Exposed in Public," 20 August. CO 1022/45.

Marston, D., and C. Malkasian, eds. 2008. *Counterinsurgency in Modern Warfare*. Oxford: Osprey Publishing.

Martin, J. 1954. Telegram to G. Templer, 28 May, CO 1030/310 no. 73.

Maxwell, W. E. 1883. "The Law and Customs of the Malays with Reference to Tenure of Land." *Journal of the Malayan Branch of the Royal Asiatic Society* 13: 75–220.

Maxwell, A., J. F. Ferguson, and R. I. Jackson. 1950. "Report of Police Mission for the Colonial Office," 16 March, CO/8481/5, BAM V/6.

McCarthy, Terry. 1998. "In Defense of "Asian Values."" *Time Magazine*, 16 March.

McClintock, A. 1995. *Imperial Leather: Race, Gender and Sexuality in the Colonial* Contest. New York: Routledge.

McClintock, A. 2015. "Greek Bailout 'a New Versailles Treaty,' Says Former Finance Minister Yanis Varoufakis." Australian Broadcasting Corporation, July 13. https://www.abc.net.au/listen/programs/latenightlive/greek-bailout-deal-a-new-versailles-treaty:-yanis-varoufakis/6616532.

McHale, T. R. 1967. *Rubber and the Malaysian Economy*. Singapore: MPH Publications.

McMichael, P., and H. Weber. 2021. *Development and Social Change: A Global Perspective*. Thousand Oaks: Sage Publications.

Mead, W. 1998. "The Real Asian Miracle; Asia Devalued." *The New York Times Magazine*, 31 May. http://www.nytimes.com/1998/05/31/magazine/the-real-asian-miracle-asia-devalued.html?pagewanted=all

Melville, A. S. 1953. "Re: Independence of MCP from Foreign Influence." Comment on Memorandum and Attachment from A.E.G. Blades, Director of Special Branch Singapore, to Commissioner of Police, Singapore, 3 December, internal file ref. SSB. 4019/19, CO 1022/46.

Memmi, A. 1967. *The Colonizer and the Colonized*. Translated by H. Greenfeld. Boston: Beacon Press.

———. 1968. *Dominated Man: Notes Towards a Portrait*. Translated by E. Levieux. Boston: Beacon Press.

Mercer, K. 2017. *The Fateful Triangle: Race, Ethnicity and Nation*. Cambridge, Mass: Harvard University Press.

Mezerik, A. G. 1965. *Malaysia-Indonesia Conflict*. International Review Service, UN Bureau.

Miller, D. P. 1996. "Joseph Banks, Empire and 'Centres of Calculation' in Late Hanoverian London." In *Visions of Empire: Voyages, Botany and Representations of Nature*, edited by D. P. Miller and P. H. Reill, 21–37. Cambridge: Cambridge University Press.

Miller, H. 1972. *Jungle War in Malaya*. London: Arthur Barker Limited.
Milner, A. 2000. "What Happened to 'Asian Values'?" In *Towards Recovery in Pacific Asia*, edited by G. Segal and D. Goodman, 56–68. London: Routledge.
Mirsky, J. 1998. "Asian Values, a Fabulous Notion." *New Statesman*, 3 April, 26–7.
Mohamad, A., and M. Caldwell, eds. 1977. *Malaya: The Making of a Neo-Colony*. Nottingham: Spokesman Books.
Morgan, S. 1996. *Place Matters: Gendered Geography in Victorian Women's Travel Books about Southeast Asia*. New Brunswick: Rutgers University Press.
Moore-Gilbert, B. 1997. *Postcolonial Theory: Contexts, Practices, Politics*. London; New York: Verso.
Moorhouse, P. J. 1952. "Colombo Plan: Federation of Malaya Chapter." Memorandum, 16 April, CO 1022/141.
Morris, O. H. 1948. "Re: Use of Banishment." Minute, 17 June, CO 717/167.
———. 1950. "Re: Treatment of Estate Labour." Letter to the RGA, 30 January, BAM II/6.
Mydans, S., and W. Arnold. 2007. "Modern Singapore's Creator Is Alert to Perils." *New York Times*, 2 September. https://www.nytimes.com/2007/09/02/world/asia/02singapore.html?pagewanted=1&_r=0.
Muggeridge, M. 1952. "The Last Chance in Malaya – I, II, III and IV," *Daily Telegraph*, 19, 20, 21 and 22 February.
Muhamad, E. (Haji). 1938. "The Malays Being Denationalized." *The Malay Mail*, 16 September.
Nakao, T. 2010. "Strong Asian Growth and Asian Bond Markets Initiative." Presentation at the OECD—ADBI 11th Roundtable on Capital Market Reform in Asia, 22–23 February, Tokyo. https://www.oecd.org/daf/fin/financial-markets/44920872.pdf
Nandy, A. 1983. *The Intimate Enemy: Loss and Recovery of Self Under Colonialism*. Delhi: Oxford University Press.
Nonini, D. 1992. *British Colonial Rule and the Resistance of the Malay Peasantry, 1900–1957*. New Haven: Yale University Southeast Asian Studies.
Noone, R. 1972. *Rape of the Dream People*. New York: Morrow.
Nougayréde, N. 2015. "If Greece and Russia Feel Humiliated, that's Something Europe Cannot Ignore." *The Guardian*, 8 June. Retrieved from http://www.theguardian.com/commentisfree/2015/jun/18/greece-russia-humiliated-europe
O'Donovan, P. 1948. "Malayan Notebook: Jungle Home Guard." *Observer*, 26 September.
Ong, B. H. 2003. *Alias Chin Peng: My Side of History*. Singapore: Media Masters Publishers.
Oppenheimer, P. 1966. "Monetary Movements and the International Position of Sterling." *Scottish Journal of Political Economy* 13: 89–135.
Orchard, F. 2021. *Bold Vision: The Untold Story of Singapore's Reserves and Its Sovereign Wealth Fund*. Singapore: Epigram Books.
Panitch, L. 2014. "The US Still Decides the Future of Capitalism, Not the G20, and Not the Brics Nations." *The Guardian*, 27 August. http://www.theguardian.com/commentisfree/2014/aug/27/the-us-still-decides-the-future-of-capitalism-not-the-g20-and-not-the-brics-nations
Parmer, J. N. 1960. *Colonial Labour Policy and Administration: A History of Labour in the Rubber Plantation Industry in Malaya, c. 1910–1941*. New York: J.J. Augustin.

Pitakdumrongkit, K. 2015. "Where to Now for the Chiang Mai Initiative Multilateralisation?" *East Asia Forum*, 28 August. https://www.eastasiaforum.org/2015/08/28/where-to-now-for-the-chiang-mai-initiative-multilateralisation/
Plummer, L. 1953. "Letter to the Editor." *The Times*, 11 December, CO 1022/45.
Polk, J. 1956. *Sterling and Its Meaning in World Finance*. New York: Harper & Brothers for the Council on Foreign Relations.
Potter, J. S. 1954a. State Executive Council notes DOS 33/16, 28 July, BAM Archives I/12.
———. 1954b. State Executive Council Notes no. 6 in NS Cnf. 3/54 SJ17,1954; No. 16 in LOJ 186/53, 22 September, BAM Archives I/12.
Purcell, V. 1945. "Report on Malaya's Political Climate 10–30 November," WO 203/5302, 3 December.
———. 1948. Letter to the *Times*, 3 September.
———. 1954. *Malaya: Communist or Free*. Stanford: Stanford University Press.
Rahman, Abdul (Tunku). 1954. "Re: Proportion of Non-Elected Officials in Government." Telegram to Secretary of State for the Colonies, 25 May, CO 1030/310.
———. 1955. "Re: Date for Independence." Telegram to Secretary of State for the Colonies, 22 August, CO 1030/70, no. 35.
———. 1956. Speech to the Federal legislative Council, 14 March 1956, CO 1030/71.
———. 1969. *May 13; Before and After*. Kuala Lumpur: Utusan Melayu Press.
Rajchman, J., ed. 1995. *The Identity in Question*. New York: Routledge
Ramasamy, P. 1994. *Plantation Labour, Unions, Capital and the State in Peninsular Malaysia*. Kuala Lumpur: Oxford University Press.
Reading, Lord. 1955. "Report on Political Situation in Singapore and Malaya." 24 October, FO 371/116941 no. 76.
Reid, J. S. 1941. "Report on the Labour Troubles in Klang." 10 May, BAM 1/18.
Ridley, H. N. 1955. "Evolution of the Rubber Industry." *Proceedings of the Institution of the Rubber Industry* 24: 114–22.
Roff, W. R. 1967. *The Origins of Malay Nationalism*. New Haven: Yale University Press.
Roitman, J. 2003. "Unsanctioned Wealth; or, the Productivity of Debt in Northern Cameroon." *Public Culture* 15(2): 211–37.
Rose, J. 2004. "In Our Present–day White Christian Culture." *London Review of Books*, 8 July, 14–7.
———. 2005. *The Question of Zion*. Princeton: Princeton University Press.
Rose, N. 1996. *Inventing Ourselves: Psychology, Power and Personhood*. Cambridge: Cambridge University Press.
Rostow, W. 1960. *The Stages of Economic Growth*. Cambridge: Cambridge University Press.
Rudner, M. 1971. *Nationalism, Planning and Economic Modernization in Malaysia: The Politics of Beginning Development*. London: Sage Research Papers.
Rycroft, C. 1995. *Critical Dictionary of Psychoanalysis*. London: Penguin Books.
'S' Troop. 1956. "RA Campaign Diary 1954–1956." WO 305/154.
Said, Edward. 1978. *Orientalism*. New York: Pantheon.
———. 1989. "Representing the Colonized: Anthropology's Interlocuters." *Critical Enquiry* 15 (2): 205–25.
———. 1993. *Culture and Imperialism*. New York: Knopf.
Sabine, N. J. B. 1942. "Criticisms of Colonial Policy in the Light of the Malayan Campaign." Memorandum, 18 March, CO 875/14/9.
Sandhu, K. S. 1969. *Indians in Malaya: Some Aspects of Their Immigration and Settlement (1786–1957)*. London: Cambridge University Press.

Savage, V. 1984. *Western Impressions of Nature and Landscape in Southeast Asia.* Singapore: Singapore University Press.
Schell, O. and J. Delury. 2013. *Wealth and Power: China's Long March to the Twenty-First Century.* New York: Random House.
Schenk, C. 1993. "The Origins of a Central Bank in Malaya and the Transition to Independence." *The Journal of Imperial and Commonwealth History* 21: 409–31.
Scott, R. 1955a. "Re: Amnesty Talks." Telegram to A. Eden, 23 October, CO 1030/27, no. 1.
———. 1955b. "Re: Risks to British Interests in Malaya and Singapore." Telegram to A. Eden, 23 October, CO 1030/27, no. 2.
———. 1956. "Defence Treaty Working Party." Telegram to Sir H. Parker, 21 March, DEFE 7/494.
Sen, A. 1999. "Human Rights and Economic Achievement." In *The East Asian Challenge for Human Rights*, edited by J. Bauer and D. Bell, 88–99. Cambridge: Cambridge University Press.
Shamsul, B., and B. T. Lee. 1988. *3 Decades of Evolution.* Kuala Lumpur: FELDA.
Sheng, A. 2016. "Review of Global Shock, Risks and Asian Financial Reform." *Journal of Southeast Asian Economies* 33 (3): 413–7.
Sheppard, E., P. Porter, D. Faust, and R. Nagar. 2009. *A World of Difference: Encountering and Contesting Development.* New York: Guildford Press.
Sheridan, G. 1997. *Tigers: Leaders of the New Asia-Pacific.* St. Leonards, Australia: Allen and Unwin.
Shin, H. Y. 2015. "The IMF and Troika's Greek Bailout Programs: An East Asian View." *Real-World Economics Review* 73: 76–91.
Sioh, M. 1998. "Authorizing the Malaysian Rainforest: Configuring Space, Contesting Claims and Conquering Imaginaries." *Ecumene* 5 (2): 144–66.
———. 2004. "An Ecology of Postcoloniality: Disciplining Nature and Society in Malaya 1948–1957." *Journal of Historical Geography* 30: 729–46.
———. 2007. "Pricing Race, Circulating Anxieties and the Fate of Malaya's Currency Reserves at Independence." *Cultural Critique* 65 (Winter): 115–39.
———. 2010a. "The Hollow Within: Anxiety and Performing Postcolonial Financial Policies." *Third World Quarterly* 31 (4): 581–98.
———. 2010b. "Anxious Enactments: Postcolonial Anxieties and the Performance of Territorialization." *Environment and Planning D: Society and Space* 28 (3): 467–87.
Sioh, M. 2018. "The Logic of Humiliation in Financial Conquest." In *Psychoanalysis and the Global*, edited by I. Kapoor, 25–47. Lincoln: University of Nebraska Press.
Smee, M. 1954. "Second Day's Meeting of Singapore Legislative Council." Script for broadcasts over Radio Malaya Blue Network, 20 February, BAM 1/14.
———. 1955. "The Nation's Committee." Script for broadcast on Radio Malaya's Blue Network, 13 June, BAM I/14.
Smith, H. 2015. "Was This Humiliation of Greeks Really Necessary?" *The Guardian*, 12 July. Retrieved from http://www.theguardian.com/world/commentisfree/2015/jul/12/was-this-humiliation-of-greeks-really-necessary
Soros, G. 1997. "Mahathir vs. Soros." *Far Eastern Economic Review*, 2 October, 32.
Spencer, O.A. 1951. "Re: Colombo Plan: Federation of Malaya Chapter." Letter to J.D. Higham, 6 December, CO 1022/141.
Spivak, G. C. 1988. "Can the Subaltern Speak?" In *Marxism and the Interpretation of Culture*, edited by C. Nelson and L. Grossberg, 271–313. Basingstoke: MacMillan Education.

Spurr, D. 1993. *The Rhetoric of Empire*. Durham: Duke University Press.

Stanley, O. 1943. Hansard Parliamentary Debates, Vol. 391 (July) col. 48.

Stenson, M. R. 1980. *Class, Race and Colonialism in West Malaysia: The Indian Case*. Vancouver: University of British Columbia Press.

Stockwell, A., ed. 1995a. *Malaya, Part 1: The Malayan Union Experiment 1942–1948*. British Documents at the End of Empire, Series B Volume 3. London: HMSO.

———. 1995b. *Malaya, Part II: The Communist Insurrection 1948–1953*. British Documents at the End of Empire, Series B Volume 3. London: HMSO.

———. 1995c. *Malaya, Part III: the Alliance Route to Independence 1953–1957*. British Documents at the End of Empire, Series B Volume 3. London: HMSO.

Stiglitz, J. 2001. *Monetary and Exchange Rate Policy in Small Open Economies: The Case of Iceland*. Central Bank of Iceland, Working Papers No. 15. https://www.sedlabanki.is/uploads/files/WP-15.pdf

———. 2006. *Making Globalization Work*. New York: W.W. Norton.

———. 2015. "A Greek Morality Tale." *Project Syndicate*, 3 February. https://www.project-syndicate.org/commentary/greece-eurozone-austerity-reform-by-joseph-e--stiglitz-2015-02

Strange, S. 1971. *Sterling and British Policy: A Political Study of an International Currency Decline*. London: Oxford University Press.

Stubbs, R. 1989. *Hearts and Minds in Guerrilla Warfare: The Malayan Emergency 1948–1960*. Singapore: Oxford University Press.

Studwell, J. 2013. *How Asia Works: Success and Failure in the World's Most Dynamic Region*. New York: Grove Press.

Sussangkorn, C. 2010. *The Chiang Mai Initiative Multilateralization: Origin, Development and Outlook*. Tokyo: Asian Development Bank Institute.

Swaine, J. K. 1952. "Re: Ambush of Special Constables." Letter from Perak Rubber Plantations, Ltd. to A. Lennox-Boyd, MP, 31 January, CO 1022/44.

Sweet-Escott, B. A. C. 1945a. "Directive to AJUF from Acting Commander of Force 136 on Conclusion of the Armistice," 13 August, WO 203/5642, no. 7/16/45.

———. 1945b. "Force 136 Policy – Malaya," 19 August, WO 203/5642, no. 1/16/45.

Takagi, Y., V. Kanchoochat, and T. Sonobe, eds. 2019. *Developmental State Building: The Politics of Emerging Economies*. Springer e-book. https://link.springer.com/book/10.1007%2F978-981-13-2904-3

Templer, G. 1952a. Telegram to Oliver Lyttelton, Secretary of State for the Colonies, and Malcolm MacDonald, Commissioner General for South East Asia, 13 March, CO 1022/139.

———. 1952b. "Re: Agricultural Policy – Federation of Malaya." Speech to Legislative Council, 19 March, CO 1022/253.

———. 1952c. Inward telegram to Secretary of State for the Colonies, 10 April, CO 1022/44.

———. 1952d. "Re: Curfew." Telegram to O. Lyttelton, Secretary of State for the Colonies, 6 May, CO 1022/54.

———. 1952e. Telegram to O. Lyttelton, Secretary of State for the Colonies, 26 May, CO 1022/56.

———. 1952f. Templer's Speech reproduced in telegram to Seccretary of State for the Colonies, 20 August 1952. CO 1022/56.

———. 1952g. Telegram to O. Lyttelton, Secretary of State for the Colonies, 15 October, CO 1022/3.

———. 1953a. Inward telegram to O. Lyttelton, Secretary of State for the Colonies, 7 February.

———. 1953b. Inward telegram to O. Lyttelton, Secretary of State for the Colonies, 1 December, CO 1022/41.

———. 1953c. Inward telegram to O. Lyttelton, Secretary of State for the Colonies, 1 December, CO 1022/42.

———. 1954a. Telegram to O. Lyttelton, Secretary of State for the Colonies, 22 April, CO 1030/309 no. 27.

———. 1954b. Telegram to O. Lyttelton, 26 May, CO1030/310 no. 72.

The Anglo-Java Rubber Company Ltd. 1952. Letter to Oliver Lyttelton, Secretary of State for the Colonies, 11 February, CO 1022/44.

The Daily Worker. 1951. 2 November, CO 1022/56.

———. 1952a 10 April, CO 1022/56.

———. 1952b. 12 April, CO 1022/56.

"The Evacuation and Detention of the Inhabitants of Tras under Emergency Regulations of Malaya." 1951. Translation from un-named Norwegian newspaper, CO 1022/135.

The Malayan Agricultural Journal. 1939. "The Malayan Rubber Planting Industry." *The Malayan Agricultural Journal* 27: 214–21.

The Malayan Post. 1946. "India for the Indians, China for the Chinese, Malaya for the Malays." 26 January.

"The Manchesters in Malaya: First Casualties in Jungle Skirmish with Terrorists." 1951. 25 September, CO 537/7262.

The Sunday Times. 1970. "Kajang Reds: Only a Radio Link-Up." 1 January, 1.

Thomas, N. 1994. *Colonialism's Culture: Anthropology, Travel and Government*. Oxford: Polity Press.

Thomson, J. T. 1984. *Glimpses into Life in Malayan Lands*. Oxford: Oxford University Press.

Thompson, R. 1966. *Defeating Communist Insurgency*. London: Chatto and Windus.

———. 1989. *Make for the Hills*. London: Leo Cooper.

Turnbull, C. M. 1989. *A History of Malaysia, Singapore and Brunei*. Sydney: Allen & Unwin Australia Ltd.

Third East Anglian Regiment, First Battalion. 1960. Diary of Commanding Officer for 'Operation Bamboo.' WO 305/960.

Thomas, S. 1948. Letter to *The Times*, 28 August.

Tronoh-Malayan Group. 1948."Interim Statement To The Shareholders Of The Tronoh-Malayan Group of Tin Mining Companies on H. M. Government Declaration of the 26th April, 1948 Regarding Malayan War Damage Compensation." 8 September, Royal Commonwealth Archives, University of Cambridge.

Trowell, M. 2018. *Anwar Returns: The Final Twist: The Prosecution and Release of Anwar Ibrahim*. Singapore: Marshall Cavendish International.

Tucker, G. M. 1983. "Fugue." In *The New Oxford Companion to Music*, edited by D. Arnold, 731–4. Oxford: OUP.

United Kingdom. 1951a. Hansard Parliamentary Debates. Vol. 490 (25 July) col. 148.

———. 1951b. "Imposition of Curfew in the Federation of Malaya." Prepared brief for the Secretary of State on the Evacuation of Tras, November, CO 1022/56.

———. 1956a. "Cabinet Conclusions on Agreement Reached at the Constitutional Conference." 8 February, CAB 128/30/1 CM 9(56)7.

———. 1956b. *Report on the Conference for the Malayan Constitution, January and February 1956*. Cmnd 9714.

———. 1957a. "Reinforcement of Singapore Revision of Joint Planning Instructions, Far Eastern Dept. 1957–1959, 'Internal Threat to Malaya and Singapore'." Report by Joint Planning Staff, 11 February, p. 4, CO 1030/655.

———. 1957b. *Agreement on External Defence and Mutual Assistance Between the Government of the United Kingdom and the Federation of Malaya*, 12 October (signed Agreement 9 July 1963), Cmnd 2094.

United Kingdom, Cabinet Colonial Policy Committee. 1955. Minutes on Forthcoming Talks between Tunku Abdul Rahman and the Communists, 28 October, CAB 134/1201 CA2(55)1.

United Kingdom, Colonial Office and the Central Office of Information. 1952. *Malaya: The Facts Behind the Fighting*. London: HM Stationary Office.

United Kingdom, Far East Committee. 1949. "Economic and Social Development in South and South-East Asia and the Far East." Report Appendix A, November, PREM 8/1407/1 EPC(49)152.

United Kingdom, Foreign Office. 1949."The United Kingdom and South-East and the Far East." Memorandum by Permanent Under-Secretary of State's Committee, October, CO 967/84, no. 69.

United Kingdom, Ministry of Defence. 1959. "Maintenance of Law and Order and Essential Services – Singapore, Far Eastern Dept. 1957–1959, internal threat to Malaya and Singapore." Memorandum to Chiefs of Staff Committee, 7 May, CO 1030/655.

Van Fleet, James. 1953. "The Way to Save Asia." *Daily Telegraph*, 19 June.

Vatikiotis, M. R. J. 1996. *Political Change in Southeast Asia: Trimming the Banyan Tree*. London: Routledge.

Voon, P. K. 1971. "The Rubber Plantation Industry in Selangor, 1899–1909: A Case Study of European Economic Penetration." *Geographica* 17: 1–18.

———. 1976. *Western Rubber Planting Enterprise in Southeast Asia 1876–1921*. Kuala Lumpur: Penerbit Universiti Malaya.

———. 1977. "Images of the Physico-Ecological Environment in Southeast Asia: Some Comments on Environmental Interpretation of Early Western Planters." *Asian Profile* 5: 286–99.

Wade, R. H. 2017. "The Developmental State: Dead or Alive?" *Development and Change* 49 (2): 518–46. ISSN 0012-155X DOI: 10.1111/dech.12381

Warner, D. 1953. Malaya's next battle for hearts and minds. *Daily Telegraph* (13 January).

Watherston, D. C. 1955. "The London Talks: Alliance Demands and the Extent to Which They Might be Met." November, CO 1030/75, no. 4.

Weber, M. 1947. *The Theory of Social and Economic Organization*. Translated by T. Parsons. New York: The Free Press.

Wheeler, C. 1995. "Malaysia: Special Report." *The Financial Post*, 26 August, 29.

White, N. 2003. "The Survival, Revival and Decline of British Economic Influence in Malaysia, 1957–70." *Twentieth Century British History* 14: 222–42.

Wickham, H. A. 1908. *On the Plantation, Cultivation, and Curing of Para Indian Rubber (Hevea Brasiliensis) with an Account of Its Introduction from the West to the Eastern Tropics*. London: K. Paul, Trench, Trubner.

Williams-Hunt, P. D. R. 1952. *An Introduction to Malayan Aborigines*. Kuala Lumpur: Government Press.

Winifrith, A. J. D. 1945. "Malayan Reconstruction Finance." Memorandum, T220/52, 19 April.
Winstedt, R. 1960. "Review of British Intervention in Malaya, 1867–1877." *Malaya* (August).
———. 1988. *A History of Malaya*. Kuala Lumpur: Marican & Sons.
World Bank. 1993. *The East Asian Miracle: Economic Growth and Public Policy*, Main Report. A World Bank Policy Research Report. New York: Oxford University Press. http://documents.worldbank.org/curated/en/1993/09/698870/east-asian-miracle-economic-growth-public-policy-vol-1-2-main-report
———. 1997. *World Development Report 1997: The State in a Changing World*. Washington: World Bank.
Wright, T., and B. Hope. 2018. *Billion Dollar Whale: The Man Who Fooled Wall Street, Hollywood, and the World*. New York: Hachette Books.
Wycherley, P. R. September, 1960. "The Singapore Botanic Gardens and Rubber in Malaya." *Malaya*, 14–21.
Young, R. 1990. *White Mythologies: Writing History and the West*. London: Routledge.
Zuckerman, M. 1998. "Japan Inc. Unravels." *US News and World Report*, 17 August 125 (7): 77.
Žižek, S. 1997. "Multiculturalism, or, the Cultural Logic of Multinational Capitalism." *New Left Review* 225: 28–51.

Index

activist state 121
Agent Orange 51
Agri-Horticultural Society 38
alienation 24–25; land 33–34
Aliens Ordinance in 1933 41
alliance 79, 82–85, 122, 124, 139; during Emergency 55; Malayan elite and MCP 45–46, 82, 85, 139; military 10; of science and capital 38
Althusserian concept of interpellation 25–26
American imperialism 79
Anderson, Benedict 95
Angkatan Permuda Insaf (API) 54
Anglo-Java Rubber Company 67
anxiety: amorphous 19; castration 12, 19, 22, 77, 81, 129; defensive 12, 19, 20, 77, 112; neurotic 21–22, 77
Asian Currency Units (ACUs) 130
Asian Development Bank (ADB) 9, 122
Asian Dollar Market 130
Asian financial crisis 1
Asian Infrastructure and Investment Bank (AIIB) 117, 32–134; members 134
Asian values 105–106, 108–109, 111–112, 116–117, 119, 121, 141

Bach, Johann Sebastian 10
Balding, Christopher 131
Baling Talks 84
Banks, Sir Joseph 37
Barisan Nasional 97, 104n1
Benjamin, Walter 94–95; montage concept 99
Bhabha, Homi 15
Bollas, Christopher 20–23, 60–61, 69, 72, 107, 110–115
botanical gardens: Buitenzorg 37; Calcutta 37; Singapore 37–38; Sydney 37; Trinidad 37
Brennan, Teresa 11–12, 16–17, 30, 107, 122–123, 137; *see also* foundational fantasy; ego's era 123
Bretton Woods 90
Briggs Plan 59–60, 62, 64
Britain's imperial economy 81–82
British India Steam Navigation Company 39
British Military Administration (BMA) (1945–46) 46–47, 49, 138–139
British plans for agricultural development: categories of land use 31; commercialized agriculture 31, 34; export crops 32; labor requirements 39–41; laws of ownership and transfer 33; proximity of railways lines 33; rubber cultivation 32–34; system of land tenure 31–32
bumiputera settler-citizens 99–101
Butler, Judith: contingent identity 26; interpellation conception 25–26, 93, 95–96, 101, 123, 130; theory of performativity 25, 93, 96, 119–120, 122–123

Campbell, Arthur 50
capitalism 15–16, 21; alienation in capitalist mode of production 24–25; disavowal and 23–24; ideological hegemony 24
carceral archipelago 62–65
castration *see* anxiety

Chiang Mai Initiative Multilateralization (CMIM) 8–9, 131–133; bilateral swap and repurchase agreements 132; capitalization 132; multilateral withdrawal agreement 132; Precautionary Line (CMIM-PL) 132
China's economic development 122
Chinese agricultural settlements 32
Chin Peng 85
Churchill, W.F.N. 50
citizenship 96
Civilizing Mission 15
collective identity 14
collective memory 12
colonial ego ideal 77
colonial/imperial aggression 108–109
Commission on Economic Growth 1
Commission on Growth and Development 121
Conrad, Joseph 31
Contingent Reserve Arrangement 134
Coyle, Diane 116
cultural and psychological guerrilla warfare 15
curfews 63
currency negotiations in Malaya 75–80; debt negotiations 76; elites' actions 77; role of race or ethnicity 76; sterling as official standard 77–79

debt, Asian financial crisis 112–118; debt and sovereignty 124, 141; debt negotiations and social position 76
decolonization 23, 44, 47, 60, 72, 75; Western popular-media depictions of 73
decolonization struggle 44
derivatives market 127–128
desires 25
developing country 4–5
developmental state 106, 121
disavowal 23–24, 60
discourses 13, 16, 94; dominance of 30; racist discourse on intellectual capability 14

East Asian countries, reserves of 117
East Asian economic success 110–111
East Asian financial crisis 1997–98 8, 105, 108, 114–117, 119, 141; application of network theory 124; liquidity crisis 125–126; losses of Asian currencies 124–125; theory of performativity 122–123
East Asian miracle 2, 4, 8, 113, 117, 121
economic botany gardens: establishment of amateur societies and clubs 38; Malacca Gardens 38; Penang Botanic Gardens 38; Singapore Botanic Gardens 37
economic growth 1–2, 10, 14, 124, 140
Eden, Anthony 83
ego ideals 16, 18, 25, 77, 129
estates, as sites of siege 52
European colonial territories, restoration of 46–47
European Payment Fund for recovery programs 81
exchange rates 5, 8, 10, 90, 115, 123–125, 127, 130, 133, 142
export-oriented manufacturing model of development 108

Fanon, Frantz 21–26, 77
Federal Land Development Authority (FELDA) scheme 26, 91–99, 137, 139–140; agricultural development 98, 103; *bumiputera* (son of the soil) settler 99–101; complementary agricultural export system 98; discipline, punishment and biopower 94; Global Ventures (FGV) 103; physical networks 99; program for settlers 100
Fleet, James Van 80
forests 49–52, 93; colonial control over space 50–51, 62; colonial exercise of power 51; as punitive space 68–69
Foucault, Michel 13–14, 30, 34, 94; biopower 94; carceral archipelago 62–65; disciplinary space 64; encoded eye 94
foundational fantasy 16–17, 28, 44, 122–124, 137; of colonial ecology 31–32; constrainment of native populations in spaces 33; framing 29–32; power relationship 36; role in colonial

identity 47–49, 57; role of finance in 35–36
Freud, Sigmund 16, 76–77, 108–109, 114–118, 126, 141; group identity 18, 108; trauma and memory 19–21, 76
Fukuyama, Francis 116

Gater, Sir George 48
Gates Foundation 15
Gay, Peter 18, 109
global capitalism 10, 23–24, 109, 129, 142
global economy 5, 8, 21, 116
globalization 6; financial deregulation in 112; homelessness of 9
government-linked corporations (GLCs) 8, 122, 125, 127–128, 130, 133–134, 142
group identity 18, 91, 108–109, 112
Gurney, Sir Henry 66, 83
Guthrie and Company agency house 35

Harrisons and Crosfield agency house 35
Harvey, David 75, 107
hedging derivatives 128
hegemonic identity 5, 47–49, 109
Herman, Judith 71, 132–133; psychological trauma 60–61; sense of helplessness and humiliation 17–21
Hertogh riots 55
Hiroshima and Nagasaki bombing 46
historical amnesia 15
Hoagland, Jim 116
homelessness of globalization 9
Hook, Derek 77
Hooker, Sir Joseph 37
Hooker, Sir William 37
humiliation 111–112, 115–117, 129

Ibrahim, Anwar 142–143
identity: agentic 26; construction 96; Western 30; *see also* group identity
identity construction through colonialism 16–17
Ikatan Permuda Tanah Ayer (PETA) 54
imperialism 4
import substitution industrialization 121
Indian Act of 1877 39
Indian Emigration Act 1922 40
Indian Immigration Ordinance 1884 39
Indian nationalism 39–41
Indian Passenger Acts of 1857 and 1859 39
insurgent East Asia 112–114
International Bank for Reconstruction and Development (IBRD) 86
International Monetary Fund (IMF) 4, 9, 21, 90, 103–115; imposed financial restructuring 106
international relations 9
interpellation 25–26, 93, 95–96, 101, 123, 142
introjection 25

Japanese economy: 1960s–1970s 121; Yen internationalization 135
Japanese Occupation of Malaya 47, 138
Joseph, May 96

kangani 40
Kasim, Siti 3
Kaum Ibu (mothers of the family) 102
Kew Gardens 37
Kew Gardens, England 36–37
khalwat 40
Klang strikes of 1941 40
Kohut, Heinz 11–12, 44, 106–107, 111, 137; differentiated between sexual desire and narcissism 17–18; framework for identity construction 35; identity construction 35; narcissistic rage 23, 110–111; selfobject concept 11–12, 17, 22, 29–30, 34, 43, 48–49, 60, 110
Konfrontasi 92
kongsis 32
Korean War 67
Krugman, Paul 105

labour in plantation agriculture: indentured system 39; issue of racial stereotyping 39; labor regrouping 67; labor troubles 40; male-to-female ratio 40; peak recruitment period 39; punishment for absenteeism 39; Tamil workers 39; wages 39; working hours 39
lactification 25
Lalang Clause 33
"land for a life" exchanges 71, 102

land tenure laws, colonial 31–32
Larkin, Philip 10
Latour, Bruno 119; network theory 122–124
Lee Hsien Loong 126
Lee Kuan Yew 126
Lee Meng 56
Lennox-Boyd, Colonial Secretary 88
libidinal economy 6, 12, 43, 106–107, 122; culture of financial decision-making 76–77; of currency reserves 75; as a process of anxiety-driven exchanges 11; value of money 75
Lyotard, Jean Francois 16

MacGillivray, Sir Donald 84–85
Malacca Gardens 38
Malaya/Malaysia 4; agricultural development 98; American commercial interests in 80; American support for 79–81; arrival of capitalism in 28; British control post independence 86–87; British foothold in 31–32; *bumiputera* settler-citizens 99–101; central bank 86; citizenscapes post independence 97–99; colonial control over space 48–52; declaration of state of emergency 1948 49; defense agreement with Britain 86; dollar earnings 81–82; elite's sense of obligation 85–86; export/import ratio with the US 81; Group Settlers Act of 1960 100; industrialization 101–102; Japanese withdrawal 48; *Kaum Ibu* (mothers of the family) 102; rubber cultivation 32–34, 38; state's economic decision-making 5; territorialization and moral scopic politics 93–96, 101–102; World War II 44–46
Malayan Communist Party (MCP) 7, 41, 43–44, 49, 53–57, 73, 85, 91, 138–139; acts of resistance 67; as a bargaining device 82–86; communications network 56, 69; control of estates 53; interpretation of Hertogh riots 55; inter-racial military force 54; issue of racial cleavages 55, 57; military resistance of 82; in open firefights 50; policy with regard to Malays 54; political clash between British and 49; psychological isolation in forests 69; shortage of food and 68–69; US against 80; women's support 55–56
Malayan counter-insurgency 93
Malayan elites 52, 60, 77, 79, 82–83, 139; alliance with MCP 45–46, 82, 85, 139; negotiations over currency exchange rates 7–8, 70, 74, 89
Malayan Emergency 1948 43, 49, 53; Briggs Plan and 59–60; as economic war for control 59–60; firing plan 63–64; house curfews 63; Malayan currency negotiations during 79–80; racial segregation 59–60; recasting of 80; regulations implemented 64–65
Malayan/Malaysia's economy 1, 10, 136, 140–142; capital control measures 126; conflict over access and rights to resources 15; conservative development program 89; domestic consumption-driven economy 126, 134; goods and services tax 127; history of 15; importance of tin and rubber 82; Mahathir era 90; Malayan export income in sterling 74; monetary policy 86–87; outflow of profits 88; plantation economy 29, 138; postcolonial condition 10–11; preferential treatment for British commercial interests 88–89; rebalancing 124–127; surplus and capital transfers 87; trajectory 25
Malayan rubber plantation 32–34, 38, 137–138; Asian-owned (Chinese) smallholdings 34; clearing houses for seeds 36; European owned plantations 34; European planters' anxieties of danger 53–54; labor requirements and immigration 32, 39–41; Ridley's innovative processes 38; role of science in 38; Rubber

Regulation Scheme 34; scientific research in 36–37; shareholding and financial control 35–36; Singapore Botanic Gardens and 37; smallholdings 34; Stevenson's Scheme 34; Western capital in 35–36
Malaya's currency reserves 8, 74; during Emergency 79; sterling exchange rate 77–79; surplus in sterling reserves 88, 139; US dollar earnings for sterling 78, 81, 87
Malay Home Guard 54
Malaysian Islamic Party or *Parti Islam Se-Malaysia* (PAS) 3, 142
Malaysian model of privatization 141
Malaysian nationalism 100
Mallet, Victor 116
Mamdani, Mahmood 92
Manichean fight of Good 60
market liquidity 134
1MDB (1Malaysia Development Berhad) scandal 136
Mead, Walter Russell 116
medical services in Malayan resettlement camps 62
Memmi, Albert 73
Mirsky, Jonathan 116
Mitchell, Sir Charles 38
Mohamad, Dr. Mahathir 3, 119, 140, 142
Muggeridge, Malcolm 80, 83

narcissistic anger 22, 107
narcissistic injury 109–111
narcissistic rage 60, 69, 109–111
narcissistic wounding 21, 23, 60, 76
national identity 14, 99; *bumiputera* settler-citizens 99–100
nation-states 12, 95–96, 121, 127; victims in 12
New Development Bank (NDB) 117, 132–134
New Economic Policy (NEP) 91, 97, 140
New Villages 62, 64–65, 72, 93, 98, 102, 139; design of 62; disciplinary space 65; Tampin Forest Reserve for resettlement purposes 62

objectification 17
O' Donovan, Patrick 52
Orang Asli settlements 31, 68, 104n2
Orientalism 13–14, 30, 76, 96; criticism of 15

Pan-Malayan General Labour Union (PMGLU) 49
performativity *see* Butler, Judith
Penang Botanic Gardens 38
People's Bank of China (PBOC) 133–134
Peradeniya botanical garden 37
Perikatan Nasional (PN) coalition 3
plantation economy 29; British plans for agricultural development 31; social relations and 29
policy activism 121
political pathologies 3
population resettlement programs 52
positive recognition 26
postcolonial identity, psychodynamics of 16–18; condition of aggression 17; economic success and economic challenges 18; self-selfobject relationship 11–12, 17; subject-object relationship 17
postcolonial Malaysia 92–93
postcolonial nationalisms 92
psychic legitimacy 3, 91–3, 96, 140
psychic resistance 16
psychoanalysis 9, 12, 16–17, 25, 109, 137
psychodrama 60
psychological alienation 24
psychological privilege 73

race riots 1969 8
racialized capitalism 75, 142
racialized dimension of global economic order 8
racial schisms 55, 57, 82
rage 22; narcissistic 23
Rahman, Tunku Abdul 83–84, 86, 97
realistic anxiety 77
Ridley, Henry 37–38
Roitman, Janet 76
Rose, Nikolas 142
Rubber Regulation Scheme 34

Said, Edward 12, 30, 36; critique of Orientalism 14, 34–35; distinction between manifest and latent Orientalism 76;

dominance of discourses 30; *Orientalism* 13; proximity to economic decisions 76
secondariness 12
Second Malaysia Plan (SMP) 97–98, 103, 140
self: grandiose self 17, 23–25, 33–35, 57–60, 110, 137, 141; self-esteem 23; stereotyped self 77
self-selfobject relationship 11–12, 17, 29–30, 34, 43, 48–49; discourses of race, class and gender 52–57; perception of forest 49–52
Shostakovich fugue 10, 137
Sime Darby oil palm estate 52
Singapore 1, 4, 123–124, 142; build-up of reserves 8; economic success of 127–130; as a financial center 130–131; financially defensive tactics and economic success 128–129; foreign reserves 127
social disempowerment 129
social hierarchy 92, 95
Soros, George 115
sovereign wealth funds (SWFs) 125, 127, 130–131; as GLCs 127; hedging derivatives 127–128; ownership and success of 131
spatial reorganization of nature 36
Stanley, Oliver 47
sterling as official standard 77–79; as Bank Rate 78; calculus of equivalence between dollars and 79; exchange rate relative to dollar 78; by gold holdings 78; Malayan contributions to sterling reserves 78, 89, 97; Malayan surplus in sterling reserves 88, 139
sterling convertibility 78, 90
sterling reserves, Malayan contributions to 77–79
Stevenson's Scheme 34
Stiglitz, Joseph 105
Stockwell, Anthony 48
subjectivity 30, 119–123, 131
Suffolk Regiment 50
The Sunday Times 59
swap mechanism 125, 134; commercial swaps 132

Tan Siew Sin 87
Tan Sri Zeti 126
Templer, Sir Gerald 57, 70, 87
theater of moral lessons: collective punishment 65; converting sites of contestation into moral representations 66; deportation 69, 71; deprivation of civil rights 65–66; designation of "black" and "white" areas 65; exhibition of dead Communists outside a police station 69; fines 66; labor regrouping 67; punishment by banishment 70–71; roadblocks 65; whipping or caning 70
theory of performativity 25, 93, 96, 119–120, 122–123; interpretation of financial strategy 122–123
Thomas, Sir Shenton 81
Trade Union Ordinance of 1940 64
trauma 43, 59, 122; aggression and anxiety 108–109; capitalism and 21; colonial and postcolonial 20; complex or repeated 52; as consequence of disavowal and alienation 23–25; control through 21; curfews 63; diagnosis 19; East Asian reaction to narcissistic wounding 23; issues of identity/culture 107–108; logic of 21–22; memory 12, 19–21, 76; in moral representations 65–71; narcissistic injury 109–111; original 19; paradoxes of 19; pathways of 61–62; psychological 60; racial privilege as 60; recognition of 19; signature of 19; through humiliating discourse 111–112
traumatic event 3
Troika 105
Truman Doctrine 83
Tsipras, Alexis 105

United Malays National Organization (UMNO) 98, 104
United Planters of Malaya Association (UPAM) 83

US: BOP 81; as superpower 79–81
US dollar 77–78; as new standard 79–81, 115
Utusan Melayu 83

Varoufakis, Yanis 105
verbal aggression 109, 137

Warner, Denis 53
Western ego 16, 30
White Man's Burden 11, 79
wish image 94
World Bank 2, 4, 90n1, 106, 113–117, 121, 128–134, 141
Žižek, Slavoj 130

FSC
www.fsc.org
MIX
Papier | Fördert gute Waldnutzung
FSC® C083411

Kolibri 360 GmbH
Ferdinand-Jühlke-Straße 7
99095 Erfurt, Deutschland
produktsicherheit@kolibri360.de